AF477791

Criminal Records

Criminal Records

A Database for the Criminal Justice System and Beyond

Terry Thomas

Leeds Metropolitan University, UK

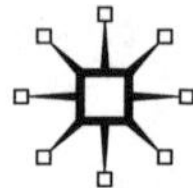

First published 2007 by
PALGRAVE MACMILLAN
Houndmills, Basingstoke, Hampshire RG21 6XS and
175 Fifth Avenue, New York, N.Y. 10010
Companies and representatives throughout the world

PALGRAVE MACMILLAN is the global academic imprint of the Palgrave
Macmillan division of St. Martin's Press, LLC and of Palgrave Macmillan Ltd.
Macmillan® is a registered trademark in the United States, United Kingdom
and other countries. Palgrave is a registered trademark in the European
Union and other countries.

ISBN-13: 978–0–230–00767–3 hardback
ISBN-10: 0–230–00767–8 hardback

This book is printed on paper suitable for recycling and made from fully
managed and sustained forest sources. Logging, pulping and manufacturing
processes are expected to conform to the environmental regulations of the
country of origin.

A catalogue record for this book is available from the British Library.
A catalog record for this book is available from the Library of Congress.

10   9   8   7   6   5   4   3   2   1
16   15   14   13   12   11   10   09   08   07
Printed and bound in Great Britain by
Antony Rowe Ltd, Chippenham and Eastbourne

Contents

List of Tables and Figure

Tables

Figure

Preface

In January 2007 a full page 'advertisement' appeared in *The Guardian* (28 January 2007) featuring a colour photograph of a run-down corner shop selling vinyl long-playing records. Inside could be seen customers standing as they browsed through the stacks of records. Outside, the words 'Criminal Records' appeared over the door, in letters a foot high.

This 'advertisement' was, in fact, an information briefing from the UK Home Office warning employers not to hire illegal migrant workers. The themed message was that if you did hire illegal migrant workers you would be as illegal as they are, and you could be fined or even face a prison sentence. The accompanying text made no mention of anyone getting a criminal record but the picture of the corner shop left no one in doubt that the imposition of a criminal record was every bit as meaningful a sanction as the fine or possible custodial sentence.

Criminal records were once a discrete item of personal information held in conditions of confidence by the police. They were used by the police and the judicial system for investigative or sentencing purposes. No one else was very much interested in them.

In the last 20 years the circulation and dissemination of criminal records has increased and their significance increased at the same time. Employers, in particular, now have much greater access to them for pre-employment screening of suitable applicants. The Criminal Record Bureau created to assist this circulation and dissemination now sits at the centre of a multi-million pound 'child protection industry' that is already spreading way beyond the protection of children's interests.

This book traces the rise and rise of the criminal record. Its production owes much to the support of colleagues at Leeds Metropolitan University – Paul Blackledge, Colin Webster, Steve Wright and Jeannette Garwood, as well as to colleagues in other universities – Joanne Smith and Bill Hebenton. Thanks are also due to staff at the Brotherton Library, University of Leeds and the British Library at Wetherby, and to Sheila Milner for word processing. Special thanks to Eileen for putting up with it all; and to Barney for showing no interest at all.

Terry Thomas

List of Abbreviations

ACPO	Association of Chief Police Officers
ACRO	ACPO Criminal Record Office
AFR	Automatic Fingerprint Recognition
ASF	Automated Search Facility
ASSET	Risk Assessment Instrument
AWF	Analysis Work Files
BRC	Back Record Conversion
CCCJS	Coordination of Computerisation in the Criminal Justice System
CICA	Criminal Injuries Compensation Authority
CIS	Customs Information System
CJIT	Criminal Justice Information Technology
CMS	Case Management System
C-NOMIS	Computer-National Offender Management Information System
COMPASS	CPS Case Management System
CPIC	Canadian Police Information Centre
CPS	Crown Prosecution Service
CRA	Criminal Record Agency
CRAMS	Case Management System
CRB	Criminal Records Bureau
CREST	Crown Court Electronic Support
CREU	Criminal Records European Unit
CRISP	Cross-Regional Information Sharing Project
CRO	Criminal Record Office
CSO	Convict Supervision Office
CTC	Counter-Terrorist Checks
DfES	Department for Education and Science
DNA	Deoxyribonucleic Acid
DV	Developed Vetting
DVLA	Driver and Vehicle Licensing Agency
EIS	European Information System
ENU	Europol National Unit
Europol	European Police Office
FBI	Federal Bureau of Investigation
FIND	Facial Image National Database

FIS	Forensic Integration Strategy
GCHQ	Government Communications Head Quarters
GCRO	Garda Criminal Records Office
HFEA	Human Fertilisation and Embryology Authority
HGV	Heavy Goods Vehicle
IBB	Independent Barring Board
IBIS	Integrating Business and Information Systems
IDENT 1	National Automated Fingerprint Identification System
IMPACT	Intelligence Management, Prioritisation, Analysis, Co-ordination and Tasking
INI	Impact Nominal Index
INTERPOL	International Criminal Police Organisation
IPCC	Independent Police Complaints Commission
I-PLX	Interim Police Local Cross Check System
IRT	Independent Review Team
ISA	Information Sharing and Assessment
ISS4PS	Information Systems Strategy for Police Service
JESICA	Justice and Emergency Services Information Communication Association
JSA	Joint Supervisory Authority
LEAA	Law Enforcement Assistance Administration
LGV	Larger Goods Vehicles
LIBRA	The National Computer System for the Magistrates Courts Service of England and Wales
LIDS	Local Inmate Database System
LOCCS	Local County Court System
MAPPA	Multi-Agency Public Protection Arrangements
MAPPP	Multi-Agency Public Protection Panels
MASS	Magistrates Courts Standard System
MO	Modus Operandi
MOPI	Management of Police Information
NACRO	National Association for the Care and Resettlement of Offenders
NAFIS	National Automated Fingerprint Identification System
NCB	National Central Bureau
NCCL	National Council for Civil Liberties
NCIC	National Crime Information Center
NCIS	National Criminal Intelligence Service

NDNAD	National DNA Database
NDPB	Non-Departmental Public Body
NFO	National Fingerprint Office
NIB	National Identification Bureau
NIM	National Intelligence Model
NIS	National Identification Service
NISIS	National Identification Service Intelligence Section
NOMS	National Offender Management Service
NPIA	National Policing Improvement Agency
NSPIS	National Strategy for Police Information Systems
NVIS	National Video Identification Systems
OCJR	Office of Criminal Justice Reform
PCV	Passenger Carrying Vehicle
PEDb	Police Elimination Database
Phoenix	Police-Home Office Extended Names Index
PITO	Police Information Technology Organisation
PLX	Police Local Cross-Check System
PNC	Police National Computer
PNCID	PNC Identity Number
PNN	Police National Network
POCA	Protection of Children Act
POVA	Protection of Vulnerable Adults
PROBIS	Probation Information System
PSV	Public Service Vehicle
PULSE	Police Using Leading Systems Effectively
QUEST	Query Using Extended Search Techniques
SC	Security Check
SCENT	Systems Custom Enforcement Network
SCOPE	CPS Computer System
SCRO	Scottish Criminal Record Office
SEARCH	Systems for Electronic Analysis and Retrieval of Criminal History Records
SEU	Social Exclusion Unit
SF	Search File
SIRENE	Supplementary Information Request at the National Entry
SIS	Schengen Information System
SSA	Social Science Association
TECS	The Europol Computer System
VIS	Visa Information System
ViSOR	Violent and Sexual Offender Register
XHIBIT	Exchanging Hearing Information by Internet Technology

YIP	Youth Inclusion Programme
YISP	Youth Inclusion and Support Panel
YJB	Youth Justice Board
YOT	Youth Offending Team

1
Introduction

The criminal courts impose sentences on people convicted of crime, and at the same time a record of that conviction and sentence is made. The criminal record thus created is the subject of this book. There is an often quoted statistic that on average one man in three in the United Kingdom will have a criminal record by his early thirties (Home Office, 1995a).

The aim here is to take a closer look at criminal records as such and to look at where the national collection of criminal records is kept, who is looking after these criminal records and to what purposes they are being put. It provides a narrative history of the origins of the UK's criminal record collection in 1869 through to the opening of the Criminal Record Office in 1913 and to the computerisation of criminal record histories in 1995; it explores the spreading use of criminal records within the criminal justice system and beyond. In looking at what constitutes 'beyond' the criminal justice system, the book particularly outlines the growing use of records for screening applicants for employment, using the Criminal Records Bureau as the mechanism for disseminating records.

Criminal records could be seen as just another item of information that can be passed around and processed in much the same way as any other item of information. If we use information technology for this purpose, we might even reduce it to mere 'data'.

In practice we tend to see criminal records as more than just information. It is certainly personal information that attaches to an identifiable individual and is therefore entitled to the various safeguards of confidentiality that have grown up to protect personal information. It is also arguably particularly sensitive personal information concerning the criminal transgressions of that individual and the associated status and stigma that accompanies a criminal record. At some point in time your fellow citizens have placed their mark on your unacceptable behaviour.

Some of our laws recognise that criminal records are a sensitive item of personal data (e.g. Data Protection Act 1998, s. 2(h)) and that the 'millstone' of having a criminal record requires laws to alleviate that burden by allowing some records to be considered 'spent' (Rehabilitation of Offenders Act 1974). Even when the original conviction has been made in the public arena of the court and reported in the media, in general terms we believe a veil of confidentiality should be allowed to fall over an old criminal record in order to allow the individual concerned to grow out of crime and rehabilitate themselves back into 'ordinary' citizenship.

The more high profile the criminal court cases that capture the public imagination, the less likely they are to benefit from any 'veils of confidentiality', and their notoriety will linger on. The press having reported the case may well have imprinted it on the public memory in a way that makes such attempts at confidentiality futile.

The national storage systems of criminal records, however, mostly consist of lower-level crimes that are not imprinted on the public memory, and in turn this begs the question of why we are storing them in the first place. In the United Kingdom there are approximately 5.5 million records held nationally. The police will say it is to help them with any future investigations and the courts will say it helps them make sentencing decisions when they know that the offender before them is not a first-time offender. Other parts of the criminal justice system may have their own reasons for wanting access to records. In recent times, employers have also raised their voice and said they want to know about old criminal records in order to safeguard their enterprise and protect the people the ex-offenders may be working with.

The use of criminal records for pre-employment screening in order to exclude 'unsuitable' applicants for work has grown inexorably over the last 20 years. The UK's Criminal Records Bureau, which opened in 2002, personifies this new usage of criminal records in order to minimise the possibility of the 'wrong' person getting work where he or she might cause problems.

A national collection of criminal records is of limited value in itself without a clear idea of what we are keeping them for and how they will be used. They are also of limited value if they cannot be successfully linked to the person they relate to. Criminal records need the additional facility of identification mechanisms in the shape of fingerprints, DNA samples or other biometric methods to make the match between the individuals and the records. Increasingly, attempts are made to make these identification matches between different countries and across international borders.

In Chapter 2 of this volume an attempt is made to outline the history of the UK national collection of criminal records, from its origins in the Habitual Criminals Act 1869 across the next 100 years and more. This is a neglected area of police history and the present attempt will hopefully encourage others to look at this history in more depth.

The focus turns to more contemporary matters in Chapter 3 where we try to locate the now computerised system of criminal record keeping in its strategy context and within the framework of the data protection laws that surround it, and highlight that, as the custodians, the police maintain the collection as a relevant, accurate and well-managed set of records.

The reasons for keeping criminal records and for what purposes they might be used are examined in Chapter 4. Traditionally they have been kept for police purposes in investigating new crimes and judicial purposes to help with sentencing decisions. Over the last 30 years these traditional uses have been supplemented by claims made on the criminal record collection by a host of new users. Initially these were still agencies within the criminal justice system (probation, prisons, courts etc.) but increasingly they include organisations beyond the criminal justice system for purposes of licensing, prosecutions by non-police agencies and other reasons.

Chapter 5 looks at the concept of the 'spent' criminal record – the record that can be considered 'extinguished' if the subject of the record has not been re-convicted for a given period of time. The idea is to assist the rehabilitation of the ex-offender, especially in terms of helping them get into employment.

In contrast, Chapter 6 looks at the demands made on criminal records by employers wishing to screen their new recruits to ensure suitability for work. Such pre-employment screening has risen in importance, and especially in the case of those whose work gives them access to children. Criminal record checks are now an embedded part of child-protection procedures and the need to safeguard the welfare of children in schools, nurseries and other settings.

The Criminal Records Bureau (CRB) puts child welfare at the heart of its activities by centralising criminal record disclosure. While the police continue to maintain the records, the CRB is now the link to employers across the country who wish to screen their new employees. Chapter 7 outlines the origins of the CRB in the Police Act 1997 and its implementation from 2002 and looks at the new phenomenon of criminal records as a 'saleable commodity'.

Although the focus of this volume is on the United Kingdom and its arrangements for criminal records maintenance and use, similar arrangements take place in other countries who maintain repositories of criminal records. In Chapter 8 the use of criminal records across international frontiers is considered, whether in an ad hoc fashion or more systematically through formalised 'transnational policing networks' like Europol and Interpol.

The final chapter attempts to bring together the various themes and developments in the maintenance and use of criminal records and consider their possible future directions. As criminal records find their way from the Police National Computer where they are stored to more and more corners of society who claim access to them for all sorts of reasons, are we witnessing the further creation of the 'disciplined society' or 'the preventive State'?

2
A Short History of Criminal Records

The British have a tradition of keeping records on themselves, from the Domesday book of Norman times through to the more sophisticated arrangements that grew up with the Industrial Revolution. The Victorians started various systems of national registration (Higgs, 2004) and in 1869 started the first national collection of criminal records. Criminal records would come to be used by the police, for operational purposes, and the criminal courts, to help determine appropriate sentences.

The courts had always needed a system to tell them if the alleged offender before them was a first-time offender or a repeat offender. In the case of the latter the earlier punishment had clearly been ineffective and something stronger was now needed. In times past, the necessary information came only from local knowledge and sometimes from the branding of offenders with a hot iron.

Branding

In the sixteenth century, branding had been a rudimentary means of letting the authorities know if they were dealing with a second-time offender. Offenders could avoid the death sentence by claiming 'benefit of clergy', which entailed being able to read a verse from the Bible. 'Benefit of clergy' was only available once, and branding of the letters 'V' for vagabond, 'T' for thief or even 'M' for manslaughter ensured due retribution for the second-time offender (Stephen, 1973: 271–274).

McLynn has suggested that such branding was always on a part of the body that could be hidden or disguised:

Clergyable felons were traditionally branded on the thumb so that they could not plead clergy again. The penalty was not to disgrace the offender; the brand could only be seen by close inspection; its sole purpose was for the benefit of the authorities.

(McLynn, 1989: 280–281)

The 1699 Shoplifting Act did allow for branding on the left cheek but the practice was not popular:

…because it was found that facial branding merely produced hardened criminals. Since no one would employ a person with the marks of criminality so clearly on his face, the first offender was forced into a life of crime.

(ibid: 281)

Branding fell into disuse in the eighteenth century and was formally abolished in 1779. Its imagery lingers on, however, and in May 2006 the headline 'Branded as Criminals' was splashed across the front page of a Sunday paper to lead into a story about inaccurate criminal records being accorded to innocent people (*Mail on Sunday*, 21 May 2006).

Henry Fielding and Patrick Colquhoun

Fielding and Colquhoun were the eighteenth-century pioneers of policing ideas which would come to fruition later in the Dublin Police Act 1786, creating a police force for Ireland and then the 1829 Metropolitan Police Act introducing the London police force.

Henry Fielding is best remembered as the magistrate who organised the Bow Street Runners as a form of policing from his Bow Street court and as the author of the novel 'Tom Jones'. In 1751 he wrote 'An Enquiry into the Causes of the Late Increase in Robbers'.

Another part of his work at Bow Street was the careful collection of information on crimes and criminals. From 1753 onwards, the court had its own:

'Register Clerk' whose duty it was 'to keep an exact Register of all Robberies committed; Descriptions of all Goods lost; the Names and Descriptions of all Persons brought before the said Magistrate who stand accused either of Fraud or Felony, or Felony, or suspected of either'.

(Radzinowicz, 1956: 46)

Conviction records were also kept and became 'the valuable register of offenders which has been so carefully preserved for many years in the public office in Bow Street' (ibid: 47). This register was added to by other neighbouring magistrates 'who constantly give notice to Mr. Fielding when they have committed any desperate rogue or suspicious man' (Pringle, 1955: 135). This early collection of criminal records for the London area was destroyed by fire during the anti-Catholic Gordon riots of 1780 (ibid: 200).

Fielding's work was taken forward by his brother John, who in 1776 suggested the Government keep formal national records (ibid: 194), and by Patrick Colquhoun, who published his 'Treatise on the Police of the Metropolis to Deal with a Crisis of Morals and Criminality' in 1795.

Colquhoun was a Scottish businessman who moved to London in 1789 where he became a magistrate. He wrote extensively on the need for less repressive laws and a more enlightened approach to help those in poverty. He advocated the need for a police force that would prevent and investigate crime as well as the need for a public prosecutor. Amongst other things, Colquhoun wanted to see the establishment of a comprehensive register of criminals and a department for receiving information about them (Radzinowicz, 1956: Chapter 9).

The momentum to create a new police force gathered pace in the opening decades of the nineteenth century, culminating in the laws that provided for a London force in 1829 and forces across the country by the mid-1850s (Reiner, 1992: Chapter 1). A police force for Ireland – then governed from London – had been created earlier with the passing of the Dublin Police Act 1786.

The beginnings of a system

The need to keep a national repository of criminal records was identified by the Victorians in the middle of the nineteenth century. At this time, the transportation of offenders to Australia and other places was coming to an end and the resort to corporal punishment and capital punishment was diminishing. The function of the prison as a 'holding' place for those to be transported or executed started to change:

> ... this breakdown in transportation created, or at least exacerbated the problem, so often posed in the press and learned journals of the period, of how to dispose of the criminal population.
>
> (Bartrip, 1981: 152)

The prison – through penal servitude – now became the punishment in itself and at the end of his or her punishment the prisoner was released back into the community. If transportation or execution represented the ultimate 'exclusion' from society for its unwanted members, the idea of release back into the community represented a form of 'inclusion' not previously recognised.

If convicted offenders were to be re-included back into society – or rehabilitated – rather than simply 'excluded', the Victorians wanted to know where they were and what they were doing. On a pragmatic level the courts still needed to know if the offender in the dock had offended before, in order to adjust the sentence accordingly.

At another level the Victorians were fearful of a class of offenders – the 'criminal class' – continuing to offend as 'habitual offenders'. Such individuals were seen as a species apart, like animals who were just there to prey on the law abiding. Sir Edmund Du Cane, a later Chair of the Prison Commission, described the characteristics of the 'habitual offender' as:

> ... entirely those of the inferior races of mankind – wandering habits, utter laziness, absence of forethought or provision, want of moral sense, cunning, dirty and instances may be found in which their physical characteristics approach those of the lower animals.
>
> (quoted in Wiener, 1990: 301)

Today's sensibilities throw doubt on such ideas and 'the more historians probe the reality of such a class, the more it is revealed to be spurious ... (and) ... largely synonymous with the poorer working class, particularly those who existed by casual labour' (Emsley, 1996: 172–173; see also Stevenson, 1986). The notion of a race or class of criminals 'other' than ourselves as the law-abiding majority remains, however, a powerful and convenient one. In May 2005, Chief Superintendent David Baines of the Greater Manchester Police warned that gangs of 'feral youth' were running wild with no fear of the police or the criminal justice system (Butt, 2005).

For the Victorians it was the street robberies of the early 1860s that caused panic. These outbreaks of 'garottings' were directly attributed – with no particular evidence – to ex-prisoners now at large in the community. The last transportation to Australia had been in 1853 and the Penal Servitude Act of the same year had increased prison sentences and introduced a rudimentary form of post-custody supervision in the form of the 'ticket-of-leave'.

The 'ticket-of-leave' idea was in turn borrowed from the penal colonies of Australia, when released prisoners there were allowed back into the local community. Now, back home, prisoners here were to be released with a 'ticket-of-leave' – a signed form informing him or her that they were on licence and subject to recall to prison if continuing to offend, associate with notorious bad characters or lead an idle or dissolute life with no visible means of support. The police were given the job of supervising the 'ticket-of-leave' offenders, who in turn had to report monthly to the police. The argument was that 'it was essential to provide society with additional security when, for the first time, it would have to face a regular threat from a large number of ex-convicts' (Radzinowicz and Hood, 1986: 245).

The police were accused of being over-zealous in their supervisory duties towards the 'ticket-of-leave' men and women and not least because there was no check on their powers of prison recall by way of a court appearance. Harassing men trying to get work only disrupted those efforts. The commissioner for the Metropolitan Police issued instructions to his officers that:

> ....the police are not to interfere with convicts on ticket-of-leave, so as to prevent their following any honest course for earning their living. Should the convicts obtain employment, the employers are not to be informed.
>
> (The General Regulations, Instructions and Orders for the Government and Guidance of the Metropolitan Police 1862, quoted in Radzinowicz and Hood, 1986: 249)

The 'garotting' panics of the early 1860s seemed to demonstrate that whether or not the police harassed 'ticket-of-leave' offenders, the system was not working. When in 1862 the Home Office asked the commissioner to name and produce reports on the 'ticket-of-leave' men in London, 'the police could not find or produce a single man of them' (ibid: 249); the same request in Birmingham produced 14 out of 100 (ibid: 250).

The Penal Servitude Act 1864 duly tightened 'ticket-of-leave' supervision by requiring offenders to report monthly to the police and notify them of any change of address or employment. What was missing from the equation was any formal way of identifying the offender who was a 'habitual offender'. Recidivists were constantly representing themselves as first-time offenders in court in order to be dealt with lightly (ibid: 251).

Pressure began to build for a system of registering known criminals. In February 1869 a deputation of concerned citizens visited the home secretary to make the argument that 'ticket-of-leave' arrangements were not working and therefore:

> ...much of new crime was committed by old criminals. If the system was to be continued there should be an efficient system of registration by which the police would know where the different criminals were located.
>
> ('The Home Secretary and Crime in the Metropolis', *The Times*, 4 February 1869)

The Social Science Association (SSA), formed in 1857, added their weight to the arguments for better supervisory arrangements. The SSA described itself as a 'Parliament of social causes' and today would be seen as an influential think tank. The Home Secretary's 'door was always open to the SSA's managers' (Goldman, L., 1986).

The response was the Habitual Criminals Bill published in 1869. An editorial in the Times outlined its contents:

> ...to make the supervision of such convicts more real, the Chief Commissioner of Police is to keep a central registry of all the licences or 'tickets of leave' guaranteed to convicts. A system of inter-communication between the different districts of the country will complete a network of supervision.
>
> ('Editorial', *The Times*, 27 February 1869)

In order to make the Bill as effective as possible, arguments were made that habitual offenders be tattooed or marked with a number or lettering to assist later identification. Colonel James Fraser, the commissioner of the City of London police, articulated the case in a letter to 'The Times':

> ...copies of these marks, transmitted from each prison to the central office of registration in London would furnish invaluable record of the history of habitual criminals and enable the police to obtain that reliable information of their antecedents which is essential to the future success of the new Bill.
>
> (*The Times*, 13 March 1869: p. 11 letters)

The tattooing idea was not taken up in the Act; it has subsequently been said that the SSA virtually 'dictated the terms of the Habitual Criminals Act of 1869' as it would later appear (Goldman, L., 1986).

The Habitual Criminals Act 1869

The passing of the Habitual Criminals Act 1869 is now taken as the starting point for the statutory collation of the United Kingdom's national repository of criminal records; in fact it only covered England, Wales and Ireland and for some reason left Scotland out. The act required that:

> ...for the better supervision of criminals a register of all persons convicted of crime in England shall be kept in London, under the management of the Chief of Police for the Metropolis, or of such other persons as one of Her Majesty's Principal Secretaries may appoint and in Dublin, a like register shall be kept, under the management of the Commissioner for Police for the Police District of Dublin Metropolis.
>
> (Habitual Criminals Act 1869, s. 5)

Duties were placed on prison governors and regional chief constables to send in information to these central repositories in either London or Dublin (1869 Act, s. 6).

The act also introduced more formal police supervision for those considered 'habitual criminals' and empowered the police to apply for revocation of their 'ticket-of-leave' if they were living by dishonest means, about to commit another crime or appeared to be waiting for an opportunity to commit a crime (1869 Act, s. 8). The act dropped the requirement for offenders to report monthly to the police and introduced the safeguard of a court hearing before any revocations were carried out.

The Metropolitan Police duly established a register as required by the act and within the first year of operation had been given 35,000 names to register, many with accompanying photographs. In effect this was all too much for them to manage and 'the material proved overwhelming, and became useless as a means of identification' (Radzinowicz and Hood, 1986: 261).

Prevention of Crimes Act 1871

The Prevention of Crimes Act 1871 re-formed the earlier legislation and at the same time repealed the 1869 Act. This time, Scotland was included in and prison governors threatened with a £20 fine if they neglected to submit the required information (1871 Act, s. 6).

On the supervision of offenders by the police, the act re-introduced monthly reporting and required changes to be notified within 48 hours.

Supervision periods became at the discretion of the courts rather than mandatory, in an effort to reduce the workload on the police. Other anomalies from the 1869 Act were addressed concerning technicalities of supervisee reporting and the information they should give (Radzinowicz and Hood, 1986: 256).

The Habitual Criminals Register

The Metropolitan Police formed a new Criminal Register Office to house the Habitual Criminals Register. The immediate problem with the register was that it was just a straightforward list of names and convictions and it was not particularly helpful as a means of identifying anyone. People could change their names or simply deny they were the person in question. The register was divided into two parts to try and make it more useful:

- an Alphabetical Register of Habitual Criminals – a bound volume of names and convictions produced annually; and
- a Register of Distinctive Marks.

The Register of Distinctive Marks was supposedly the key to identification. The body was divided into nine general areas such as face/head, thighs/legs, and so on, and any distinguishing marks duly recorded (Cole, 2001: 27). It was, in a way, a search for natural markings that might once have been achieved by branding or tattooing; it probably also supported the view that the 'habitual criminal' was of a race apart and therefore easily identifiable from appearance. In 1875 the Italian criminologist Cesare Lombroso furthered this view that criminals were somehow physically different (Lombroso, 1875).

In theory, the police officer first consulted the 'Register of Distinctive Marks' and with a successful hit then went to the 'Alphabetical Register of Habitual Criminals' for the complete criminal record. In practice it was a laborious and ineffective system, not helped by the 'Alphabetical Register' being an annual bound publication rather than any form of card-index more easily kept up to date. The Metropolitan Police thought it was a 'comparatively useless' system (Petrow, 1994: 84) and 'a police memorandum of 1872 complained that the register was not being used enough by police' (Smith, 1985: 121). In the provinces the police hardly consulted it at all, preferring to start keeping their own records (Petrow, 1994: 121). Even large conurbations like Liverpool, Manchester, Birmingham, Sheffield and Bristol were found – by 1872 – to have made no enquiries at all of the new register (Radzinowicz and Hood, 1986: 262).

A total of 150,000 names were on the Alphabetical Register by 1875 but only 1000 had ever been successfully identified from it (Radzinowicz and Hood, 1986: 261–262). The 1874 Lushington Report for the Home Office declared the registry 'a comparative failure' and suggested that it be transferred from the Metropolitan Police to the Home Office (ibid: 163). The registry was duly transferred to the Home Office, Prison Department, in 1877, where it remained until 1896 (Moylan, 1934: 190).

An exercise carried out in March 1893 suggested that the move had made little difference. Twenty-one officers were asked to search the 'Register of Distinctive Marks' to identify 27 prisoners. The officers spent a total of 57½ hours searching and managed to identify only seven of them, taking an average eight hours for each identification (Higgs, 2004: 97).

During the 20 years in which the Home Office took over as custodians of the criminal record collection, the Metropolitan Police developed their own record system and – like the provincial police – hardly ever consulted the national register, and 'thus two branches carried on the work of registration, working in parallel with little inter-communication' (Petrow, 1994: 85–86).

A Criminal Record Office

If the register on its own was proving ineffective it had to be remembered that it had been conceived as just one part of the new arrangements for supervising the 'ticket-of-leave' offenders. By looking at those other parts of the arrangements, we can see how the register became an integral part of the Criminal Record Office (CRO) formed in 1913.

A Convict Supervision Office (CSO) was created within the Metropolitan Police in 1880 and it was this office, consisting of a chief inspector and three sergeants, that attempted to supervise offenders in the community. The CSO also compiled and maintained the separate registry of criminal records for London that ran parallel to the national registry kept by the Home Office, in order to assist them in their supervisory work. The CSO's criminal record system has been described as 'systematised in a manner and to an extent not hitherto attempted' (Petrow, 1994: 86).

In 1883 this office also produced the *Police Gazette* that had been started back in 1828 and based on the even earlier work of John Fielding at Bow Street. The *Gazette* was a confidential report to all forces containing details of people wanted, new crimes committed and offenders being discharged from prison (Critchley, 1978: 209). The *Police Gazette* is still produced today from New Scotland Yard.

It was the problem of identification that remained intractable. The Register of Distinctive Marks was slow and laborious and the police were still resorting to their old identification practice of going to prisons to observe the prisoners at exercise and literally committing their faces to memory. 'It was inadequate and thoroughly haphazard' (Radzinowicz and Hood, 1986: 263). The answer lay in the new developing 'sciences' of fingerprinting, anthropometry and better photography, and it would be these endeavours that would bring criminal records, identification and supervision together in an embryonic CRO.

The big struggle was between fingerprinting and anthropometry. Fingerprinting was an emerging science that had still to be tried and tested and anthropometry was a more time-consuming system developed in France that involved measuring parts of the body to produce a unique set of measurements. A Home Office departmental committee Chaired by Charles Troup in 1894 hedged its bets and recommended that both systems be developed; fingerprinting was the favoured system but it lacked a systematic means of classification.

Edward Henry now provided the means of classifying fingerprints. Henry had developed his system in India and now, as assistant commissioner, brought his ideas to New Scotland Yard. Henry won the police over and later convinced the government's 1900 Belper Committee, set up to inquire into 'The Method of Identification of Criminals by Measurements and Fingerprints'. Fingerprints had won the day and anthropometry would fall into disuse (Henry, 1900; Joseph, 2001; Sengoopta, 2003: 177–182; McCartney, 2006: 6ff).

The Metropolitan Police opened their Fingerprint Office in 1902 and 'the attendance of police officers at prison identification parades (was) dispensed with' (Commissioner of Police for the Metropolis, 1903: 8). The Fingerprint Office was subsequently merged with the office holding the register of 'habitual criminals' – now back from the Home Office – and the Convict Supervision Office. In 1913 it was given the name of the CRO for the country and:

When, today, therefore, we speak of criminal records, we cannot readily differentiate them from the identification methods by which they are made practicable. Indeed, in most police departments, criminal records and identification devices are but part of one huge inter-related system, approachable from many angles.

(Fosdick, 1915: 319)

In general terms the CRO presaged the emergence of a new bureaucratic type of police officer located at New Scotland Yard and 'exhibiting an unshrinkable passion for processing statistical information and extolling the objective value of his work in homing in on the habitual criminal' (Petrow, 1994: 83).

The supervision of ex-offenders by the police was effectively ended by Home Secretary Winston Churchill in 1910. Verdicts on how successful supervision had been were generally negative. According to one offender at the time, 'if a man is determined to do wrong all the supervision in England will not prevent it. They cannot always watch a man' (cited in Petrow, 1994: 80).

> ...on balance police supervision, while theoretically valuable, had been practically useless. It helped the police manufacture a criminal class, without really deterring criminals or diminishing crime.
>
> (ibid: 82)

The inter-war years

The dual role for the CRO of registering the known offenders and collating information to help identify offenders continued into the 1930s. Organisationally, the work divided into that of maintaining Central Registration Records on the one hand and Central Identification Records on the other.

- Central Registration Records

This was the continuation of the original Register of Habitual Criminals now held on a card-index system. Local police forces and prisons submitted their conviction records to maintain the system. They had also to submit a Descriptive Form on the offender – including a photograph if possible – and a full set of ten fingerprints. The fingerprints were stored in the Main Register of Fingerprints, often referred to as just the Main Fingerprint Index or the Main Index. Together, the conviction record, full set of fingerprints and the Descriptive Form constituted the national criminal records of all known offenders.

A review of these arrangements was made by the Home Office in 1938. The review emphasised the 'most essential requirement for efficient working of the central record system (was)...the maintenance of smooth and cordial co-operation between the Criminal Record Office and the individual forces' (Home Office, 1938: para. 279; see also Appendix 19 for ways in which this could be improved).

- Central Identification Records

The CRO's second function was to help identify offenders through its Central Identification Records; in particular to help to identify those responsible for new crimes. These records, in turn, broke down into four groups:

(a) The Crime Index

The Crime Index classified criminals by their behaviour or modus operandi (MO), such as burglary, larceny, fraud and so on, as a means of identification. The idea of MO lists had been developed by Major Llewellyn Atcherley, chief constable of the West Riding, as early as 1908. In 1913 Atcherley published a booklet for his officers called 'MO in Criminal Investigation and Detection' (cited in Fosdick, 1915: 346). The Crime Index now had a sub-set of records known as the Method Index (for more on the Crime Index see Moylan, 1934: 198–200).

Another sub-set of records within the Crime Index listed personal characteristics of criminals, including deformities, marks and other peculiarities based on the earlier Register of Distinctive Marks.

(b) The Single Fingerprint Index

In 1930 a Single Fingerprint Index had been started to run alongside the full Main Fingerprint Index. The Single Fingerprint Index was a much smaller database consisting of the fingerprints of persons who have been guilty of any form of breaking and entering offence. At the end of 1935 it contained the prints of 2836 criminals compared to about half a million in the Main Fingerprint Index; a further 1000 were stored in the Scenes of Crime Collection on unknown individuals (Home Office, 1938: para. 268).

(c) Photograph Collections

This collection was arranged according to methods and 'contained photographs of the most important criminals listed in the Method Index' (ibid).

(d) The Wanted Index

This index was made up from reports submitted by forces; it included people known only by their descriptions, who might be responsible for a series of crimes across the country. The index hoped to link them up.

A good deal of anecdotal history of these times has been passed down in the form of memoirs and autobiographies of retired police officers. Some of these memoirs have a distinct rose-tinted hue to them and Scotland Yard often painted as a super-efficient machine that 'always gets its man'. The CRO is an integral part of this mythology providing a veritable 'Who's Who of criminals' (Moylan, 1934: 188).

Put together, the criminal record now consisted of:

> ...the complete and workable dossier of a criminal. This consists of his past record – his past achievements so far as can be ascertained in the world of criminality – the where, when and how of his misdeeds, his photograph in two positions, full and side face, and his fingerprints. In addition to this you also have him detailed in the (Crime) Index, which contains all kinds of curious information about him, his personal habits, tastes, indulgences, weaknesses, customs, peculiarities of body and mind and of course his particular line.
>
> (Adam, 1931: 133; see also Woodhall, 1936: 137–138)

The Metropolitan Police raised awareness of the CRO amongst Officers in 1936 by publishing a booklet entitled 'Catching Thieves on Paper'.

Officers of the CRO were said to be so knowledgeable that they even knew names by memory, and hardly had to look them up. Reginald Morrish, a former chief inspector with the Metropolitan Police, noted this 'amazing memory' of the CRO officers:

> I have telephoned them on many occasions, and have been surprised to find that at times they have been able to give me at once the real identity of the criminal I have been seeking.
>
> (Morrish, 1940: 43)

The records held some 770,000 names by 1924 (Commissioner of Police for the Metropolis, 1925: 14), so these memories must have been quite extraordinary.

Another former chief inspector recalled the CRO officers' use of the Crime Index to help him track down a murderer in Essex:

> There could not possibly be many men in the country who could carry out such awful violence. The Record Office at the Yard was there to help us. 'Give me' I asked 'a list of criminals who are known to use violence'. They gave me such a list. The first name I read on it was 'Frederick Guy Browne'.
>
> (Berrett, 1932: 13)

Browne was the murderer.

Local, group and regional CROs

The London CRO held a position of primacy as the agency mandated by statute to collate criminal records. In practice, more localised record systems now grew up at local, group and regional levels.

(a) Local CROs

In order to report records to London, local forces had of necessity to deploy officers and open specialist offices just for this purpose. Inevitably this led to forms of local CROs in some police forces with records on local criminals being duplicated and shared locally. Often these local offices became more valuable to their forces than the London-based one, which could be seen as distant and somewhat irrelevant. In Scotland the inspector of constabulary noted such offices to be found in Edinburgh, Glasgow, Aberdeen, Dundee, Perth, Greenock, Ayr, Dumfries, Stirling, Elgin and Inverness as early as 1904 (HMIC, 1905: iv).

One early pioneer of local records in England was Major Llewellyn Atcherley, the chief constable of the West Riding police in Yorkshire and the pioneer of analysing modus operandi. Atcherley opened his own CRO in Wakefield in 1908, recording local convictions and publishing the West Riding's own 'information' comparable to the national *Police Gazette.*

In practice, local CROs were organised in force headquarter offices and divided their work along the same divisions as London with Registration Records and Identification Records. There was variation in how organised they were, with some forces seeing it as a way to avoid contact with London altogether and some as a necessary – but minimal – local complement to London (Home Office, 1938: para. 215).

(b) Group CROs

Some forces had no CRO of their own but joined up with other forces to share a group CRO. Sometimes a large urban centre would offer this service to local satellite towns of smaller populations. At this time the United Kingdom had approximately 200 forces. County and borough forces having their respective headquarters in the same town might form group CROs.

The Home Office recognised the usefulness of group CROs and noted the way it generally encouraged better 'working together' across force boundaries (ibid: paras. 235–238).

(c) Regional CROs

An even bigger area could be covered by a series of forces electing to work through a regional CRO or 'clearing house' for information on criminals. An early proponent of such arrangements was Major Atcherley in Yorkshire.

Atcherley's West Riding was geographically so large it divided into 22 divisions and the experience of sharing records and information on crime over this area was now used to inform an even wider regional sharing. The Inspectorate of Constabulary reported:

> ...a somewhat new system, based on a simply understood classification of crime; and since the beginning of the year, with the co-operation of several neighbouring County and Borough Police Forces, (Atcherley) has established a 'clearing house' at Wakefield, which will no doubt lead to good results.
>
> (HMIC, 1914: 3–4)

These regional arrangements were not based on statute like the national system, but were an expedient exercise in decentralisation to speed up access to information and build confidence in the new bureaucratic skills of record keeping. Forces as far apart as Scotland and the south Midlands reportedly involved themselves with the Wakefield scheme (Devlin, 1966: 505). The information travelled along set 'routes' to assist the police in tracing mobile criminals.

When Major Atcherley moved on from chief constable to become an H. M. Inspector of Constabulary, he continued to be an advocate for 'clearing-house' arrangements. In his annual report for 1931 he said:

> Where a Clearing House institution has been at the disposal of neighbouring forces, the state of detection has correspondingly improved. I venture to express the hope that this organisation may be extended so as to reach other forces in a similar way.
>
> (HMIC, 1932: 7)

A year later he was able to identify eight co-ordination districts in England and Wales (HMIC, 1933: 12).

The Clearing House system was now seen as a means of detecting the 'travelling' criminal as car use and road networks improved. Informally it was a continuing recognition of problems in accessing the London records and the unreliability of their content. The Home Office formally endorsed the importance of local and regional CRO's or 'clearing-houses' in its 1938 review as long as they all recognised the primacy of the London CRO. The review recommended the West Riding 'clearing-house' be used as a model to develop similar arrangements for Liverpool, Birmingham, Cardiff and Bristol (Home Office, 1938: paras. 251 and 259).

'Schedule one offenders'

The Children and Young Persons Act 1933 covering the civil and criminal law relating to children contained a schedule at the end listing offences it was possible to commit against a child. The schedule was to help the police and others to implement the act. Over the years the Schedule One list – as it became known – has been added to and the 'Schedule One status' of those who have committed these offences passed into the language and folklore of child-protection professionals. The terminology is still used today, although the Home Office has recently decided that it is outmoded (see Chapter 3).

In strictly legal terms the Schedule One status did not mean very much, and did not, of itself, invoke any statutory consequences in terms of sanctions or interventions. All this status or label did was alert practitioners that this person has committed one of the designated offences in the schedule. It was effectively another form of identification. Child-protection procedures and legal interventions *may* have been brought into play but they were independent of the Schedule One status. All it meant was that an individual with a criminal record fell within a defined category.

Post-war years

After the Second World War the romanticised view of the central CRO continues to appear throughout the 1950s until the seeds of criticism start to show through in the 1960s. This was the era of the fictional 'Dixon of Dock Green' who 'embodied the quintessential beloved British bobby, and still stands as a regularly evoked ideal' (Reiner, 1992: 58).

Firmin described Scotland Yard as an organisation that puts everything down on paper and as a result has the reputation of 'an organisation that never forgets':

> The Criminal Record Office … contains the secrets and life histories of nearly a million people, any single one of which can be turned up in the space of a few minutes.
>
> (Firmin, 1949: 58)

The 1930s' adage that this was all about 'catching thieves on paper' continued to be quoted (Martienssen, 1953: 37) and Sir Harold Scott, the commissioner of the Metropolitan Police from 1945 to 1953, continued the 'Who's Who' simile:

> ...a national and international registry of crimes, a 'Who's Who' of their perpetrators, a means of enabling new crimes to be traced to old criminals, several crimes to be traced to the same person, and old criminals to be recognised with certainty when they are re-arrested.
>
> (Scott, 1954: 122)

The officers working in the CRO were noted to have the same memory for names and details that had existed pre-War, and 'as soon as a crime is reported, they are usually able, without looking at their cards, to name several "likely starters" ' (ibid: 125). The picture painted is that of a polished machine going smoothly about its business as 'a national library of wrongdoing' (Howard, 1953: 180) or even 'the greatest library of crime in the world' (Barr, 1962: 17).

As for the actual content of a file:

> ...in a limp folder of fawn coloured forms is recorded the criminal's name, date and place of birth, description, distinctive peculiarities, aliases, photographs and particulars of crimes, convictions and sentences. With all its cross referencing and cross checking, a CRO file is almost a biography.
>
> (Barr, 1962: 17)

Cross-referencing still took place to the Crime Index. The Crime Index with its modus operandi records had been transferred to punch cards:

> ...and the position of the hole indicates his habits, the method he uses, his favourite time for pulling off a job, the plans he normally makes for a getaway and a score of similar points. Turning up an individual card is a matter of seconds only.
>
> (Firmin, 1949: 60)

In 1952 the Home Office received a report from a Chief Constables' Working Party on 'Crime Circulations and Clearing Houses' and accepted what was, in effect, a belated endorsement of the 1938 Departmental Committee on Detective Work and Procedure (Home Office,

1938), the further implementation of which had been interrupted by the War (Home Office, 1952).

Meanwhile a more critical picture of the CRO at Scotland Yard was beginning to emerge:

> ...before and during the war, reporting to CRO by local police forces was less complete than it has been since...In consequence, a middle-aged recidivist's early convictions are very elusive, unless he himself is both communicative and gifted with total recall.
>
> (Walker, 1965: 245)

Reflecting on his career in the 1960s and in the context of new technological breakthroughs, a former director of administration at New Scotland Yard believed:

> ...the detection of crime and the apprehension of criminals have been greatly impeded by the inability to get much needed information quickly, even though it is almost certainly on record...(it was)...essential to set up a central bank of information readily and quickly accessible...this can only be done by installing an extremely powerful computer.
>
> (Walker, 1970)

In the early 1970s the CRO opened its doors to the American academic James Rule to report on its activities. Rule has also produced a less than romanticised picture in his account of the daily activities of the CRO (Rule, 1973: Chapter 2).

Rule found a CRO with 2.5 million names recorded on a Nominal or Criminal Names Index held on small slips in loose-leaf binders in alphabetical order and with a CRO number attached. This index led to the Criminal Records Files themselves, all filed numerically by their CRO number, and created in date order as required.

The Criminal Record File sub-divided into three parts:

1. The Criminal Record: the straightforward listing of the conviction history from the first to the most recent, complete with court, conviction sentence and relevant dates.
2. The Descriptive Form: including a description of the individual and a photograph as well as the circumstances of the arrests and details of the arresting officer and his force.

3. The Antecedents History: a statement of a person's background and history to be presented in court following a conviction along with the history of any previous convictions. This statement may contain details of a person's family, employment history, financial situation and associates.

> (Fictitious examples of these three forms are reproduced in Rule, 1973: 52–55)

The CRO was also responsible for cross referencing the Criminal Record File to the Fingerprint Office – as the main way of identifying offenders – and for maintaining other indices such as the Wanted and Missing Persons Index. A 'Distinguishing Marks File' was still held on known criminals – Firmin had called it the 'deformities' file (Firmin, 1949: 60) – and the Crime Index had become the Modus Operandi or Method Index, in turn sub-dividing into (a) an index of known criminals and (b) an index of unsolved crimes (Rule, 1973: 58–59). The former was said to be now further broken down into 800 headings of various crimes and associated traits (Laurie, 1970: 206).

Rule was yet another observer who felt disposed towards the 'library' simile describing the CRO as giving 'the distinct impression of the stacks of a closed-access library':

> Circling around and through the stacks is a system of trolleys, which move the files from the stacks to their destinations and return used files, and requests for new ones, to the staff.
>
> (Rule, 1973: 49)

Rule believed that the system was not as efficient as some police officers would like to believe. Responses to requests for information 'were often very slow' (ibid: 47) and this fact had in turn helped maintain the regional offices and local CROs as more accessible facilities:

> ...even requests by telephone or teleprint are subject to long delays, when all lines to the London headquarters are engaged...and one regional official even reports obtaining 'No trace' reports on persons known with certainty to have criminal records, suggesting that the frustrated staff of the London Offices have simply refused to check the files as requested.
>
> (ibid: 69)

Computerisation was seen by Rule as being the way forward and although he could foresee obstacles to computerising the whole of the Criminal Record Files it was 'concrete and realistic' to begin with some of the simpler indices (ibid: 86).

Regional Criminal Record Offices

In the 1950s the term 'clearing house' was replaced by that of Regional Criminal Record Offices and formal recognition was accorded by the Home Office and H. M. Inspectorate of Constabulary. By 1956 regional CROs had been established in Wakefield, Birmingham, Manchester, Liverpool and Preston, and following the recommendation of the 1952 Chief Constables' Working Party, financial arrangements were put in place by the Home Office to help more regional CROs come into existence (HMIC, 1957: para. 61).

New regional CROs were opened in Bristol in 1958 (HMIC, 1959: para. 57), Cardiff and Durham in 1959 (HMIC, 1960: para. 55) and the Scottish Criminal Record Office (SCRO) was opened in 1960. What impact these developments had on morale at New Scotland Yard we can only speculate, but in 1962 they themselves were party to trying to organise a regional CRO from their London offices to serve the south-east of England, known as 'no. 6 District'. This so-called Number 6 District Crime Bureau opened in October 1962 as something just less than a regional CRO and:

> ... cannot operate to the extent of a Regional Criminal Record Office, but is in a position to make good use of the facilities available in the Criminal Record Office New Scotland Yard and is fulfilling an increasingly useful function in the policing of no. 6 District.
>
> (HMIC, 1964: 49)

Later, the constituent constabularies making up District 6 created their own Group Record Offices to replace the arrangements based at Scotland Yard. These Group Record Offices also fell short of regional CRO designation but were more locally based in Winchester (for the Hampshire police), Brighton (Sussex), Maidstone (Kent) and Guildford (Surrey) (HMIC, 1968: 46).

According to Rule, the regional office was a duplicate of the London office but did allow for easier access and 'experiment(s) with different techniques of organisation of filed material':

...but every variety of information filed at New Scotland Yard has its counterpart in the regional offices, and the similarity even extends to the physical appearance of the installations. The banks of telephones, the telex machine, the rows of filed cards...are equally distinctive of the regional offices and of New Scotland Yard.

(Rule, 1973: 59–60)

Rule also thought the regional offices took work off the national centre with its 'enormous accumulation of information and ever-increasing demand for service' (ibid: 68) and only with the advent of computerisation would the police be able 'to convert all records, regional and national, from criminal record offices...to computer storage in a single central location' (ibid: 85).

Since 1869 and the origins of the centralised criminal record collection, there had been a process of decentralisation taking it back to the provinces. Only the promise of computerisation from the 1970s onwards would take it back to anything approaching a centralised system. In 1974 the Police National Computer (PNC) came online and in 1977 an index to the names in the criminal record collection was added to its functions (for more on the PNC, see Chapter 4).

The National Identification Bureau

In order to better reflect the nature of the work now being carried out, the central CRO and the Fingerprint Office were amalgamated into the National Identification Bureau (NIB) in 1980. The criminal records themselves were now being transferred to microfiche from their old card and paper index base, albeit not without some difficulties ('Criminal delays at Scotland Yard', *The Observer*, 6 September 1981). The Method Index was still kept as a manual system.

A further addition to the PNC was that of Convictions History in 1985 for all new conviction records coming to notice after 1 January 1981. The Home Office believed this 'should greatly reduce the need for forces to telephone the National Identification Bureau' and produce 'savings in time and effort at force level' (Home Office, 1984: para. 2). Local forces still had the laborious job of reporting information on manual forms to the NIB; the NIB74A form with details of an arrest or summons and the NIB74B for the final decisions from court (see Home Office, 1991: Annex B and C for the format of these forms).

The terminology developed of 'reportable' offences that had to be sent in to the NIB. Reportable offences were generally those that could incur a prison sentence (whether or not they had) plus other offences designated as needing to be reported. Just to confuse matters the Regulations listing what these other offences were, called them 'recordable' (e.g. National Police Records (Recordable Offences) Regulations 1985, SI 1985/1941). To that extent 'reportable' and 'recordable' offences appeared to be synonymous terms at this time, but when all criminal records became computerised from 1995 onwards the term 'reportable' became historical. Officers across the country could now record them, themselves, directly on to the PNC without any reporting to the NIB (see Chapter 3). Pre-1995 the NIB acted as a central conduit through which all these forms from around the country passed. It enabled the officers working there to act as a form of quality control over what went on to the PNC records.

Conclusions

Once the Victorians had decided they needed a system of recording criminals it was not long before a rudimentary national repository of criminal records was started. The statutory underpinning of the new collection of records – or 'register' as it was initially called – was the Habitual Criminals Act 1869 and the Prevention of Crimes Act 1871.

The criminal records collection was allied with the identification work of the fingerprint office to create the first national CRO in 1913. Local and regional offices later developed which sometimes duplicated the collection held nationally in London. Given the limited communications systems of the time, this was accepted as necessary and even encouraged and the criminal records system effectively decentralised itself over the next 50 years.

In the 1960s the advent of the computer and information technology suggested that decentralisation was not as important as it had been. The creation of the PNC in 1974 was followed by a limited application being added to it for criminal names in 1977, and the establishing of the NIB in 1980. The foundations had been completed for the building of the centralised criminal record system as we know it today.

3
Contemporary Criminal Record Maintenance

As the 1980s came to an end the police held a hybrid collection of criminal records on computer and microfiche. Mostly this was held centrally at the NIB with indexes and some conviction records available through the Police National Computer. The 1990s would see a growing dissatisfaction with this state of affairs and the full computerisation of all records on to the PNC by the turn of the century. The NIB would become the National Identification Service (NIS) and downsized to a much reduced residual role, as police officers across the country were now able directly to input the records they held.

The Police National Computer (PNC)

The Police National Computer came on line in 1974 and within a decade it would have a central role in the maintenance of the national criminal record repository.

From the mid-1960s onwards, the Home Office and police forces had started to discuss the possibility of putting police records on to computer. A Home Office letter of 6 December 1965 advised forces of the feasibility studies taking place and a 1969 circular brought them up to date on progress and drew police authorities into the debate (Home Office, 1969). Vehicle details would be the first category to go on the Police National Computer, as the project was now called, followed by an index to fingerprints and then the Criminal Names Index; the project would be based in Hendon, North London, and secure communications networks would link it to an anticipated 670 terminals across the country (ibid).

Walker estimated a need for 800 terminal points to bring instant information to 'the constable on a lonely beat' (Walker, 1970). He also warned of the possibility of releasing 'suppressed demand', a phenomenon already experienced in the United States of America. In the past, if the police knew information would not be available or it would take too long to get hold of it, they would simply not request it. Now that it would become much more readily available the demand could be expected to rise by as much as five times (ibid).

The Police National Computer went live in 1974. It was an apocryphal story that its name was not the National Police Computer because the Home Office did not want any 'national' associations with anything to do with policing. Hiding that word in the middle of the computer's name was the best that could be done.

Since its inception the PNC has been progressively developed and enhanced 'from a record keeping service to a sophisticated source of intelligence' (PITO, n.d.: 1). Different indices or applications were progressively added over the years including Stolen Vehicles (1974), Fingerprints (1976), people Wanted or Missing (1978), Property and Property Descriptive Search (1991) and so on (for more on the early days of the PNC see Bunyan, 1977: 85ff; Campbell, 1980; Campbell and Connor, 1986: Chapter 8).

Work began on adding the Criminal Names Index to the PNC in 1977 and was completed the following year when the system went live. The Index was a simple cross-referencing device linking to the existing manual records held by the CRO. Dr Shirley Summerskill for the Home Office told the Commons that this could involve a total of 3.8 million names but allayed any fears of an emerging Orwellian database by reassuring the House that the PNC would only be replicating what was already being done manually:

> ...the computer will store information at present kept on paper in New Scotland Yard about crime, criminals and their associates...the system will not become operational until next year.
>
> (Hansard HC Debates, 2 December 1977, cols. 445–446)

All new Conviction Histories coming to notice after 1 January 1981 were also added to the PNC in 1985. Local forces passed their records manually to the NIB who input them to the computer.

This new work for the PNC was taking its toll on the original 1974 model, and by the late 1980s arrangements were in hand to upgrade it. Not least this would enable *all* criminal record information to go on the

PNC. Gordon Wasserman, under-secretary of state at the Home Office, made the case:

> Although we have all the criminal names on PNC1 as well as the previous convictions of persons convicted since 1981, we do not have the entire national collection of criminal records. PNC2 will give us this collection as a single, comprehensive computerised system.
>
> (Wasserman, 1989)

The upgraded PNC 2 was said to be faster, more secure and able to present information more clearly and with the use of colour for the first time (Grundy, 1990). It now linked to over 2600 terminals, 200 printers and 41 police local computers through key switching points in the Midlands, the North of England, Scotland and Wales (Home Office, 1991; see also Hansard HC Debates, 3 February 1992, cols. 104–114 for a rare Parliamentary debate on the PNC). The full criminal record – the Phoenix Application – was put on to the PNC in 1995 (see below).

In 1996 the PNC management was taken over by PITO (Police Information Technology Organisation) and after further upgrading was accessible to some 30,000 terminals by 2006 (PITO, 2006; for more on PITO see Chapter 4). The PNC is now available through mobile terminals placed in police cars and in some forces through personal hand-held computers to all officers. In West Yorkshire, for example, 2500 officers have access to the PNC and other local intelligence, including the electoral registers for the constituent local authorities of West Yorkshire, through hand-held computers (West Yorkshire Police, 2006).

As the PNC has developed and grown in stature, its customers have also grown. In 1992 Parliament was told that only the Driver and Vehicle Licensing Agency (DVLA) and H. M. Customs and Excise had direct access to the PNC for 'read only' purposes, although plans to improve the speed of communications between the PNC and individual forces 'could be extended later to other agencies in the criminal justice system' (Hansard HC Debates, 3 February 1992, cols. 109–110). Today this position has changed. Apart from servicing the needs of the 43 police forces in England and Wales, the eight forces of Scotland and the Northern Ireland Police Service, other smaller police forces and specialist units have direct access to the PNC as do a number of non-police agencies – some of them beyond the criminal justice system – who have demonstrated a need for access.

A list of some of these other forces, specialist units and non-police agencies has been compiled in Table 3.1. This is not presented as

Table 3.1 Agencies having direct access to the Police National Computer

British Transport Police
Civil Nuclear Constabulary (previously the UK Atomic Energy Authority
    Constabulary)
Isle of Man Police
States of Jersey Police
Guernsey Police
Ministry of Defence Police
Royal Military Police
RAF Police
Secret Intelligence Service
Security Service
National Ports Office
National Identification Service
National Criminal Intelligence Service
National Crime Squad
Scottish Crime Squad
Scottish Criminal Record Office
Northern Ireland Criminal Record Office
Regional Criminal Intelligence Offices
Port of Dover Police
Hendon Data Centre
Police Staff College, Bramshill
Police Information Communication Technology Training Services (PICTTS),
    Leicester
Immigration Service
H. M. Revenue and Customs
Post Office
Financial Services Authority*
National Health Service*
Department of Trade and Industry*
Office of Fair Trading*
Central Summoning Bureau (Dept. of Constitutional Affairs)
Department of Work and Pensions* (previously Dept. of Social Security)
Criminal Records Bureau
Forensic Science Service
Motor Insurance Database
H. M. Prisons (some of them)
National Enforcement Service
Drivers Vehicle and Licensing Authority
Schengen Information System

* for prosecution purposes only
Sources: Hansard HC Debates, 22 March 1995, col. 200; 18 April 1995, cols. 87–88;
26 April 1995, cols. 566–567; 5 February 2002, col. 858W; 8 July 2003, col. 716W;
15 July 2003, col. 278W; 4 July 2005, col. 63WA. *PITO News*, Issue no. 8 (pp. 14–15);
no. 9 (p. 3); no. 29 (p. 11); no. 30 (pp. 8–9); no. 35 (pp. 8–9). Home Office (2003a)
Annex B Group 4

a definitive list but as examples of how wide the dissemination of information on the PNC has reached. Access is agreed by an ACPO (Association of Chief Police Officers) 'PNC Access Application Panel' and 'PNC Data Access Agreements' duly drawn up; those with direct access must comply with the ACPO Information Systems' 'Community Security Policy' (ACPO, 2003).

Most of these recipients of PNC-held data have 'read only' access and no facility to update. Some only have access to one database such as the DVLA with its access to vehicle information and some only have access to names of people with a criminal record rather than the full record from Phoenix (as explained at Hansard HC Debates, 18 April 1995, cols. 87–88).

A customs officer, for example, has described how they use the PNC:

> .. we're able to use the PNC to gain background information ... what we want to know is if someone we suspect – say of drugs smuggling – has a criminal record or if a vehicle has any markers against it. So we have limited access to the PNC databases for vehicles and names.
>
> ('PNC keeps Customs and Excise in the picture',
> *PITO News*, 14 December 1998)

A total of 1638 customs officers out of 25,000 reportedly had access across the United Kingdom (ibid).

In prisons, access has proved particularly useful with the assessment and categorisation of newly arrived prisoners; 38 prisons had access by 1999 (Prison Service Order 1999, no. 0905).

The spreading use of the PNC has been facilitated by the PITO Directorate in charge of the computer (see Chapter 4 for more on PITO). The 'Phoenix Links' project sought out new customers after 2001 and this later became known as the PNC Application Integration Infrastructure. According to PITO's director of operational services at the time:

> ... we saw the need some years ago to develop a new approach for the implementation of system-to-system links between PNC and the increasing number of applications that were beginning to arise on third party systems.
>
> (quoted in 'Jurors technology breaks new ground',
> *PITO News*, Issue 30, 2002)

Exactly how many agencies have a direct link is uncertain as no definitive list appears to exist. A four-page document describing non-police users of the PNC as at 29 April 2002 was produced at an Information Tribunal hearing in 2005, but this document has not been made public. The list was shown to David Smith, the assistant information commissioner, during the hearing:

> ...it is fair to say that Mr. Smith expressed some surprise...at the length of the listed organisations (and)...he asked the not unnatural question 'is it really necessary for all these organisations individually to have access?'
>
> (The Chief Constables of West Yorkshire, South Yorkshire and North Wales Police and the Information Commissioner, Information Tribunal, 2005: at para. 126)

When asked in Parliament how many *individuals* (as opposed to agencies) have access to the PNC, Home Office ministers always say the information is not available (see, e.g. Hansard HC Debates, 22 January 2004, col. 1440W and 9 February 2006, cols. 1436–1437W).

Apart from exact numbers and lists of those with access, the spreading use of the PNC could be feeding a culture that says this information is not that confidential after all. Informal access may be growing alongside the formal. Co-operation between the police and housing departments, for example, has been encouraged to tackle crime and anti-social behaviour. In Nottingham, a housing official has explained how they get information from the PNC, working from the same premises as the police:

> ...we actually had a PNC terminal here, so I could literally go to the sergeant and say 'have you got anything on this individual?' and within a matter of minutes...he could give me information on that individual.
>
> (cited in Burney, 2005: 126)

Housing departments have no direct access to the PNC but working together and sharing information has made access fairly easy. The use of vehicle-based terminals and hand-held terminals arguably makes the 'policing' of confidentiality even more difficult.

In April 2006 the government announced its intention to replace the PNC as such by a new Police National Database costing £367 million and due for implementation by 2010. While this new database was under development, funding would be made available 'to update the hardware platform of the PNC (to) ensure it remains fit for purpose until the Police National Database is fully in service' (Hansard HC Debates, 19 April 2006, cols. 18–19WS).

Data quality – 'a terrifying condition of inaccuracy'

The House of Commons Home Affairs Committee had started an enquiry into the work of the Crown Prosecution Service in 1990 when, in the course of that enquiry, it received evidence about the quality of data held in the national collection of criminal records. The committee decided to divert its energies to 'undertake a short inquiry into (criminal records and) their maintenance and use'; the Law Society, for example, had told them the records were in 'a terrifying condition of inaccuracy' (House of Commons, 1990a: paras. 1–3).

The problem was located in the reporting of information to the NIB for inclusion in the national collection. On average it was taking 77 days for the police to supply arrest information and court results on their NIB74A and NIB74B forms. This delay was in turn attributed to the fact that no one had clear ownership of the work. The courts and the Crown Prosecution Service had the court results but the police were the only ones who could input them to the records held at the NIB. Various forms of liaison existed but the outcome was clumsy and laboured and this was the 'heart of the complaint' with as many as '30,000 records still incomplete after two and a half years' (ibid: para. 8). The committee saw the answer as full computerisation on to the PNC, followed by giving the court clerks, rather than the police, the job of directly inputting court results to the national collection (ibid: para. 11). More controversially it suggested taking criminal record maintenance away from the police and giving it to a new independent agency (ibid: para. 41).

In 1990 this recommendation for computerisation was still a relatively long-term resolution of the problem. In the meantime it was suggested that the Lord Chancellor's department lay down time limits in which court clerks had to get information to the police (ibid: para. 10).

The government was generally welcoming of the committee's report, which it saw as supporting its own long-term plans to computerise the entire national collection of criminal records. It also accepted some of the short-term recommendations such as new target times for inputting information to the NIB. It was not convinced of the need for a new independent agency to take criminal record maintenance off the police but it was prepared to commission an immediate scrutiny study to examine how the needs of the police, courts and others could best be met (Home Office, 1990a).

The Home Office Scrutiny Report

A team from the Home Office carried out the required 'scrutiny' study. They confirmed the parlous state of the data quality in the national collection, describing it variously as being 'in a very unsatisfactory state' (Home Office, 1991: para. 19) and in 'a very fragile state' (ibid: para. 106). Their recommendations on the way forward were divided into long-term and short-term proposals.

In the long-term, the Scrutiny Report felt only computerisation was going to resolve the problem, and that computerisation had to be not just for the police but carried out for the whole of the criminal justice system. The aim would be to make the records available to multiple users online (ibid: para. 23). This was going to have to be a well-led disciplined strategy, building on the upgrading of the PNC2 and the already running Coordination of Computerisation in the Criminal Justice System (CCCJS) (see Chapter 4), and in turn the aim included a number of objectives:

- the national collection should go on the PNC and local Criminal Record Offices be closed down;
- police cautions should be added in;
- the present record content remain broadly unchanged;
- all existing elements of a record should be maintained;
- access to speculative search of the collection and to those parts that extended beyond criminal history should be subject to statutory control;
- a new national agency should take over the national collection from the police following computerisation;
- that agency should be self-funding from fees charged to users; users would include the police.

(Home Office, 1991: para. 48)

The proposed new national agency represented a change of direction for the Home Office and it was given the working title of the 'National Criminal Records Agency' with responsibility for England and Wales with links to Scotland and Northern Ireland.

The Scrutiny Report found the Scottish system, organised around the SCRO, to stick out something like a sore thumb. In contrast to the system for England and Wales, and its 'fragile state', the criminal records office for Scotland was strong and well developed. Scottish chief constables were understandably found to be hesitant about any new UK national developments 'until they were satisfied that it provided a service as good as or better than that available through SCRO' (ibid: para. 26). The SCRO system was already 'fully computerised and provides the capability of speculative search' (ibid: para. 25). The only negative the Scrutiny Report could come up with was that the SCRO systems were 'relatively old' and would soon need upgrading; otherwise 'the English should not be too proud to borrow good ideas from Scotland' (ibid: para. 29).

In the short term, the Scrutiny Report suggested a number of measures to improve data quality within the existing manual system. An Advisory Committee was suggested to oversee the work of the NIB and monitor compliance with new target deadlines for inputting information. The police, it was proposed, should input all arrests within 5 days and court results within 10 days; the courts were given a deadline of 3 days to get results to the police (ibid: Annex M).

The government made a statement in response to the Scrutiny Report, saying it needed more time for 'detailed consideration'. The only recommendations immediately endorsed were that cautions should be part of the record and the idea of a new national agency holding the national collection *was* now accepted having been discounted a year before in responding to the Home Affairs Committee Report. The government reply also re-stated the view that this new national agency should organise and manage the national collection 'for the benefit of the Criminal Justice System as a whole' (Hansard HC Debates, 22 October 1991, col. 531WA).

On the question of local and regional CROs, the Scrutiny Report had recommended that they be closed as no longer necessary, now that information technology was so advanced. The report estimated some 2.8 million records kept in London were simply being duplicated and maintained in the provinces 'at a salary cost of £2.2 million' (Home Office, 1991: para. 2(c)). This money could be saved if local offices were closed, although H. M. Inspectorate of Constabulary would need to be vigilant 'to monitor any tendency for local record systems to re-germinate after they have been abolished' (ibid: para. 59).

As for those records only maintained locally – minor crimes and cautions – the government agreed with the Scrutiny Report that they would in future have to be stored in London:

> ... in order to eliminate the need for local record systems, the national computerised records system will have to hold information on a wider range of offences.
>
> (Hansard HC Debates, 22 October 1991, col. 531WA)

Phoenix

The Scrutiny Report and the government's statement gave impetus to the Home Office and the police work already started on converting the national collection of criminal records into a computerised form. The PNC was to host the collection on a new application to be known as Phoenix (Police-Home Office Extended Names Index).

Initial inquiries were made of a firm in the Philippines to carry out this conversion process but members of Parliament were not impressed. Not only did they dislike the idea of confidential criminal records leaving the country but they had heard worrying reports about the firm in question. Saztec Philippines were said to have a militaristic organisation, including staff uniforms, and to prefer non-union employees of which 10 per cent were deaf mutes. On their 1-day off a week, staff were required to visit patients in psychiatric hospitals, including those described as 'criminally insane' (Cohen, 1992).

A more acceptable contract was agreed with the UK-based company PCL to carry out what was now referred to as the Back Record Conversion (BRC) exercise. All the records held on microfiche by the NIB would be transferred to the PNC Phoenix application, which would replace the old Names Record or Index started on the PNC in 1977. Four elements of information were to be held:

- Nominal/Descriptive – a person's name and description
- Offence processing – arrest, summons, remand, conviction
- Wanted/Missing persons
- Disqualified drivers

The NIB itself would have a reduced role and would no longer act as the central point through which NIB74A and NIB74B forms would be filtered. The NIB was also to be re-named as the NIS.

Local forces would in future become responsible for the accuracy and completeness of information added to Phoenix and information could be input and accessed by officers across the country at any of 10,000 terminals; today the figure is put at 30,000 terminals. Each name on the database had a PNC Identity Number (PNCID no.) and if necessary a Criminal Record Office Number (CRO no.) allocated by the new NIS cross-reference with fingerprints, a Search File Number (SF no.) if no fingerprints were held, and an Arrest/Summons Reference Number to refer to a specific arrest or summons.

Phoenix formally went live on 22 May 1995 although the police readiness for it was questioned in some quarters. When Home Secretary Michael Howard spoke at the Police Federation conference the same month, delegates reportedly laughed when he spoke of the level of training and preparation that had preceded the arrival of Phoenix (Graham, 1995).

The BRC exercise was also proving laborious and time consuming. The microfiche record had to be scanned and then sent to the contractors – PCL – for keying, then returned to the police for quality assurance and the resolution of any other problems before finally being loaded on to Phoenix. The BRC was slow and cumbersome and over a year later only 286,000 records had been entered from a total of over 5 million (Hansard HC Debates, 16 July 1996, 33WA). A degree of dissatisfaction set in and the PCL contract – worth £8.6 million – was ended by mutual agreement ('PCL loses criminal records job', *Computing*, 26 September 1996).

The Home Office cited 'technical difficulties, complex equipment and the nature of the records' as the reason for slow progress, and a senior police officer said that, even when loaded on to Phoenix, some records just came out as 'gobbledegook' (Tendler, 1996a). The number of records converted stood at 320,000 by November 1996 (Hansard HC Debates, 5 November 1996, col. 438) and over 3 years later had only risen to 500,000 (HMIC, 1999: para. 6.20). Despite all the publicity attendant on Phoenix going live in 1995, the truth was that the police were still handling 'some 8000 microfiche enquiries on a weekly basis' over 4 years later, and the Home Office funding for the BRC was about to run out (ibid).

The Metropolitan Police Service, NIS – see below – took over the BRC but had to do it on a 'come to notice' basis. In other words, the microfiche records were converted as and when other police forces or agencies needed the old records or an offender with an old record was newly arrested or charged. By August 2005 just over 1.28 million records had still not been back record converted (personal communication, 16 May 2006). New offenders with no previous records were, of course, going straight on to Phoenix.

The National Identification Service

The NIS was formed at the same time as the criminal record collection was computerised on to the Phoenix application of the PNC in 1995. The NIS replaced the earlier NIB. From its inception the NIS has experienced a prolonged period of change and an ever-reducing workload; by 1999 it had lost approximately 33 per cent of its staff (HMIC, 1999: para. 6.19).

The organisation and functions of the NIS is outlined on their website which is a part of the Metropolitan Police Service website (www.met.police.uk/). The NIS structure broadly divides into three, covering criminal records, fingerprints and general resources.

On the criminal records side the NIS still has responsibility for the microfiche collection of records that has not been put on to Phoenix and since June 2001 it has responsibility for the BRC exercise to put these records into electronic form. Some 60 staff are allocated to this BRC work.

The NIS also keeps the Phoenix application on the PNC names database up to date. H. M. Prison Service provides details of custodial sentences' ending or prisoners being released on licence. Other agencies such as the armed services, Interpol and other government departments input information as appropriate. The NIS makes approximately 160,000 updates a year, to complement the major part of the updating that now goes on by all 43 police forces across the country.

The NIS provides intelligence and non-conviction information to the CRB to enable the CRB to complete Enhanced Disclosures on people living in the London area (see Chapter 7). This work is carried out by the 110 staff of the NIS Character Enquiry Centre. A further 16 members of staff work in the Vetting section, providing criminal records and other information for national security vetting purposes (see Chapter 4). Individuals wishing to exercise their 'subject access' rights under the Data Protection Act to see what information the police are holding on them are also dealt with by the NIS.

The Method Index remains the responsibility of the NIS and is now referred to as the National Method Index and kept on the Method Office Computer. In December 2002 the National Method Index was joined to the section of NIS publishing the weekly *Police Gazette* to form the NIS Intelligence Section (NISIS).

The National Fingerprint Office is a self-contained entity within the NIS. Individual forces have been able to process and store fingerprints on the national collection through the electronic 'Livescan' system and NAFIS/IDENT 1 since 2001 and the NFO now provides assistance to forces in this task and maintains the National Fingerprint Archive for fingerprints stored before 2001.

The Sex Offender 'register'

In 1997 a sub-set of criminal convictions was created that would become known as the Sex Offender 'register'. Unlike the 1933 arrangements for the list of 'Schedule One offences' (offences against children) the 1997 list – or 'register' – had specific legal duties attached to it.

The Sex Offender 'register' was to enable the police and other authorities to keep better track of where known sex offenders lived, in the hope of preventing further offending and acting as a deterrence towards those on the 'register'. Some local authorities had been known to be compiling their own 'do it yourself' criminal records databases for known offenders in their area in the interests of better child protection; the Home Office had made it known that it was not altogether happy with such arrangements (Home Office *et al.*, 1991: paras. 6.52–6.54). Manchester City Council was one authority that admitted it was trying to put together a database along these lines ('City aims for sex fiend file', *Manchester Evening News*, 5 September 1996).

The official sex offender 'register' came online 1 September 1997 and obviated the need for local authorities to compile their own lists. Anyone convicted of one of the designated offences would in future have to notify the police every time they changed their address or their name; failure to do so would be an offence in itself (Sex Offender Act 1997; now Sexual Offences Act 2003, ss. 80–93; see also Thomas, 2004).

The idea of the 'register' came from the *United States of America* and the Home Office originally proposed that 32 offences should be designated as requiring 'notification' (Home Office, 1996a). The Sex Offenders Act 1997 would later reduce this to just 12, although it had to add in the different offences applicable in Scotland and Northern Ireland – something the original 1996 White Paper had overlooked. Since then further offences have been added in by the Sexual Offences Act 2003 and the list now stands at 35 (England), 25 (Scotland) and 32 (Northern Ireland) (see 2003 Act, Schedule 3); as stated above the 'register' is simply a sub-set of criminal records held on the PNC (ACPO, 1997: paras. 5–6). On 20 October 2006, 29,973 names were on the sex offender register (NPS, 2006).

The 'register' can be interrogated on the PNC by software known as QUEST (Query Using Extended Search Techniques) to reveal, for example, the number of offenders living in a particular geographic area (Orr-Munro, 2001). The 'register' has also now been supplemented by a new national information system available to the police and probation services called ViSOR (Violent and Sex Offender Register). The ViSOR contains information on offenders including descriptive details, activity logs, risk assessments, a photographic library and modus operandi; it is linked to the PNC and thus directly to criminal record information (Home Office, 2005a).

Schedule One Offenders – an update

Schedule One of the 1933 Children and Young Persons Act listed offences it was possible to commit against children (see Chapter 2). In 2005 the Home Office suggested the term 'Schedule One Offender' be discontinued.

The fear has been that some contemporary practitioners and professionals have been overly directive with Schedule One offenders by suggesting that their status alone means they 'have to do this' or 'they cannot do that'. One Home Office commissioned report has said, for example, that:

> …conviction for any sex offence against a child carries *heavy consequences* in terms of imposing Schedule One status under the Children and Young Persons Act 1933.
>
> (Home Office, 2000a; emphasis added)

The point is made again that any such consequences would require new legal applications and are not an automatic result of the Schedule One status.

Even the very labelling of the Schedule One offender is a hit-and-miss affair. In prison it is now formalised under Home Office guidance and requires the prisoner to be informed by the governor during their sentence. The prisoner must formally sign an acknowledgement that they know they have been so designated and that probation and the local authority social services will be informed of their release back into the community along with details of the address at which they will be going to live at. Any other consequences will be for the 'social service department alone to decide' (H. M. Prison Service, 1994: Annex C, para. 4). No such formalities exist within, say, the probation service for people who receive non-custodial sentences for offences against children.

The Home Office has been concerned that many of today's childcare practitioners do not know the origins of the 'Schedule One status' and are even 'unsure of which offences are included in Schedule One' (Home Office, 2005b: para. 4).

In 2004 a multi-agency working party began looking at the whole concept of the Schedule One and just how useful it was. The Home Office was concerned that a focus only on a person's past – in terms of a criminal record – was not necessarily the *sole* factor that should be looked at in terms of possible future behaviour. They cited the Risk of Sexual Harm Order that could now be applied for, to stop adults 'grooming' children even if the adult had no criminal record at all (Sexual Offences Act 2003, ss. 123–129). An interim Home Office circular to the police and directors of social services suggested the terminology be dropped and replaced with the phrase 'a person identified as presenting a risk, or potential risk, to children' (Home Office, 2005b: para. 4). Later guidance confirmed that the term was no longer to be used and advised practitioners that it had been replaced by the more succinct phrase 'risk to children' (H. M. Government, 2006: paras. 12.4–12.5). Of course by disconnecting the terminology from the anchor of a known criminal record, the scope of who might present a risk to children was greatly extended.

Data quality – continuing problems

The accuracy and completeness of the national criminal record collection has been a continuing problem for the police. We have noted the findings of James Rule and others in the 1970s and of the Home Affairs Committee report and subsequent Scrutiny Report in the early 1990s. In 1994 magistrates were still complaining that 'the problem of obtaining up to date information about a defendant's previous convictions is nationwide' (*The Magistrate*, February 1994 50(1): 20).

The police for their part were at least able to find some humour in the situation. Examples of mistakes and double entendres in the records made their way to the tabloid press. They included:

'When being spoken to, his left eye glides to the centre of his face where it is stopped by his nose'.

('Baffling case of gliding eyeball', *Daily Mirror*, 22 April 1993)

We were told:

'The Yard's National Identification Bureau which receives police arrest forms from all over the country, has had a good laugh over the clangers. It admits some officers aren't too particular when they're taking down particulars'.

(ibid)

The Home Affairs Committee and the Scrutiny Report had pinned their hopes on the advent of computerisation to achieve better quality data and the arrival of Phoenix in 1995 seemed to hold out the promise of better things to come. In practice, the problems of data quality have continued.

In 1996 an internal PITO report criticised the levels of data quality within the criminal record collection and the lack of urgency on the part of the police to do anything about it (PITO, 1996), and 2 years later a report commissioned by the Home Office Police Research Group confirmed the poor state of affairs (Russell, 1998). Not only was data quality poor but the police were failing to utilise the benefits of computerisation to make better use of the criminal record collection to reduce and detect crime.

The Police Research Group report laid part of the blame on the 1995 computerisation exercise itself and the procedural arrangements for inputting data on to Phoenix and the fact that 'no two forces have in place identical working practices' (ibid: 26). Whereas in the past, the NIB had acted as a central point and could exercise some 'quality control' over input; computerisation meant information was coming in from all quarters across the country with no national standards of accuracy, completeness or timeliness. The replacement NIS had relinquished any such role.

Poor information recording practices included police officers recording data in the wrong place or providing insufficient or irrelevant information. Instances were cited of officers 'making up' data if it was not known or could not be remembered, before passing it for entry to the PNC; such information was usually seen to be the 'non-essential' information (ibid: 8).

Additional problems occurred when external agencies still failed to play their part. A number of forces cited delays in receiving criminal conviction information from Magistrates' Courts and Crown Courts. Despite the 3-day deadline magistrates courts were now supposed to be meeting (Home Office, 1991: Annex M) delays were still being experienced of between 'two and ten days (and) in some instances extending to as much as three or four weeks' (Russell, 1998: 29). Crown Courts were even worse, with delays of 2 weeks being normal and some instances of delays lasting 6–18 months:

> (One) force had not received a Crown Court result for over twelve months. This only came to light when a person came in to a police station to register as a sex offender.
>
> (ibid: 31)

In turn, poor records could be re-produced in court where they caused additional problems:

> Our backlog was so bad, judges were complaining the force's records were not up to date. In one case the Superintendent was called to account in court. The offender had served three years for rape and this had not yet been recorded.

and

> We reported no previous history for the offender. We subsequently discovered he had six previous convictions sitting in our backlog of records. But the offender had already been bailed.
>
> (ibid: 33)

The Report recommended senior officers get more involved and ACPO produce national standards on timeliness and data. A national format for information input – Phoenix Source Documents – was also recommended as was a 'Phoenix awareness' module to be introduced at various levels of police training (ibid: 41–42; see also Thomas, 2001).

The ACPO responded to the criticisms (see also Simons, 2000) with its own 'Compliance Strategy for the Police National Computer' (reproduced at HMIC, 2000a: Appendix I). The strategy endorsed the need to improve data quality and further emphasised the need to be seen to be acting ethically and professionally with the pending implementation of the Human Rights Act 1998 and the Data Protection Act 1998. Added to this was a concern to be maximising the potential of the PNC for investigative and intelligence purposes in the era of 'intelligence led policing' (ibid).

Police officers were now expected to comply with Timeliness Performance Indicators and to input Phoenix Source Documents on arrests and charge within 24 hours, with 90 per cent expected to be done in that time; this could include just initial details known as 'skeleton records', but they had to be fully entered within 5 days. A 100 per cent of all court results had to be entered within 72 hours of coming into police possession. Further performance indicators covered the content of the Phoenix Source Documents and included the requirement to include 'methods' or modus operandi (in 90 per cent of cases), location of offences postcode (95 per cent) and descriptive marks such as scars, abnormalities, and so on (95 per cent) (ibid: 132). H. M. Inspectorate of Constabulary followed up this initial report in 2000 with further reports over the next

2 years. The inspectorate carried out compliance exercises on individual forces and evidence of improvement was found (HMIC, 2002).

In January 2005 the performance indicators of the ACPO 'Compliance Strategy' were replaced by a new statutory 'Code of Practice for the Police National Computer' in order to ensure the data quality of criminal conviction records (for more on this code, see below).

The identification of offenders

A collection of criminal records – however well maintained – is of limited use without a means of identifying the person you want. The Victorians had realised this when they started the original Habitual Criminals Register (see Chapter 2) and their solution had been the Register of Distinctive Marks and later the use of fingerprints. In the 1980s fingerprints still held sway as the main form of identification used by the police, but it would now be joined by new techniques including DNA sampling.

Fingerprints

The central Fingerprint Office had come under the umbrella of the NIB in 1980 to maintain a central collection of fingerprints. Local forces kept their own records, and sometimes shared a 'fingerprint bureau' with other forces. In 1988 the Audit Commission was critical of the police use of fingerprints, and noted variable usage around the country and low motivation amongst officers engaged in the work. The answer lay in new technology and 'high speed, computerised automatic fingerprint recognition and retrieval' (Audit Commission, 1988: 2).

Attempts to automate the matching of prints with scenes of crime had started in the 1970s, but despite the promptings of the Audit Commission, the Home Office seemed happy to leave things to the market to provide. One senior scientist felt this was cynical:

> ...those of us who have worked many years to see that our police forces are equipped with effective, modern, crime-fighting techniques know that commerce left to its own devices will develop the wrong equipment for the wrong reasons and usually mislead police forces into thinking they need it.
>
> (quoted in Kirby, 1990)

In 1992 a consortium of 37 police forces decided to go it alone and bought into the IBM Automatic Fingerprint Recognition (AFR) system.

The move was ill-fated and in 1995 the arrangement collapsed and officers went back to the old systems of manual matching (Hayward and Cusick, 1995). The Thames Valley Police even suggested the old system was better and 'the number of identifications since the AFR was stopped has been excellent' (Hillier, 1995). IBM later settled the matter legally with a £1.2 million out-of-court payment to the consortium ('Police finger IBM for £1.2m settlement', *Computing*, 24 April 1997).

The Home Office had formed the PITO in 1996 and it was this agency that now stepped in and led negotiations with the US company TRW and its partners to supply the police with the new National Automated Fingerprint Identification System (NAFIS). Nottingham Constabulary were the first force online in 1998 and all forces were using NAFIS by 2001 (PITO, 2001). By that time technology had replaced the old rituals of ink, pads and messy fingers with the electronic taking of fingerprints through 'Livescan' (for more on PITO see Chapter 4).

When the NAFIS contract ended in March 2004, PITO signed a new 8-year contract worth £122 million with the Northrop Grumman Company to develop identification techniques through the IDENT 1 programme. The PITO intention was to develop yet more ways of identification to complement fingerprints, including:

- Facial Images National Database (FIND) – a national collection of photographs;
- National Video Identification Systems (NVIS) – to create video 'identification parades';
- PALM – using palm prints and marks for identification;
- LANTERN – enabling mobile checking of fingerprints at scenes of crime.
  (see 'PITO seals IDENT 1 deal' and 'How NVIS and FIND will find the criminals', *PITO News*, 2005, no. 38: 10–11)

The police reportedly held 6.42 million sets of fingerprints stored on IDENT 1, including 19 per cent of the UK male population (Nuffield Council on Bioethics, 2006: 12).

Fingerprints have achieved a high level of certainty as a unique way of identifying people. A case in Scotland, however, has recently shaken that certainty. Shirley McKie's fingerprint was allegedly found at the scene of a murder in Kilmarnock in January 1997. Ms McKie was a serving police officer but she had never been present at the scene of this crime. Her subsequent denial that it could be her print somewhat confused the trial of the man subsequently convicted for the murder and 2 years later, she herself was arrested and charged with perjury.

The perjury trial heard conflicting evidence from fingerprint experts that Ms McKie's prints did actually match those at the crime scene, and the charges were eventually dismissed. The case threw open the possibility that experts in fingerprint matching were actually not as good at their work as had been believed. The Scottish Executive later paid Ms McKie £750,000 compensation now that her police career had been ruined and some called for a public inquiry into the whole business of fingerprint matching (O'Neill, 2006; Robertson, 2006).

DNA samples

Although identification by fingerprints had taken a knock, the advent of DNA identification techniques did seem infallible. Samples of DNA (Deoxyribonucleic acid) taken from an individual provided a unique 'barcode' to that person, and the terms 'DNA fingerprinting' and 'DNA profiling' came into usage. Work on this biological information – or bioinformation – for crime investigation purposes had started at the University of Leicester during the mid-1980s and was now taken up by the Home Office and the idea of a national DNA database of offenders was put forward (Kirby, 1989). Samples taken from saliva, blood, skin, hair or semen from individuals would be matched to samples taken from scenes of crime.

The UK National DNA Database (NDNAD) was opened on 10 April 1995, holding samples from serious and violent offenders and was heralded as the first of its kind in the world. Criminal records on the Phoenix database were duly marked to show if a DNA sample had been taken (Home Office, 1995b: para. 58).

The NDNAD experienced some teething problems when samples were wrongly matched with scenes of crime (Bennetto, 1995) and when the police experienced, what they considered to be, a very slow service (Tendler, 1996b). Lawyers started to raise questions about civil liberties and how DNA evidence should be presented and analysed in court (Redmayne, 1998; McCartney, 2006). The press had heralded the advent of DNA as almost a 'magic bullet' to solve crime but it only assisted the identification of someone at a scene of crime or other place; further corroborative evidence was always needed to prove any allegation of criminal activity.

In more general terms, however, both politicians and the police were excited by the prospects held out by DNA. Laws were introduced to facilitate the collection and retention of DNA. A spokesman for the

Police Superintendents' Association even suggested the entire population should go on the database and not just known criminals (Campbell, 1998) and Prime Minister Tony Blair announced an initial £34 million for the expansion of the NDNAD (Home Office, 1999a) and followed this up with a further £109 million a year later; the Prime Minister opined 'I believe the civil liberties argument is completely misplaced' (Home Office, 2000b; Watt, 2000). The numbers on the NDNAD stood at 750,000 in 2000.

The DNA Expansion Programme started in April 2000 and the police were now able to use the techniques on volume crime, such as burglary, and vehicle crime and not just murder and serious sexual offences. With some resonance with the Victorians' wish to have all habitual offenders on a register, the aim now 'was to hold a DNA profile for all active offenders' in the country; this was put at an estimated 2,500,000 and this target duly achieved by 2004 (Home Office, 2005c: para. 3).

The same year that the DNA Expansion Programme started, the police were revealed to be keeping thousands of illegal DNA samples. An H. M. Inspectorate of Constabulary report found 'as many as 50,000 (samples) may be found on the database when they should have been taken off' following acquittals or other non-prosecution decisions (HMIC, 2000b: para. 2.23). Although the revelations stirred up some press interest, the Inspectorate report – in more prosaic terms – felt the way forward might be to 'revisit the legislation' so that such samples could be retained 'to aid future investigations' (ibid: para. 2.31). Another way of putting this might be to say 'let's legitimise the illegal activities of the police'.

In fact the courts were already being asked to consider the question of DNA retention. A man charged with burglary in 1998 was brought to court but acquitted. Before his trial a DNA sample had been routinely taken and later, a match was found with a sample taken from a rape victim in 1997. The man was duly charged with the rape and brought to court, where the prosecution case collapsed because the DNA sample being used as evidence should have been destroyed following the acquittal on the burglary charge. The attorney general appealed against the decision to the House of Lords, who agreed that the sample should have been admissible on grounds of common sense (*R* v. *B* Attorney-General's Reference no. 3 of 1999, The Times Law Report, 15 December 2000; Pickover, 2001).

The Criminal Justice and Police Act 2001 s. 82 duly amended the law to allow the police to retain DNA samples – and fingerprints – from people either not prosecuted or acquitted. The Criminal Justice Act 2003

s. 63 further opened the door to more fingerprints and DNA samples by allowing the police to take them from *anyone* who has been arrested on suspicion of a recordable offence.

In Sheffield, Michael Harper was arrested and charged with an offence which was subsequently dropped by the prosecuting authorities. He asked the South Yorkshire police to destroy the DNA sample they had taken. When they refused he sought remedy in the courts for breach of his privacy under Article 8 of the European Convention on Human Rights. The case was dismissed in the Appeal Court on the basis that DNA was about 'identification' and not 'personal information' that might be construed as a privacy issue. Lord Justice Sedley pointed out the benefits of retention and that 'from a policing and law enforcement point of view the unconvicted population is not uniformly beyond suspicion' (*R* v. *Chief Constable of South Yorkshire and others* [2002] 1 WLR 3223).

The director of the campaign group Liberty said he was 'disturbed' by the decision:

> ...the government has never had the courage to force all of us to give DNA samples. However, it is content for those innocent of any crime but who happen to have been caught up in the criminal justice system to have their DNA profile retained indefinitely.
>
> (Liberty, 2002)

The Marper case was dismissed again by the House of Lords, where Lord Brown of Heaton under Heywood argued:

> ...the more complete the database, the better the chances of detecting criminals, both those guilty of crimes past and those whose crimes are yet to be committed...the larger the database the less call there will be to round up the usual suspects.
>
> (*R* v. *Chief Constable of South Yorkshire* (Respondent) ex parte Marper (FC) (Appellant) Consolidated Appeals, Session 2003–2004 [2004] UKHL39 at para. 88)

Mr Marper was understood to be taking his case to the European Court of Human Rights in Strasbourg. At the start of 2006, some 200,000 people were on the National DNA Database who had never been charged or cautioned for any offence; 8000 had been matched to old crimes and the government believed the policy was 'justified'. The NDNAD now held 3 million samples in total (Hansard HC Debates, 17 February 2006, cols. 117–119WS).

The police themselves were more wary of the database when it came to giving samples of their own DNA. The Police Elimination Database (PEDb) was set up in 2000 to ensure that DNA samples inadvertently left at crimes scenes attended by the police did not get muddled up with those of any offenders. Many police officers refused to give samples on the grounds of privacy and the fear that it could be used against them for disciplinary matters (Connor, 2001). It has now become a condition of service for personnel who have joined the police service since 1 August 2002. Similar arrangements were later made for fingerprinting police officers (The Police Regulations 2003, Regulations 18 and 19 SI 2003 no. 527).

The Home Office final verdict on the DNA Expansion Programme was that 'DNA has significantly boosted the probability of crime detection' (Home Office, 2005c: para. 34). The programme itself was then (in 2005) subsumed into the new Forensic Integration Strategy (FIS) designed to take forward 'the UK's global lead on the use of DNA to all forms of forensic intelligence' (ibid: para. 90; see also Hansard HC Debates, 9 May 2006, col. 199W). In October 2006 Prime Minister Tony Blair added his voice to the idea that *the whole population* could usefully be put on the DNA database (Jones, 2006).

Developments in the collection and retention of DNA, and fingerprints from an earlier age, have taken place without sustained public debate. McCartney has summed up the process:

> ...the legislative developments concerning fingerprints and DNA sampling have all been in a similar vein; extending the circumstances in which samples may be taken and the type of samples able to be taken without consent, relaxing restrictions on who can authorise sample collection and who can take the samples, as well as authorising the retention of samples in all circumstances, for the purposes of building national databases for use in speculative searches.
>
> (McCartney, 2006: 18)

DNA in particular has been seen as the magic 'solution' to all crimes even though it can only ever be part of the evidence to prove criminal activity by identifying someone as being at the scene. In 2006 some critics were making their voices heard and the beginnings of a public debate were being attempted (McCartney, 2006; Nuffield Council on Bioethics, 2006; Surveillance Studies Network, 2006).

The legislative framework

The original criminal record collection, having been started in 1869 by the Habitual Criminals Act and its successor the 1871 Prevention of Crimes Act, seems to have been somewhat neglected by the law for most of the twentieth century. Serving police officers did have to sign the 1911 Official Secrets Act which prohibited any state employee from communicating information to any 'unauthorised person' and thus put in place legal constraints on officers to keep criminal records confidential. But any other legal framework was conspicuous by its absence.

The 1871 Prevention of Crimes Act was effectively repealed by the 1967 Criminal Law Act (s. 10, Schedule 3), resulting in no statutory legal underpinning at all for the criminal record collection for the next 17 years. The Police and Criminal Evidence Act 1984 put the collection back on a legal footing by providing that:

> ...the Secretary of State may by regulations make provision for recording in police records convictions for such offences as are specified in the Regulations.
>
> (Police and Criminal Evidence Act 1984, s. 27(4))

The wording of this sub-section, using the word 'may', implies that it still only empowers the police to keep criminal records rather than placing any statutory duty on them to do so.

The definition of convictions in the sub-section was later amended by the Crime and Disorder Act 1998 (s119 and Schedule 8, para. 61) to include cautions, reprimands and final warnings.

The secretary of state produced the first regulations in 1985 as The National Police Records (Recordable Offences) Regulations (SI 1985 no. 1941) and these were periodically updated with similarly named regulations in 1989 (SI 1989 no. 694), 1997 (SI 1997 no. 566), 2000 (SI 2000 no. 1139) and 2003 (SI 2003 no. 2823). The regulations gave rise to the notion of 'recordable offences' falling within their definition and 'non-recordable', outside of the regulations. In essence a 'recordable offence' was any conviction for an offence imprisonable in law, plus any others that the home secretary decided to add on. The 2003 Regulations, for example, added 'begging' and illegal 'cab or taxi touting' to the list of 'recordable offences'. Before 1995 'recordable' offences were also 'reportable' to the NIB; now they are literally only recordable.

The 1974 Rehabilitation of Offenders Act s. 9 had made it an offence for anyone handling criminal records as part of their official duties to make those records available to unauthorised third parties and similar language concerning 'authorised' and 'unauthorised' disclosures was used in the re-vamped 1989 Official Secrets Act. Of more direct concern to the confidentiality of criminal records was the passing of the Data Protection Act 1984.

The developments in information technology taking place in the late 1970s meant a growing awareness of computers and their possibilities. The positives of easy storage and fast retrieval of information were balanced by the negatives of computers as a threat to privacy. The Younger Report (1972) looked at all aspects of privacy and its possible 'invasion' and the later Lindop Report (1978) focused in on data protection and information privacy.

The Lindop Report in 1978 touched on the subject of criminal records (ibid: para. 8.08) and the PNC. Evidence was received that the PNC was not going to be linked with any other central government departments (ibid: para. 8.14) and that there were no plans to computerise the criminal record collection (ibid: para. 8.15). The report was more concerned with police attitudes that they should be exempted from any possible future data protection legislation (ibid: 8.29) and that the present inquiry was unnecessary. The report singled out the Metropolitan Police Service for being particularly unhelpful to their enquiries (ibid: para. 8.03).

Opinion was slowly gathering to demand a data protection law (see, e.g. Home Office, 1975a) and after the Council of Europe's convention on the subject was passed (Council of Europe, 1981) the United Kingdom was obliged to produce an act (Home Office, 1982).

The Data Protection Act 1984 applied only to computer held information and embodied the council's eight data-protection principles:

1. data should be obtained and processed, fairly and lawfully;
2. data should be held only for one or more specified purposes;
3. data should not be disclosed in a manner incompatible with that purpose;
4. data held should be adequate, relevant and not excessive;
5. data should be accurate;
6. data should not be retained longer than necessary for purpose;
7. persons should be able to have access to data held on them;
8. data should be held in conditions of appropriate security.

> (The full text of these principles can be seen in the Data Protection Act 1984 Schedule 1; they are slightly adjusted in the Data Protection Act 1998 (which replaced the 1984 Act) with

> principles 2 and 3 merged into one and a new principle 8 added
> that data should not leave the European Union unless the receiving
> country has adequate data protection laws)

The new post of Data Protection Registrar would oversee the 1984 Act. Chief constables were required to register as data users and publicly state the purpose or purposes for which the data was to be held or used. When criminal records were fully computerised in 1995 through the Phoenix application, the Home Office reminded chief constables of their obligations:

> ... the owners of the data on Phoenix (referred to as 'data users' in the Data Protection Act) are the police forces who use it, as represented by their Chief Constables. They are ultimately responsible for ensuring that data protection and security obligations are met, including the control of access to the PNC, the accuracy of the data held, and the implementation of legal and regulatory controls.
>
> (Home Office, 1995c: para. 8)

The 1984 Act also had provisions specifically to cover criminal records by allowing the secretary of state to make 'additional safeguards' for personal information relating to criminal convictions (Data Protection Act 1984, s. 2(3)(d)). This recognition that criminal records were a particularly sensitive form of personal information was made again in the 1998 Data Protection Act (s. 2(g)) that replaced the 1984 Act. No secretary of state has ever made any such 'additional safeguards'.

The Council of Europe that originally instigated the laws on data protection for computer-held information went on to produce further guidance specifically for the police. The council's formal Recommendations no. R(87) 15 filled in a gap in the 1981 convention that had allowed the police certain exemptions from data protection and gave more detailed guidance on implementing the data protection principles (Hayes, 2005). The UK government accepted almost all of the recommendations but after lobbying by the police entered a 'derogation' which effectively exempted it from two of the principles. One concerned the need to tell individuals when the police held data on them as soon as any police activities would no longer be prejudiced. The Home Office said this was 'unrealistic and impractical'. The second was the collection of data solely on the basis of a particular racial origin, religion, sexual behaviour or political opinion; the Home Office cited the investigation and detection of paedophiles as a reason for this reservation (Council of Europe, 1988: paras. 2.2 and 2.4; Hansard HC Debates, 15 October 1990, col. 717).

In 1995 the European Union put its weight into the data protection question and produced its own directive for its Member States to complement and enhance that of the Council of Europe. The directive required new national data protection laws because it was designed to cover *all* records, including manual ones, and not just computer-held information. The police were again given certain exemptions (see Article 3(2)), but on criminal records the directive stated that:

> ...processing of data relating to offences, criminal convictions or security measures may be carried out only under the control of official authority, or if suitable specific safeguards are provided under national law... However, a complete register of criminal convictions may be kept only under the control of official authority.
>
> (EC Directive, 1995: Article 8(5))

The new UK Data Protection Act based on the directive received its royal assent on 16 July 1998 and was implemented from 28 February 2000. Manual records were now covered as well as computerised ones and data users were now renamed as 'data controllers'.

Criminal records were also referred to in the legislation that would lead to the creation of the CRB (see Chapter 7). The Police Act 1997 outlined how three levels of conviction disclosures would be made to employers on applicants for work giving 'the prescribed details of every conviction of the applicant which is recorded in central records' (Police Act 1997, s. 112(2)(a), s. 113(3)(a) and s. 115(6)(a)). Central records were in turn defined as 'such records of convictions held for the use of police forces generally as may be prescribed' (s. 112(3) and s. 113(5)).

Improper disclosures

Within this legal framework, improper disclosures of criminal records have taken place for various reasons and have been singled out by the deputy Chair of the Independent Police Complaints Commission (IPCC) as a long term problem:

> ...the misuse of PNC data...has been a consistent problem during the last twenty years – and still poses a challenge today for the new IPCC. The types of cases in which abuse occur include using the

PNC to gain evidence for civil proceedings, to find evidence about a partner's estranged husband, or to check out a daughter's latest boyfriend. There is also the perennial problem of data being sold to private detectives.

(IPCC, 2004)

In fact reports of criminal record information being improperly passed to private detectives or security officers – many of them ex-police officers – goes back further than 20 years. In 1968 Anthony Gardner, MP, asked for an assurance in the House of Commons that such transactions with private detectives did not take place and was told by the Home Office that it could not possibly take place (Hansard HC Debates, 8 February 1968, cols. 209–210).

The 1972 Younger Report also homed in on private detectives being able to easily obtain police criminal records. The report received evidence that 'a practice of exchanging mutually useful information had developed on a quid pro quo basis'. The police denied such exchanges took place and not least because 'any police officer concerned would risk severe punishment under the Police (Disciplinary) Regulations' (Younger Report, 1972: para. 436).

Draper, in her study of private detectives, also found evidence of criminal records passing along this ex-police officers' old-boys' network, but was hopeful that the Rehabilitation of Offenders Act 1974 s. 9 was going to stem the flow along with the more rigorous self-policing of the police (Draper, 1978: 156–158).

Sporadic reports of criminal records on the PNC being disclosed improperly continued to surface throughout the 1980s. *The Observer* newspaper ran an exclusive story on how they could get criminal record information through 'childishly simple methods' involving impersonating police officers on the phone. They found 'the most elementary safeguards are being ignored' (Leigh, 1981). Nottinghamshire police reportedly tightened their procedures in direct response to this story (Lundin, 1981).

In 1989 five private investigators and three police officers were found guilty of collectively abusing confidential PNC information at Winchester Crown Court ('Policemen guilty of conspiracy over computer information', *The Independent*, 3 February 1989). In June 1996 two Metropolitan Police Officers were found guilty of improper use of the PNC to check out the boyfriend of an estranged partner (Steele, 1996), leading to H. M. Inspectorate of Constabulary to call for tighter safeguards (Bennetto, 1996a).

When the Information Commissioners Office (ICO) made its own investigation of the trade in illicit personal information, criminal records and the PNC were found to be just one sector of the trade. Professional 'investigators' were obtaining information from numerous organisations by either bribing officials who worked in them, or by making telephone calls pretending to be authorised users of the information and persuading officials to disclose it. The demand for this information was coming from newspapers, finance companies and local authorities tracing debtors and criminals intent on fraud or witness and juror intimidation. A customer could be charged up to £500 for an illegal criminal record check (ICO, 2006: para. 5.35).

All of these activities had been made illegal in 1994 with amendments to the original Data Protection Act made by the Criminal Justice and Public Order Act 1994 s. 161; the law now is in the Data Protection Act 1998 s. 55. Police officers were among those known to commit 'section 55 offences' and the ICO reported regular contact with the police on these criminal activities:

> The ICO Investigations Unit liaises almost weekly with police forces, often at their request for advice. The unlawful disclosure of information from police systems is an issue of particular concern, as many professional standards units within the police are investigating corrupt practices by serving officers.
>
> (ibid: para. 4.6)

We might surmise that the problem is even wider than police officers when considering all the other agencies that have access to the PNC (see above). The ICO now proposed the increasing of sanctions to include custodial sentences for 'section 55 offences'; at this time only non-custodial sanctions were available (ibid: paras. 7.6–7.8). A government consultation paper took this idea forward (DCA, 2006a).

The ACPO Codes of Practice

During the 1980s the police devised their own internal Code of Practice covering the work of the PNC. This code was not made public other than to members of Parliament, where it could be seen in the House of Commons Library (Hansard HC Debates, 9 March 1984, cols. 721–722WA). A public version did appear in 1987 as the Association of Chief Police Officers' 'Code of Practice for Police Computer Systems' (ACPO, 1987) which was updated in subsequent editions (ACPO, 1995,

2002). Each edition was endorsed by a foreword from the data protection registrar – and later the new post of information commissioner. In the 2002 edition the commissioner said she was:

> …encouraged by the efforts that are being made to bring about improvements but…as modern day policing increasingly relies on sophisticated information systems there must be a strong commitment to properly maintaining those systems. Adherence with this Code is an essential part of delivering that commitment. It is in this light that I am keeping under review the question of PNC data quality.
>
> (ibid: 3)

Codes had been specifically encouraged by the EU Directive of 1995 (EC Directive, 1995: Article 27).

All of the three ACPO codes follow the format of the eight data-protection principles and explain how the police comply with them. Expounding the principle of not retaining information for longer than is necessary, the codes incorporated the ACPO 'General Rules for Criminal Weeding on Police Systems'. The 2002 edition of the code, for example, states that all recordable offences should be retained for 10 years and then deleted if there was nothing further to record. There could be departures from this rule in the case of serious or persistent offending and anyone with three convictions would have their record retained for 20 years from the date of the last entry. Others might have their records retained for life or until they reached the age of 100; these included:

- offenders receiving a total of six months or more imprisonment;
- people found unfit to plead by reason of insanity;
- convictions involving indecency, sexual offences, violence or the possession or supplying of Class 'A' drugs;
- conviction for an offence where the victim was a child or other vulnerable person;
- conviction for a terrorist offence.

(ACPO, 2002: 21)

Police cautions of adults were to be deleted after 5 years if there was no further record, unless the victim had been 'a vulnerable person'. Reprimands or Final Warnings given by the police to children and young people might also be deleted after 5 years if there were no repeat incidents (ibid: 22).

The problem with the ACPO Code of Practice was that it remained just that – a Code of Practice. It had no statutory force and was policed by the police themselves subject to the wider regulation of the Data Protection Act and the promptings of the information commissioner appointed under that act. In 2005 the commissioner did question the length of time the police were retaining some criminal records.

The case concerned three individuals who believed their records should not have been retained for as long as they had been because the records' disclosure to third parties outside of the criminal justice system had been prejudicial to them. One 34-year-old had lost a job, for example, and another 24-year-old was denied US citizenship on the basis of juvenile convictions. The individuals had turned to the information commissioner, who had decided to impose enforcement notices on the three police forces concerned under section 40 of the Data Protection Act 1998. The notices required the police to delete the conviction data because its retention convened the third and fifth data-protection principles that personal data be adequate, relevant and not excessive and that it should not be kept for longer than necessary. The police in turn appealed to the Information Tribunal on the grounds that they had acted within the ACPO Code of Practice.

The Information Tribunal upheld the right of the police to have retained the records as the sentences totalled more than 6 months' custody for two of the individuals concerned while the third individual was booked for an offence of violence. As such the 100-year rule was found to be in order for the retention of these records. At the same time the tribunal did think the police were wrong to have disclosed the records to third parties and therefore the enforcement notices were amended to reflect the fact that the 100-year rule should apply only to police retention in this case. Future cases would have to be dealt with on their merits (*The Chief Constables of West Yorkshire, South Yorkshire and North Wales Police* v. *Information Commissioner,* 2005).

The tribunal ruling set in train a re-think on the way police information – especially criminal records – might be disclosed to third parties like employers and licensing bodies. Agreed, third parties did have a right to see criminal records for screening purposes (see Chapters 4, 6 and 7) but perhaps they did *not* have the right to see full records, especially when they were old. An ACPO 'DNA and Fingerprint Retention Project Team' were asked to look at this question and came up with the idea of a 'step model'. A distinction would be made between information needed for police operational purposes and information made available to other users; the latter information could be 'stepped down' and not disclosed (see below).

Further criticisms of the ACPO Code came from the Bichard Report set up in the wake of the murders of two children in Soham, Cambridgeshire, in 2002. The report looked at record keeping by the police in Cambridgeshire and Humberside where Ian Huntley, the convicted murderer of the children, had lived and also the vetting practices and information sharing that had taken place between the police and other agencies (Bichard Report, 2004).

The Bichard Inquiry found a number of problems with the ACPO Code and not least on matters of review, retention and deletion of records. It found scope for differing interpretations between police forces, and confusion between the concept of 'review' and 'delete'; this confusion not helped by the use of the word 'weed' to cover both activities (Bichard Report, 2004: para. 4.41). The report proposed two new Statutory Codes of Practice (ibid: rec. 5 and 8; for more on the Bichard Report see Chapter 7).

Statutory codes and guidance

The continuing problems of data quality on the PNC and the specific recommendations of the 2004 Bichard Inquiry Report in fact led to a flurry of activity that produced three statutory codes and associated guidance on the management of police information. These documents looked at all aspects of police-held information – not just criminal records – to try and raise the standards across the country at both local and national levels.

(a) Code of Practice: the Police National Computer
This code was produced in line with the Police Acts 1996 and 1997 (as amended by the Police Reform Act 2002) and was implemented from 1 January 2005. It relates only to the Names Index on the PNC and therefore has direct relevance for criminal records. The code is specifically aimed at the PNC data-quality questions and seeks to improve the timeliness and integrity of the data; in so doing it replaced the ACPO PNC Codes of Compliance (Home Office, 2005d).

The new statutory code specifically refers to the widening use of the PNC by other agencies as a reason for ensuring data quality (see above and Chapter 4) and therefore making the need for accurate and timely records all the more important (ibid: paras. 28–29). An initial arrest, report or summons – now referred to as 'an event' – has to be on the PNC within 3 days and 75 per cent of final results have to be on within 7 days (ibid: paras. 30–31). Chief officers have to integrate PNC data-quality compliance into their performance review and inspection programmes and the work of the PNC inputting staff has to be regularly checked (ibid: paras. 44–50).

(b) Code of Practice: National Intelligence Model

This code was made under the same legal provisions as the PNC Code and was implemented from 12 January 2005. It sought to achieve the basic principles and minimum common standards of the National Intelligence Model (NIM) drawn up in April 2003 (Home Office, 2005e; for more on the NIM see Chapter 4).

(c) Code of Practice: Management of Police Information

This code has a similar statutory basis to the two referred to above and was implemented from 14 November 2005. The Management of Police Information (MOPI) Code ranges over all forms of information held by the police for purposes of policing and aims for more consistent obtaining, recording, storing, reviewing and deletion of information; it also looks at the police sharing of information with other agencies (Home Office, 2005f). The code is accompanied by two volumes of guidance.

The 'Guidance on the Management of Police Information' was published by ACPO in April 2006 and 'the Code and this guidance together form a package that chief officers will have regard to under the terms of the (Police) Act (1996)' (ACPO, 2006a: 5). The need to establish a clear 'policing purpose' is again highlighted as the cornerstone of effective police information management and sections of the code outline how information should be collected, recorded and evaluated. The need for police protocols – or Information Sharing Agreements – with other agencies when sharing information is also emphasised. Criminal records on the PNC are briefly mentioned as just one category of personal information held, and readers of the code are re-directed to the 2005 Code (see (a) above) and yet further guidance specifically on the 'retention' of PNC records.

The 'Retention Guidelines for Nominal Records on the Police National Computer' is the second ACPO publication and is also 'part of the guidance issued under the Code for Management of Police Information' (ACPO, 2006b: para. 1.2). These guidelines replace the earlier ACPO 'General Rules for Criminal Weeding on Police Systems' as from 31

March 2006; the 'General Rules' had been incorporated into the ACPO Codes. The origins of the new 'Retention Guidelines' were outlined in the Information Tribunal hearing during 2005 (The Chief Constables of West Yorkshire, South Yorkshire and North Wales Police and the Information Commissioner, Information Tribunal, 2005: paras. 46–55; see above).

The main innovative feature of the 'Retention Guidelines' was the so-called 'Step Down Model'. The 'Step Down Model' was introduced specifically to address problems encountered when the police provided criminal records to third parties, especially to the CRB and employers using the records to screen job applicants (see Chapters 6 and 7). It seemed unfair that someone could be refused employment based on convictions and cautions in the dim and distant past. The 'Step Down Model' introduced a system of denying such criminal record information to employers if certain criteria were met, but not deleting it from the records, should the police ever need it in the future (Readhead, 2006).

The criteria now drawn up for restricting access to non-police users of records were based on:

- the age of the subject;
- the final outcome;
- the sentence imposed; and
- the offence category.

Offences were categorised in the 'Retention Guidelines' from serious (Category A) to less serious (Category B) to minor (Category C). The age of the subject was a simple division between adults and youths (under 18), the 'outcome' a division between custodial and non-custodial sentences and the 'sentences' being a division between 6 months and longer and those under 6 months (ACPO, 2006b: passim). Planning for incorporation of the 'step down model' into police – CRB co-operation was continuing throughout 2006 with a view to introduction later that year (personal communication, 14 September 2006).

Conclusions

The current maintenance arrangements for the UK national collection of criminal records have evolved around the growth of information technology in the last decade of the twentieth century. The Phoenix application added to the PNC in 1995 has given the United Kingdom a 'criminal justice record service' with a growing range of users.

The Phoenix application, containing the national collection of records, was constructed against a backdrop of continuing criticism of the quality of the records kept. Too many records were incomplete or inaccurate and computerisation was seen as one way of improving the data quality. In practice this did not happen straight away and further interventions have been needed to get on top of the problem. New statutory Codes of Practice have been introduced to finally bear down on the data-quality problems of police-held information. The ACPO still produces its own complementary code on data protection (ACPO, 2006c).

Alongside the development of Phoenix and its management, the police have been given access to new forms of identification. Apart from the traditional use of fingerprinting, they now have the National DNA Database as a form of identification based on body samples, said to be unique to each individual, and experiments continue with biometric forms of identification, national photograph collections and palm prints.

As maintenance and retrieval of criminal records has improved, arrangements have been made to improve data quality and ensure appropriate management and regulation of the databases. At the same time identification of individuals has become more sophisticated. None of those developments should be taking place in a vacuum, however, and we need to turn now to questions of what we do with the records and forms of identification we now have at our disposal through information technology and advances in science.

4
Criminal Records – Their Role and Purpose

The original purpose of collating criminal records was to help track and supervise offenders coming out of prison, who were no longer transported abroad or executed (Chapter 2). Later the purpose would become refined down to policing purposes and judicial purposes: policing purposes to aid police investigations – 'catching thieves on paper' – and judicial purposes to let the courts know if a convicted person had offended before. The judicial purpose has subsequently grown to include prosecuting agencies, prisons and the probation service, who all need records to complete their task.

When the Phoenix application to the PNC was created in 1995, it was pointedly given the sub-title 'the Criminal Justice Record Service' to reflect the fact that it was meant to be 'for the whole of the criminal justice system' (Home Office, 1995d). It was intended for agencies such as 'the Benefits Agency, Post Office, H. M. Customs and Excise and the RSPCA (who) all have legitimate requirements for information from Phoenix' (ibid).

The spreading use of criminal records for vetting purposes, whether for employment or licence screening, now sees Phoenix-held information being disseminated even more widely.

This chapter divides into two halves, considering firstly, the traditional uses made of criminal records within the criminal justice system by the police and the judicial process, and secondly, the increasing number of agencies now using the records outside of the criminal justice system. The specific question of using criminal records for pre-employment screening purposes is considered in Chapters 6 and 7.

Criminal records within the criminal justice system

The rationale for starting a national collection of criminal records was to help the police and the courts when a person with old convictions kept coming to their notice. The habitual offender was the Victorians' *bête noir* that needed to be recorded, identified and noted. The courts needed records to help decide on sentences; the police, to help them with new investigations and the detection of offenders.

The policing purpose

Police investigations

The police officer confronted with a new crime to investigate now looked to the criminal record collection and its accompanying means of identification as part of the tools of his or her trade. The theory was that they would reveal similar crimes committed by a known person or modus operandi that linked crime scenes to given individuals.

Whether the practice was as neat and tidy as the theory is less certain, but over the years the criminal record has been joined with the modus operandi, fingerprints, DNA, palm prints and other innovations to try and give the officer as coherent a picture as possible. The information from the scene of crime, or witnesses, may not lead to a definitive 'match' with information on file, but even partial matching could lead to degrees of a positive or negative match, which in turn could lead to search of other sources and for corroborative evidence (McCartney, 2006: Chapter 2).

Police officers themselves have been criticised for seeing criminal records as just a historical record and the PNC as a record-keeping device rather than the records being part of an active means of investigating crime and detecting criminals. The move towards more 'intelligence led' policing in the 1990s tried to raise the status of criminal records as being part of the information available to the police to assist investigating officers (see, e.g. Audit Commission, 1993). New concepts like 'routine activity theory' and 'repeat offenders' (see, e.g. Trickett *et al.*, 1992) and techniques such as Comparative Case Analysis (later re-named as Crime Pattern Analysis) also pushed officers into re-thinking the information they held as a potential tool to aid investigation.

When criminal records became available through Phoenix, further attempts were made to encourage officers on the ground to make better use of them. The weekly journal *Police Review* ran a series of 10 articles on the PNC between 1 November 1996 and 10 January 1997 in an attempt to help raise awareness of its potential. The first one bemoaned the fact that 'most operational staff are unaware of the depth of data (the PNC) holds' (Thompson, 1996) and pointed out that the names database:

> ...can now hold up to 200 pages of information and can provide wide-ranging intelligence from convictions to shoe size, aliases to addresses.
>
> (ibid)

The Hendon Data Centre, which had oversight of the PNC at that time, produced 20 posters for distribution to police stations across the country, encouraging officers to use the computer more as an investigative tool.

If police officers were sceptical so were others. Apart from being a cue to 'round up the usual suspects' when a crime had been committed it was not altogether obvious how an old criminal record did help investigate new crimes. The campaign group Liberty, for example, pointed out that the Data Protection Act which normally allows individuals to see what information organisations hold on them ('subject access') also allowed the police to deny such access if it would interfere with an ongoing investigation:

> ...given that criminal records contain only factual information on charges or offences, it seems questionable whether the subject access exemption available to the police should ever apply.
>
> (Liberty, 1991: para. 2.7)

The struggle to get police officers to use the PNC as an investigative tool continued. In July 1998 the new QUEST software was introduced specifically to help officers use the PNC more effectively.

> 'Quest' unlocks the full potential of the Phoenix application and realises its role as an investigative tool. Provided the information entered into Phoenix is up to date and complete, QUEST will find who you are looking for.
>
> (PITO, n.d.: 9)

Three years later a publicity campaign was launched to raise awareness of QUEST. According to a manager from PITO (see below):

> ...too many officers are unaware of QUEST's capabilities – particularly its investigative side.... some officers tend to view PNC as just a record

keeping and reference tool . . . QUEST enables them to do much more than that.

(Orr-Munro, 2001; see also HMIC 2002: paras. 6.1–6.6)

At the end of 2005 *Police Review* repeated their 1996 exercise with another 10 articles (14 October 2005–9 December 2005) explaining the benefits of the PNC as an investigative tool. The police service was told it 'needs to wake up to the investigative opportunities they are missing out on' (Evans, 2005).

The National Intelligence Model

This exhortation to get the police to use criminal records and the PNC more to help with new investigations was part of the wider movement in the 1990s towards intelligence-led policing. With a growing perception that the police were failing to reduce crime, 'intelligence-led' policing was seen as a way forward. Instead of reacting and investigating to find who might have committed the latest new crime, the idea now was to gather intelligence on people known to commit crime and on areas where criminal activity was known to be high. This pro-active policing focused on the criminals, their anticipated behaviour and certain geographical 'hot spot' areas rather than on just the new crime (Audit Commission, 1993; Maguire and John, 1995).

This emphasis sought to turn information into usable intelligence. The police have adopted a '5 × 5 × 5' format to enable this process. The source of the information is assessed as being:

1. Always reliable
2. Mostly reliable
3. Sometimes reliable
4. Unreliable
5. Untested source.

A similar fivefold evaluation is then made of the actual content of the information:

1. Known to be true without reservation
2. Known personally to the source but not to the person reporting
3. Not known personally to the source but corroborated
4. Cannot be judged
5. Suspected to be false.

A final fivefold assessment is made to attach a 'Handling Code' to the information that guides officers on the degree to which the information should be disseminated:

1. dissemination to the UK police service and to other law enforcement agencies
2. dissemination to UK non-prosecuting parties
3. dissemination to foreign law enforcement agencies
4. dissemination within originating force/agency only for a given time period
5. dissemination to an agency bound to observe conditions as specified.
        (for more on the $5 \times 5 \times 5$ format, see ACPO, 2006a: Appendix 2)

Information is then turned into intelligence for police to act upon if appropriate. Criminal records could later be added to the intelligence 'package' as required.

The NIM was finalised in 2003 by staff at the National Criminal Intelligence Service (NCIS), and endorsed by ACPO and the Home Office. It was seen as a managerial tool that laid out the constituent parts of any effective police intelligence system. It looked at how you obtained information, stored it, used and analysed it to turn it into intelligence. The NIM was particularly concerned with ensuring standardisation and compatibility between forces as a precursor to having a national intelligence IT arrangement to communicate nationally between forces. A Code of Practice accompanied the NIM (Home Office, 2005e; see also Chapter 3).

Police Information Technology Organisation (PITO)

A recurring problem for the police had been in the ability to exchange information between local forces. The early 'clearing houses' and 'regional criminal record offices' had been one way of doing this, but by the late 1980s the police needed to adopt the emergent information technologies if they were going to stay ahead of the game. The PITO created in 1996 was the agency charged with improving the police use of computers to exchange information.

Various reports in the late 1980s had identified the problems of individual forces developing their own localised IT systems that worked for them but not necessarily anyone else. The metaphor of 'islands' and 'silos' of information began to be used (Wilmot Report, 1987; Home Office, 1988a). Interfaces could be engineered to link these 'islands' together but what was really needed was a national strategy that all forces could agree on and work towards.

A National Strategy for Police Information Systems (NSPIS) was published in 1994 by the Home Office, ACPO and the Police Authorities. The strategy document was broken down into 10 separate strategy papers, covering the overall framework, data flow models, the existing environment, technical infrastructure, and so on (Home Office *et al.*, 1994). PITO was the agency designed to ensure implementation of the NSPIS.

The PITO started life as a part of the Home Office but achieved its own legal status in 1998 as a government Non-Departmental Public Body (NDPB) through the Police Act 1997 Part IV. Apart from implementing the NSPIS, it had oversight of the PNC, and its BRC exercise, advised on procurement of new IT systems and helped local police systems learn from each other and carry forward 'best practice'. Within the NSPIS vision the aim was to ensure better inter-working within forces and better inter-operability between forces and with other agencies of the wider criminal justice system.

The question of procurement was particularly pressing because there was a belief that the police – in common with other government departments – were not very good at dealing with the private sector who supplied the IT equipment and software that was needed. For their part, the private sector had formed – in 1994 – their own consortium of suppliers to the police and others in the justice system known as JESICA (Justice and Emergency Services Information Communication Association).

JESICA was a sub-group of INTELLECT, the trade association for hi-tech industry, and in 2006 JESICA represented the interests of over 140 information systems, services and consultancy companies operating in the criminal justice and emergency services (all listed on the INTELLECT web site www.intellectuk.org/).

The PITO divided its work into directorates or 'business areas' that included:

Integration and Technical Authority – looking at forces being able to work together and across the criminal justice community.

Communications – looking at the Police National Network (PNN) as a secure form of communications between forces and initiatives like AIRWAVE, a new digital radio communications system.

Identification – developing electronic fingerprinting (NAFIS and IDENT 1), FIND, LANTERN (mobile finger-printing facilities), NVIS, biometric identification, etc.

Operational Services – ensuring direct delivery of services, including the PNC, NAFIS/IDENT 1, ViSOR and links to the Schengen Inform-ation System (SIS) (see Chapter 8 for more on the SIS).

The PITO's perennial problem was that of trying to get so many different forces across the country to work together. Many had tried and trusted systems – or 'legacy systems' – that they were happy with. The PITO had limited executive powers and the NSPIS could seem distant and remote. In 2001 PITO started work on a new strategy document. Programme Valiant was a 6-month project 'carried out by a core team based in PITO and a partnership of experts in police IT from around Britain' ('We'll have the technology', *PITO News*, Winter 2001: 6). The work on Programme Valiant was premised on the belief that:

> ...the current National Strategy for Police Information Systems cannot deliver the service's requirements. With police systems gener-ally fragmented and inadequate, officers do not feel supported by IT in their efforts to deliver a fast, effective response.

> (ibid)

Programme Valiant metamorphosed into the Information Systems Strategy for the Police Service (ISS4PS). Initially published in 2002 the strategy document came in two volumes looking at 'Understanding ISS4PS' (vol. One) and 'Implementing ISS4PS' (vol. Two) (Home Office *et al.*, 2002). The ISS4PS was later re-vamped and 'refreshed' to guide the police in the direction of a national 'integrated information envir-onment' ('Refreshing the Parts...', *PITO News*, Winter 2005: 12–13). This was in contrast to the increasingly left-behind NSPIS approach that favoured national standard IT applications for discrete areas of police activity. The Police Federation dismissed NSPIS in evidence to the Home Affairs Committee as 'the debacle of the National Strategy for Police Information Systems' (House of Commons, 2005: vol. 2, Evid-ence p. 138).

More specific to policing was the publication of the first National Policing Plan (Home Office, 2004a) and the Home Office's Police Science and Technology Strategy (Home Office, 2004b) as well as the Bichard Report on the shortcomings of police information sharing arrangements revealed in the case of the Soham murders of 2002 (Bichard Report,

2004: for more on Bichard, see Chapter 7). Policing was to be more directly led into the twenty-first century:

> ... the consensual approach that underpins (police governance) works well most of the time. Sometimes however, national and local priorities are not fully reconciled and delays in decision making arise that impact the common good... this has happened with information sharing across forces where, despite a clearly identified and accepted national imperative, progress has in practice been very slow.
>
> (Home Office *et al.*, 2002: 11)

Just 6 years after achieving its legal status the future of PITO was now drawn into question. An 'end-to-end' review of its performance was announced in January 2004 (Hansard HC Debates, 14 January 2004, cols. 30–31WS) and the McFarland review duly reported that PITO was not trusted by the police, who were reluctant to be 'told' what to do:

> (PITO) lacks clear definition or purpose, results in confused lines of responsibility and is almost certainly poor value for money.
>
> (Home Office, 2005g; see also Collins, 2005)

The Police Federation were as dismissive of PITO as they had been of NSPIS: 'We are not convinced that with 600 staff and a budget of £350 million the Police Information Technology Organisation provides value for money' (House of Commons, 2005: vol. 2, 130).

A Home Office White Paper on the future of policing had by now proposed a National Policing Improvement Agency (NPIA) and suggested that such an agency would inevitably 'mean significant change' for PITO (Home Office, 2004c: para. 5.49). Clause 1 of the Police and Justice Bill published in January 2006 abolished PITO and established the new NPIA. The new agency was to deliver in the following three core areas:

- good practice development – refinement and codification of core policing processes and competencies;
- an implementation support function – working with forces and others to implement swift change on key mission critical policing priorities; and
- operational policing support.

This would include support on matters of IT and the procurement of IT; NPIA would have powers 'to require forces to implement mission critical objectives' (ibid: para. 5.48).

The judicial purpose

The Crown Prosecution Service (CPS) needs criminal records to decide whether or not to prosecute or to oppose bail, and to inform the defence of the record of any prosecution witnesses. They may wish to invoke the 'bad character' provisions of the Criminal Justice Act 2003. The National Probation Service may need access to records in connection with Pre-Sentence Reports, and other risk-assessment exercises. The courts need criminal records to make decisions about bail and to help make decisions on sentencing, The Prison Service may need them for allocation decisions within the prison estate.

1. Antecedents

Antecedents are lists of criminal records and cautions provided to judges and magistrates towards the end of trial – following a finding of guilt – to help them make their sentencing decisions. Although a person is on trial for a particular charge and the court has been hearing the 'facts of the case', there is inevitably a degree of disapprobation directed at the offenders themselves. At its most simple, the first-time offender may get a lighter sentence than someone with an existing criminal record.

The rules governing the provision of antecedents to courts have traditionally been laid down in court Practice Directions (see, e.g. Practice Direction (Crime: Antecedents) ([1993] 1 WLR 1459), Practice Direction (Crime: Antecedents) [1997] 4 All ER 350) and some Home Office circulars (see, e.g. Home Office, 1978). Following a recommendation of the Auld Report (2001: 512–513) the rules were consolidated for all courts in new Criminal Procedure Rules 2005 (SI 384).

The police have been asked to produce a summary of convictions and cautions from the PNC for both Crown and Magistrates Courts; they are asked to complete supplementary forms for any convictions not on the PNC (on form MG16) and for any cautions not on the PNC (form MG17). The police produce seven copies of the antecedents for the Crown Court; two go directly to the Crown Prosecution Service and the Crown Court forwards two of their five to the Probation Service and defence, respectively. Five copies are produced for the Magistrates Court, all going straight to the CPS, who in turn distribute to the Probation Service (1), defence (1) and the courts (2). A copy of the antecedents accompanies any individual leaving the court for a custodial sentence to inform the relevant receiving institution.

In order for the court to maintain the presumption of 'innocent until found guilty', criminal records are not normally disclosed during a trial unless the 'bad character' provisions are invoked (see below). The prejudicial effect of hearing about such conviction records is a principle of the British justice system laid down in the Criminal Evidence Act 1898 s. 1 and summed up by one judge as 'one of the most deeply rooted and jealously guarded principles of our criminal law' (*Maxwell* v. *DPP* [1935] AC 309, 317; see also Lord Sankey in *Woolmington* v. *DPP* [1935] AC 462).

In the past some courts have found improper ways of getting round this principle to let magistrates know when a defendant has a record:

> ...at one time it was not unusual for a prosecuting advocate or police officer to arrange his papers on the desk or in his hand in such a way that magistrates could see the familiar lists of previous convictions...they may not have been able to read the detail, but the message was clear. The transmission of such a message by that soundless display was not always accidental.
>
> (*Magistrate*, July 1986, 47(2): 107)

Apart from the mechanics of getting the criminal record to court, the actual use of previous convictions in deciding on a sentence has been the subject of some debate amongst penal theorists. In general terms, sentencing theory has taken two approaches to its subject area, with sentencing decisions based on 'utilitarian' approaches or theories of 'retribution' (see, e.g. Hudson, 1996).

The 'utilitarian' approach has sometimes been referred to as the 'welfare' approach and concerns matters of rehabilitation and treatment. Its focus may be said to be on the criminal – as opposed to the crime – and the character of that criminal, and its aim is to reduce the possibilities of any 'future crimes' that he or she might commit. Young offenders in particular, are said to warrant this approach. The welfare approach tries to take into account as much information as possible about the offender, including the full criminal history record they might have.

The 'retributive' approach looks more at the crime than the criminal and bases sentences on how serious the crime is and what might be a proportionate punishment. The retributive approach is a 'just deserts' model matching the punishment to the criminal act. It is less concerned with reducing 'future crimes' and more concerned with the crime that has taken place – the 'past crime' – and what sentence is appropriate to it (von Hirsch, 1986). As the 'retributive' approach is less concerned with the offender, so too it is less inclined to look at the previous criminal record.

In post-war years these two approaches have broadly covered the 1945–1990 period (utilitarian) and the 1990 onwards period (retributive). In practice the two have often blended together rather than appearing in any 'pure' form. A first-time offender with no previous convictions could argue their behaviour is out of character and therefore deserving of a more lenient sentence. A persistent offender with a criminal record might argue that they have already been punished for their previous crimes, but most courts would think a heavier sentence is due because of the ignoring of the earlier sentences – increased culpability – and the loss of the status of the first-time offender. In practice, courts could consider aggravating and mitigating factors, and the persistent offender experiences a progressive loss of mitigation that the first-time offender enjoys.

Professor Martin Wasik, the Chair of the Sentencing Advisory Panel (at the time of writing), has long been a student of the use of criminal records in sentencing; he has elaborated on their significance by outlining eight factors that might be taken into account:

(a) the number of previous convictions;

(b) the similarity of previous convictions (implying that perhaps some are irrelevant to the current concerns);

(c) the frequency of convictions (as recognised by the 1974 Rehabilitation of Offenders Act and the concept of 'spent' convictions – see Chapter 5);

(d) the seriousness of previous convictions (again recognised by the Rehabilitation of Offenders Act);

(e) the previous sentences (and their impact);

(f) the staleness of previous convictions (as recognised by the Rehabilitation of Offenders Act);

(g) the age of the defendant at the time of previous convictions (the 1974 Rehabilitation of Offenders Act halves the rehabilitation time for young offenders);

(h) previous convictions may indicate a certain kind of character and influence a 'risk assessment for the future'.

(Wasik, 1987)

The Criminal Justice Act 1991 s. 29(1), taking a 'just deserts' approach, tried to actively reduce the influence of old convictions in sentencing. Sentencers were effectively being asked to look only at the current offence and its seriousness (although s. 29(2) rather ambiguously did allow the courts to look at previous convictions in some circumstances). The Criminal Justice Act 1993 s. 66 ended this rather short-lived experiment by repealing s. 29(1), and the impact of previous convictions on sentencing was again permitted.

In 2001 there was evidence that the government wanted the criminal record to play an even greater part in sentencing. The Halliday report took the same line that the Victorians had taken, that crime was committed by an identifiable group of people. For the Victorians these were the 'habitual offenders' and now they were 'persistent offenders' and it was they who 'commit a disproportionate number of crimes and account for a disproportionate number of sentencing occasions', and

> ...the doctrine of 'progressive loss of mitigation' raises an important question of policy: what effect should a bad criminal record have on the severity of sentence following a further conviction?
>
> (Halliday Report, 2001: para. 1.14)

The Halliday Report wanted more attention paid to the criminal record and that the record should be a more integral part of the principles governing severity of sentence:

- severity of punishment should reflect the seriousness of the offence (or offences as a whole) and the offender's criminal history;
- the seriousness of the offence should reflect its degree of harmfulness, or risked harmfulness, and the offender's culpability in committing the offence;
- in considering criminal history, the severity of sentence should increase to reflect a persistent course of criminal conduct, as shown by previous convictions and sentences.

> (ibid: para. 2.40)

Critics have questioned where this new approach comes from because there is no 'real articulation of the rationale for the proposed shift of emphasis towards previous offending' either in the Halliday Report itself or other Home Office pronouncements (von Hirsch, 2002). As for the idea that there is a small group of hard-core persistent offenders, 'probably no more than 100,000 strong' (Halliday Report, 2001: para. 1.28) and that is why criminal records should be more closely scrutinised by sentencers, 'no basis has been offered for this supposition' (von Hirsch, 2002).

2. Evidence of 'Bad Character'

There are some very specific circumstances where criminal records can be introduced as evidence during a trial. The Criminal Justice Act 2003 Part II, Chapter 1 consolidated and extended the law in this area with its provisions known as 'evidence of bad character'.

The idea that the law needed amending was put forward by the 1993 Royal Commission on Criminal Justice (Runciman Report, 1993: Chapter 8, paras. 29–34) and the brief passed to the Law Commission, who produced a Consultation Document (Law Commission, 1996) and then a final report on the subject (Law Commission, 2001). The name of the game was to balance the input of relevant criminal records *during* a hearing against the danger of prejudicing the magistrates or jury; the ultimate fear was that the presumption of innocence could be eroded.

The existing exceptions to the rule allowed evidence of bad character when the behaviour comprised 'similar fact' or patterns of behaviour that demonstrated a propensity or disposition similar to the current charge. The defendant who attacked the character of a witness could also leave themselves open to disclosure of their bad character. All this was at the discretion of the judge.

The Law Commission's two reports went into the arguments for and against before coming down in favour of changes to the law and more openness to courts' hearing of criminal records during a trial. The Auld review of the criminal courts recognised the complexities and illogicalities but preferred to wait for the deliberations of the Law Commission before making any recommendations (Auld Report, 2001: paras. 11.112–11.120). The government brought the idea further forward in its White Paper 'Justice for All' (Home Office *et al.*, 2002: paras. 4.54–4.59) and the Criminal Justice Bill 2003 put the proposals before Parliament.

The arguments had been fierce. The campaign group 'Justice' thought the new laws would have an adverse effect on the fairness of proceedings and although the submission of criminal records would not be automatic:

> ...the proposed regime is intended to and will lead to the relatively frequent admission of evidence of the defendant's bad character. The commonplace admission of, for example, the defendant's previous convictions may lead a jury to convict on the basis that it is 'more

likely' that he is guilty rather than on the strength of the evidence that proves he is guilty of the offence charged.

(Justice, 2003: para. 12)

The consequence could be the police rounding up the usual suspects and not looking for sufficient other evidence to put before the court (ibid: para. 14). People with a criminal record were more likely to be questioned by the police and if the court heard the record, the person was more likely to be convicted again and get a longer record, meaning the next time there was a similar crime in that area they were again the first to be questioned (see also McEwan, 2002).

Two research studies carried out by Oxford University seemed to support these speculations. A study of mock jurors found them to be more negative to a defendant on hearing of a criminal record (Law Commission, 1996) and a similar study of magistrates revealed a similar effect (Law Commission, 2001: Appendix A). The researchers concluded that 'these findings do not offer confidence that the rules on admitting previous convictions can be safely relaxed for magistrates any more than for juries' (ibid: Appendix A, para. A.38).

Lord Falconer steered the proposals through Parliament for the government and cited examples of situations he wished to avoid, including that of a doctor accused of raping a patient. The jury were unaware of his criminal record of indecently assaulting six patients, the fact that he had been struck off and that he was being brought to court each day from prison; in court he was still routinely addressed as 'doctor' (Dyer, 2003). The Criminal Justice Act duly received its Royal Assent in November 2003 and the new 'bad character' disclosures were able to start on 15 December 2004, for offences of theft and sexual offences against a child under 16. The principles of how the disclosures should be brought into a trial were laid out in the case of *R* v. *Hanson* (2005) (EWCA Crim 824).

3. Probation Service

Probation officers are entitled to receive criminal record histories to help them write Pre-Sentence Reports for courts; before 1991 these reports were known as 'social enquiry reports'.

In the 1970s agreements were drawn up between the probation service, the police and the Home Office as to how the police would make available criminal records to the writers of the reports (Home Office, 1971: paras. 14–15) and confirmed in later circulars (Home Office, 1983: para. 3; Home Office, 1998a). Probation officers have not always been happy with the service they have received from the police, complaining in the past that they were often 'unable to obtain accurate information about previous convictions of offenders on whom we are required to report...(and)...increasing inaccuracy among the records we do receive' (House of Commons, 1990a: Appendix 5).

4. H. M. Prison Service

When a new prisoner arrives at his or her first prison of residence the accompanying court antecedents sheet/criminal record helps to determine which prison they might be allocated to and how they might be classified in terms of security needs. This process has historically not always worked well and Walker reports that in the 1950s new prisoners were often asked, 'have you served a prison sentence before?' The question might appear as a general welfare question but was really because the prison authorities did not know if the prisoner had a criminal record and had served time in custody or not (Walker, 1965: 247). As we saw in Chapter 3, direct links between prisons and the PNC have put prison access to criminal records on to a new level.

Information technology and the criminal justice system

As information technology has progressed, it has become clear that the criminal justice system and its constituent agencies have been somewhat left behind. If it was to work as a 'system', arguments were now made that there needed to be a smooth transfer of information on offenders moving from police to CPS to courts, probation and prisons, forming a consistent information trail from custody to release, and this movement had to be facilitated by electronic means.

A Home Office proposal to have information circulating within the criminal justice system using information technology was first put forward in 1986 (Goldman, H., 1986). In 1989 a joint initiative between the Home Office, the Lord Chancellor's Department and the Crown Prosecution Service was started, called the Steering Committee on CCCJS. The Steering Committee was concerned with maximising the benefits of computerisation across the criminal justice system as a whole rather than with any one agency. The three main departments involved brought to the table representatives from the Magistrates Courts, Prison Service, Police and Probation Service (Home Office), the Crown Court (Lord Chancellor's Department) and the Crown Prosecution Service (Waugh, 1991).

The CCCJS Steering Committee provided a forum for understanding the existing information flows and routes and developing the necessary infrastructure. An early concern was to achieve a common set of data standards, such as case numbers, codes for offences, court disposals and remand status, to facilitate interchange. A series of seminars inviting a wider audience took place between October and December 1992 and identified some of the obstacles to progress. Anxiety was expressed that no one had 'ownership' of the new approach and security of data was a perennial problem. Concerns also arose over the independence of each contributing organisation to be able to still make their own decisions. As for getting more publicity for the CCCJS there was some ambivalence; it was important that organisations and decision makers knew about it but it was also:

> ... important not to create *public unease* by publicising too early, or be accused of secrecy by publicising too late. Civil liberties bodies must be approached (but) ... It is difficult to know exactly when to go public on the question of data protection, but there is no reason to stop work on a project because there might be civil liberties implications.
>
> (Home Office, 1993a; emphasis added)

Progress on the CCCJS remained glacially slow throughout the 1990s; meanwhile, the various constituent agencies of the criminal justice system all experienced their own trials and tribulations in adapting to the new world of information technology. The Probation Service, for example, launched its PROBIS system in the mid-1980s and replaced this with CRAMS in the 1990s, which in turn was reviewed in 1999 with a view to 'redeveloping' it; ultimately the inclusion of probation into the newly formed National Offender Management Service (NOMS) led to the adoption of the C-NOMIS information system.

The Magistrates Courts had dipped their toe in the IT waters in 1989 with a system called MASS but this was replaced in 1997 by LIBRA. LIBRA did not fare much better and was in turn closed down in 2002 amidst some acrimony (NAO, 2003); the Chair of the House of Commons Public Account Committee denounced it as 'one of the worst IT projects I have ever seen' (quoted in Collins, 2003).

The Crown Courts did somewhat better with the CREST system introduced in 1991 to carry out basic back office tasks and produce common forms, and the County Courts with their LOCCS system. The Crown Prosecution Service had an early system called SCOPE and followed this up with the COMPASS case management system – now simply referred to as CMS – and H. M. Prison Service had the unhappy acronym of LIDS (Local Inmate Database System) as the name of their IT system.

At the end of the 1990s the CCCJS project was replaced by the IBIS initiative. The IBIS (Integrating Business and Information Systems in the Criminal Justice System) continued the aim of developing an information systems and information technology strategy for the criminal justice system and looking at what was required to manage the change. The IBIS immediately produced a Medium Term Strategic Plan that placed criminal records at the centre of the proposed new systems:

> Access to accurate, up to date information on Phoenix, the national criminal records database, is key to the improvement of public protection. Custody sergeants and courts making decisions on bail ... fines, community or custodial sentences, and prison governors deciding on the correct category of prison for an individual – are all reliant on the information on previous convictions being up to date.
>
> (IBIS, 1999: 12)

The changeover from the CCCJS to IBIS came too late, and within a few years the writing was already on the wall for IBIS. A collective two-volume report from the Inspectorates of Prisons, Probation, the Police, the CPS, the Social Services and the Courts Services Inspectorate highlighted inconsistencies and gaps in information flows between agencies of the criminal justice system, and recommended:

> ... the Home Secretary consider using the powers available to him to ensure that casework information IT systems which promote the best interests of the criminal justice system are adopted.
>
> (CPSI *et al.*, 2000: vol. 1, para. 1.17)

A separate report published later the same year made the same point with respect to the Probation Service (HMIP, 2000: paras. 3.20–3.21).

In a wider context the government was now generally committing itself to greater engagement with information technology. It was to play a major part in modernising the whole of government (Cabinet Office, 1999: Chapter 5) and at a European level the United Kingdom pledged itself to the Lisbon Agenda of March 2000. The Lisbon Agenda emerged from a 'special' meeting of the European Council that wanted to make the European Union the most competitive and dynamic economy in the world through the power of the information technology revolution.

Rather than any 'public unease' being caused by these attempts to join up the criminal justice system using information technology, the lack of progress was now denounced as 'a public disgrace':

> ... that parts of the system are still, in the first decade of the twenty-first century, effectively relying upon manual systems to support some of their key tasks is a public disgrace ... it is remarkable that one still cannot reliably expect to send an e-mail direct to a justice's desk, to a Crown prosecutor or to a prison governor.
>
> (Auld Report, 2001: 354)

Prime Minister Tony Blair declared that 'many of our criminal justice IT systems are still in the dark ages' (Blair, 2002) and an Audit Commission report estimated £80 million was being wasted annually on court adjournments, delayed and 'cracked' trials; 'cracked' trials were those where pleas changed at the last minute, or the prosecution offered no evidence and the trial just petered out (Audit Commission, 2002: para. 2). A White Paper on reform of the system made a commitment to new and better IT to join-up the agencies involved:

> ... police, CPS, courts, probation and prisons will be able to exchange case file information electronically and provide victims with secure access to the exchange to be able to track the progress of their case on-line.
>
> (Home Office *et al.*, 2002: para. 9.64)

At the Treasury some £650 million – it would later rise to £1 billion – was found to invest in case management IT across the criminal justice system over the next 3 years (H. M. Treasury, 2002) and a working group formed of senior civil servants from the Home Office, Department of Constitutional Affairs and the Attorney General's Office to take forward the new joined-up thinking.

This Criminal Justice Group, as it was called, would become the Criminal Justice Information Technology (CJIT) group and it was CJIT that would be properly funded to take forward the work of the CCCJS and IBIS.

On a wider front the complete reform of the criminal justice system was now taken forward by the formation of the National Criminal Justice Board, Chaired by the Prime Minister, and 42 Local Criminal Justice Boards across the country. It was part of the Prime Minister's declared aim to stop fighting twenty-first-century crime with nineteenth-century institutions and arrangements. A new Office of Criminal Justice Reform

(OCJR) was created in 2004 to service the National Criminal Justice Board, and CJIT was now located within that office.

The CJIT brought into being the Criminal Justice Exchange, which was to be the platform for the secure exchange of information between the agencies of the criminal justice system. One of its first success stories was the introduction of the Crown Court link up through the exchange called XHIBIT (Exchanging Hearing Information by Internet Technology). The XHIBIT could provide hearing information from the courts, within minutes, to the police, CPS, prisons, probation, Youth Offending Teams (YOTs), NOMS and even victims. All 99 Crown Courts had XHIBIT by April 2006 and the police welcomed its arrival as a means of speeding up the inclusion of court results on to the PNC (DCA, 2006b). Later a national case progression system, linking Crown Courts, Magistrates Courts, the CPS and defence solicitors was piloted. This system – known as PROGRESS – would have progress officers ensuring cases were never unduly delayed (OCJR, 2006).

Criminal records beyond the criminal justice system

Criminal records were now also moving beyond the criminal justice system. Here we note their expanding use by agencies that have no direct affiliation to the traditional criminal justice system.

National security

Government employees in sensitive positions concerned with national security such as the Government Communications H. Q. (GCHQ) or the Security Services themselves are screened for their posts. The origins of this so-called positive vetting are normally traced back to the late 1940s and the start of the 'cold war'. Worries about access to classified information that could be passed to the 'enemy' particularly attached themselves to atomic energy and atomic weapons development programmes. Positive vetting included a criminal record check and references, but also required more rigorous interviewing and checking of extended family, political leanings, sexuality and a search for 'character defects' (Hennessey and Brownfield, 1982).

Positive vetting was fine-tuned during the 1960s and the 1970s but in essence remained unchanged. Hollingsworth and Norton-Taylor talk of 'normal vetting' having the add-on of 'positive vetting'; 'normal vetting' involving 'a sweep through the Criminal Records Office as well as a check with Special Branch and MI5 files' to see what is known (Hollingsworth and Norton-Taylor, 1988: 24). Linn also refers to 'negative vetting', with the addition of positive vetting (Linn, 1990: 18–21; see also Radcliffe Report, 1962).

In 1990 the government announced the result of a review of positive vetting which broke the idea up into a hierarchy of vetting. Normal or negative vetting would constitute the foundation of checks, and this was now broken into two levels – reliability checks and counter-terrorist checks. On top of that there were to be three levels of positive vetting, becoming ever more rigorous or intensive as levels of access to sensitive information increased:

- Positive Vetting (Secret)
- Positive Vetting (Top Secret) and
- Enhanced Positive Vetting.

> (Hansard HC Debates, 14 July 1990, cols. 159–160W;
> see also Lustgarten and Leigh, 1994: Chapter)

A few years later the system was further changed to try and make it more streamlined. A review started in March 1994 was completed later the same year and in future, positive vetting was to give way to developed vetting with a two-tier hierarchy:

- Security check – comparable to the old positive vetting (secret)
- Developed vetting – comparable to the old enhanced positive vetting and positive vetting (top secret)

The security check (SC) clearance was again the common starting point that developed vetting (DV) was added on to as required. The SC clearance included 'a check against the National Collection of Criminal Records and relevant departmental and police records' (Hansard HC Debates, 15 December 1994, cols. 764–766).

Counter-terrorist checks (CTC) were to continue as a third level of vetting for anyone likely to be working in proximity to public figures who might be at risk of attack or where there was access to sensitive information; this included those granted unescorted access to certain military, civil and industrial establishments considered possible terrorist targets. For completion of a counter-terrorist check, 'Criminal record information may...be taken into account' (ibid).

The former reliability checks were now to be known as basic checks, including 'verification of identity, and written references (confirming) recruits are reliable and trustworthy'. These basic checks were to be augmented by DV or SC as necessary (ibid).

National security checking has remained at this level and six organisations carry out the necessary investigations – the Security Service, the Secret Intelligence Service, GCHQ, the Defence Vetting Agency, the Foreign and Commonwealth Office and the Office of Civil Nuclear Security. All have access to the criminal record collection as part of their work. In terms of their overall performance, variations in the intensity of the vetting by these different agencies have been noted, and attempts to achieve greater uniformity are being made (Intelligence and Security Committee, 2005: paras. 47–50).

Criminal Injuries Compensation scheme

The Criminal Injuries Compensation Authority (CICA) that administers compensation payments to victims of violent crime may make a reduced payment to applicants with a criminal record. All applicants are subjected to a criminal record check and payment may be reduced or withheld if:

> ...the applicant's character as shown by his criminal convictions (excluding convictions spent under the Rehabilitation of Offenders Act 1974 at the date of application or death) or by evidence available to the claims officer makes it inappropriate that a full award or any award at all be made.
>
> (CICA, 2001: para. 13(e))

Victims of violent crime are expected to be 'innocent' victims and not someone who has caused work for the criminal justice system in the past or whose lifestyle has contributed to their victim status. The rationale was spelt out in the original White Paper that proposed the Criminal Injuries Compensation scheme back in the 1960s (Home Office, 1961: paras. 31–37).

The CICA guide to the current scheme elaborates the position, and advises that the Authority will use its discretion. More recent and more serious offences will count for more than old and trivial offences and a system of 'penalty points' has been devised based on this formula. As the penalty points for a given criminal record add up, so too does the percentage reduction in possible claim (CICA, 2004: Part 4, paras. 19–24).

Licensing approvals

A number of positions involving a need to be licensed now require disclosure of a criminal record in order to obtain that licence. There is a clear overlap here between employment screening (see Chapters 6 and 7) and the obtaining of a licence which gives you the right to certain employment.

- People acting as security dealers require a licence to practice to ensure the probity of their dealings (Prevention of Fraud (Investments) Act 1958, Financial Services Act 1986), and licenses are required to trade in alcohol either as a landlord or off-licence trader (Licensing Act 1964, s. 6). Licences were once issued by magistrates, but they are now issued by local authorities (Gambling Act 2005).
- In order to obtain a Public Service Vehicle (PSV) licence or a Heavy Goods Vehicle (HGV) licence to drive a bus or lorry, applicants had to have their criminal records checked (Transport Act 1968, s. 35(1) and 36(3)). The terminology has now changed to Passenger Carrying Vehicle (PCV) and Larger Goods Vehicles (LGV).
- Licenses are required by casino workers and staff in bookmakers' offices (Gaming Act 1968, s. 34, Schedules 5 and 9; now the Gambling Act 2005), as are those running amusement arcades (Lotteries and Amusement Act 1976) and outlets for National Lottery tickets to ensure the probity of their activities (Lottery Act 1993).
- Taxi drivers need a licence from their local authorities and since 1992 a criminal record check is part of the application (Road Traffic Act 1991, s. 47; see also Department of Transport, 1992).
- There had been a long campaign to screen the growing numbers of people working in the private security industry, from private investigators through to 'door supervisors' (or 'bouncers'). Licences were introduced by the Private Security Industry Act 2001, and these were issued by the Security Industry Authority and included a criminal record check. A list of offences likely to lead to a licence refusal for some jobs has been compiled (SIA, 2006: 55–65); and as part of the prison privatisation project it became necessary to check the backgrounds of workers from the private sector.
- Motor salvage operators have to be screened under the Vehicles (Crime) Act 2001 and the Motor Salvage Operators Regulations 2000 (no. 1916).

Non-police prosecuting agencies

Criminal records are made available to a number of agencies – besides the police – who have prosecution powers. The Financial Services Authority, the National Health Service, the Office of Fair Trading and the Department of Trade and Industry all have such powers. At the Department of Work and Pensions, for example, six solicitors' offices in Leeds, Liverpool, Birmingham, Cardiff and two in London have direct PNC access to help build cases for prosecution of fraud cases ('PNC reduces burden on police and saves DSS time', *PITO News*, 8 December 1997).

Youth offending

In order to 'help' children and young people who have committed crimes, rather than just punish them, arrangements are in place to promote liaison between the police and other agencies, which encourages the exchange of information. As far back as 1927 the Home Office reported informal discussions between police, probation and social workers as to whether or not some young offenders actually needed to be prosecuted (Oliver, 1978: Chapter 2).

The 1969 Children and Young Persons Act formalised some of these arrangements requiring the police to inform local authorities every time a young person was arrested and to discuss with them the need for prosecution. In practice, the provisions of 'discussions' were never implemented but many police and local authorities still set up their own non-statutory schemes of 'juvenile-liaison' to consider the children they were both dealing with; Home Office guidance existed on how this might be carried out (Home Office, 1970: paras. 92–97).

New Labour laws eventually took these informal arrangements and made multi-agency work with young offenders a statutory requirement when it created YOTs. The new YOTs comprised social workers, police, probation officers and others, and to ensure a smooth exchange of information between the agencies the law now empowered such exchanges wherever it was contributing to the aims of the act, that is, the reduction of crime (Crime and Disorder Act 1998, s. 115).

Other multi-agency arrangements that followed were non-statutory but still required the necessary exchange of information. Youth Inclusion Programmes (YIPs) and Youth Inclusion and Support Panels (YISPs) both involved police, social workers and others in working with young people, including children under 10 and below the age of criminal responsibility, to prevent their offending.

Criminal record information held by the police would of necessity be prime information for most of these multi-agency exercises. In the YOTs, for example, the (ASSET) risk assessment instrument required input of a range of factors helpful in predicting the likelihood of future offending, including criminal record history of the young persons themselves and also criminal family members. The ASSET is used to help define a 'core profile', and help decide on bail decisions and final warning decisions (Baker, 2005; see also YJB/ACPO, 2005).

Child safety and welfare

Criminal records have been made available to local authorities concerned with child welfare for many years. Originally this was for vetting applicants to become foster parents or adoptive parents (see, e.g. Public Health Act 1936, s. 210(c)) and from the 1970s to help local authority social services departments and social workers to protect children from abuse. In more recent years the sharing of information has been to safeguard children in a wider sense, including the concept of 'children in need' introduced by the Children Act 1989 and indeed the latest thinking that 'every child matters' (Parton, 2006).

The police have made criminal records available to local authorities through the mechanism of the child-protection conference. The conference is a multi-agency meeting convened to pool information on a child, family and household where there are possible child-protection questions arising. It is attended by social workers, doctors, health care professionals, teachers and the police. The original guidance to the police on how they should input criminal records to conferences confirmed the confidentiality of records and that they 'should only be disclosed to professional colleagues involved in the case' (Home Office, 1976: para. 11).

The Home Office guidance also said that the police should only make available 'any relevant previous convictions' concerning a person involved in the care of a child or member of the same household, and that normally it would be sufficient to do this orally (ibid: para. 8). No guidance was given on how the police might determine relevance, and no explanation offered on why it should only be orally, given that all such conferences were immediately minuted. The Inquiry Report into the death of a child in London highlighted the problem of 'relevance' when it found one police officer who would have made certain records available to a child-protection conference and another who would not (London Borough of Lambeth, 1987: 148; see also Hebenton and Thomas, 1992).

On the uses made of disclosed criminal records the Home Office advised further caution because 'not all criminal convictions are recorded' (Home Office, 1976: para. 13) and that in interpreting criminal records, conferences should remind themselves that 'a record of previous convictions may not be a true guide to present conduct' (ibid: para. 14).

Child-protection conferences are non-statutory arrangements guided only by Home Office circular. The original Home Office circular of 1976 is still applicable although more general advice has been updated. In 1999 all professionals attending a conference were asked to 'bring with them details of their involvement with the child and family, and information concerning…the capacity of the parents to safeguard the child' (DoH *et al.*, 1999: paras. 5–62). The courts have recognised the circular status of this guidance that 'does not have any legal status' but have emphasised that 'the consequences of inter-agency co-operation is that there has to be free exchange of information between social workers and police officers' (comments by Butler Sloss LJ in Re G (a minor) [1996] 2 All ER 65 at 68).

The Children Act 1989 does make reference to information exchange and lists agencies that have a duty to assist local authorities carrying out child abuse investigations (s. 47(9)–(11)). The list includes health authorities, housing authorities and others, but not the police. This was because of the idea of police independence and the Home Office not wanting to be seen as directing the police to do anything. On the other hand, as David Mellor for the Home Office said during Parliamentary debate on the bill, 'police refusal to co-operate on any matter would be indefensible' (Hansard HC Debates, Standing Committee B, 6 June 1985, col. 342). The most recent guidance states that:

> (the police) are committed to sharing information and intelligence with other organisations where this is necessary to protect children.
> (H. M. Government, 2006: para. 2.101)

As the Children Act 1989 was implemented in the 1990s, it became apparent that much of the work was concentrating on the 'sharp-end' of child welfare in terms of child abuse and child protection at the expense of a more preventive approach looking at the wider welfare needs of what the act called 'children in need' (DoH, 1995). Attempts were made to re-focus on this wider group of children and to move away from the forensic requirements of just looking at child protection. Put simply this meant early intervention in order to avoid situations deteriorating into child abuse and the need for child protection. This movement of policy and practice not only took the need for information gathering and sharing with it, but also:

> …went along with an ambitious longer term aim of improving management information and its collation by central government,

with the overall aim of implementing an integrated children's system. Such a system would clearly be far more wide ranging, complex and inclusive than the earlier child protection system, which it would replace.

(Parton, 2006)

The government put forward its proposals in the significantly named Green Paper '*Every* Child Matters' (Chief Secretary to the Treasury, 2003; emphasis added). The Green Paper had widespread implications for future social work with children and families, but for present purposes it is the improvement of information collection and sharing that we should note. The idea was to create 'information hubs' to store electronically information from all agencies having contact with all children, including the police:

> …systems would hold records for every child or young person resident in a local authority area. This would be important in enabling practitioners to ensure that no children or young people are overlooked. Information would be updated by practitioners in response to changes in the child's life.

(ibid: para. 4.7)

The idea of 'information hubs' was taken forward by the Children Act 2004 s. 12, which gave the legislative underpinning for the 'information databases' to be created on all children. The database would hold the names of other practitioners or professionals working with that child or indicate which other agency had an interest in the child. It would not allow each agency to have open access to each other's files. These new arrangements are now referred to as contact point and are anticipated to come online by late 2008 (Hansard HC Debates, 8 December 2005, cols. 114–116WS).

Multi-Agency Public Protection Arrangements

Liaison between the probation service and the police service has been ongoing in a generic manner for many years. More recent arrangements have focused on adult – and juvenile – offenders likely to be considered 'dangerous' in terms of violent or sexual offending, and liaison has been formalised between the probation service and the police and extended to include other agencies.

The West Yorkshire Police and their counterparts in the West Yorkshire Probation Service are examples of two agencies who started regular meetings as far back as 1986, when 'it was clear both agencies were holding relevant information and if the two were married up then certain events could be prevented' (MacDonald, 2000; see also Kemshall and Maguire, 2001). These informal arrangements took on a new significance following what became known as the 'North Wales decision' and the introduction of the sex offender register in 1997.

The 'North Wales decision' referred to the courts upholding the right of the North Wales Police to disclose criminal record information to members of the public in the interests of crime prevention. The information was on the presence of two people with offences against children living in the locality. The two people concerned appealed to the courts to rule the police actions to be unreasonable; the appeal was lost (*R* v. *Chief Constable of North Wales Police* ex p. AB (1997) Times 14 July; *R* v. *Chief Constable of North Wales Police* ex p. Thorpe (1998) Times 28 March).

In saying the police were in order to release this information the courts added that this should not mean a 'blanket' disclosure of conviction records was acceptable but only when there was an identifiable risk to the public by specific individuals. The court decision was inevitably tied in to the implementation of the sex offender register from 1 September 1997 and the fact that all those on the register might be seen to pose a risk. Informal co-operation between police and probation started to intensify to help with risk-assessment and risk-management exercises.

The Criminal Justice and Court Services Act 2000 ss. 67–68 put these arrangements on to a formal statutory basis with the police and probation now designated as the 'responsible authorities' and other agencies being asked to assist them. The new arrangements were to be known as Multi-Agency Public Protection Panels (MAPPPs) or Multi-Agency Public Protection Arrangements (MAPPA). Information sharing was at the heart of these arrangements, and although never explicitly stated in Home Office guidance this would also mean criminal records:

> ... the local arrangements made are based first and foremost on information sharing between agencies. Information needs to be shared on all the relevant offenders ... in many cases the sharing of information to inform the risk assessment will be the only inter-agency action required.
>
> (Home Office, 2001: para. 9(b))

The 'relevant offenders' were defined as those on the sex offender register, other violent offenders and indeed any other person who might present a risk of harm (Criminal Justice and Court Services Act 2000, s. 68; Home Office, 2002a: paras. 24–29).

These MAPPAs were in many ways the mirror image of the Area Child Protection Committees or Local Safeguarding of Children Boards and their Information Sharing and Assessment (ISA) arrangements. The MAPPAs would oversee adults in the name of 'community public protection' and the latter would oversee children in the name of child protection. In practice, it has been pointed out that the relationship is not quite as simple, with the two systems having been arrived at through separate policy developments and the MAPPAs looking mostly at dangerous men in the community and the Local Safeguarding Children Boards, at children and women as their primary carers. On top of that there were no straightforward mechanisms to exchange information between the two systems and 'while both aimed to improve the sharing of information, the potential for misunderstanding and misinformation seemed considerable' (Parton, 2006: 137).

In 2003 the H. M. Prison Service was drafted in as a third 'responsible authority' on the MAPPAs and the list of agencies expected to co-operate was extended. This list now included YOTs, local education authorities, housing authorities or social service authorities, social security officials, employment and training officials, registered social landlords, health authorities, Primary Care Trusts, NHS Trusts and providers of electronic monitoring services (Criminal Justice Act 2003, s. 325; see also Hewitt, 2004).

Conclusions

The uses to which criminal records have been put have widened over the years. The traditional use – by the police for policing purposes and the courts to assist with sentencing purposes – has been added to in a number of ways. This has led to information technology being used to facilitate the exchange of criminal records around the agencies of the criminal justice system, including the probation service, the prison service, the Crown Prosecution Service and the courts themselves. This CJIT programme is still being developed but envisages a far more electronically joined-up criminal justice system than we have seen before.

It is also clear that criminal records are being used more by agencies outside and beyond the criminal justice system. Some of these agencies have used records for a long time. Agencies who need to vet staff for national security purposes are long-time users, as are the administrators of the Criminal Injuries Compensation Scheme. More recent users are local authorities for child-welfare purposes and child protection, and YOTs working with young people 'in trouble' with the law. The use of criminal records for pre-employment screening has seen a massive growth since 1986 and it is that particular use of criminal records that we turn to in Chapters 6 and 7.

5
The 'Spent' Criminal Record

When an offender's period of punishment ends, there begins a process of resettlement or rehabilitation back into the community. Accommodation, family support and employment are all important parts of this transition. Employment in particular has been singled out as a key factor in successful re-integration. According to one former home secretary, 'a job is the best help that any ex-offender can get to avoid returning to crime'. The existence of a criminal record, however, transcends the period of resettlement and remains as a block to successful rehabilitation, as a possible stigma and specific obstacle to employment.

In order to assist the ex-offender in the process of re-settlement most Western countries now have systems of removing criminal records from the formal record after given periods of time during which there has been no further offending. In the United Kingdom we have the 1974 Rehabilitation of Offenders Act with its concept of the 'spent' conviction for certain offenders. In 2002 the government started a review of this act with a view to updating its provisions.

Resettlement

The process of resettling an offender back to full status as a citizen after a period of punishment is a social process that may take some time. Hopefully the process also leads to the ending of criminal activities – or desistance from crime.

McWilliams and Pease (1990) offer the model that rehabilitation in its wider sense takes place when the punishment ends. The offender has all his or her rights of citizenship returned to them and from a de-graded status – during the time of punishment – they are restored to a re-graded position alongside everyone else. Rehabilitation in this sense does not imply any reform or change – which may or may not have taken place – but only that the punishment and its consequences have come to an end.

Others have looked more closely at why people stop committing offences:

> The processes by which people stop offending and are 'resettled', 'reintegrated', 'rehabilitated' 'reformed' and so on, have only of late received very much attention. All of these 're' words imply that this group of people are in some way returned ... to some state that previously they had occupied.
>
> (Farrall and Calverley, 2006: xii)

The factors that have now been identified as leading to desistance from crime are loosely divided into the 'external' and the 'internal'. External factors include the 'package of adulthood', made up of a home, work, relationships and children, together with treatment interventions including, say, probation supervision or the cessation of drug use. The internal factors include emotional changes in the way the offender sees him or her self and tries to cast off an old identity in favour of a new more pro-social identity (Maruna, 2001; Farrall and Calverley, 2006).

Employment has consistently been identified as a key factor in resettlement and desistance from crime. It provides status, income and social groupings that lead people into a law-abiding life. Some research suggests that employment reduces the risk of re-offending by between a third and a half (Uggen, 2000; SEU, 2002: Chapter 8). Efforts are made in prison to give prisoners work skills, training and education and links are increasingly made to bridge the transition from prison back to employment in the community (see, e.g. HMIP/HMIP, 2001: paras. 6.22–6.50; DfES *et al.*, 2005).

The work that agencies put in with ex-offenders to try and find them employment is well intended. But even where it does take place, the continuing presence of a criminal record hangs over everything like the 'spectre at the feast'. According to one imprisoned person:

> I would get out and for the first few weeks I would ... try and get a job, but obviously with a criminal record, if you were honest and said, yes, I've got a criminal record, then, there's the door basically.
>
> (quoted in SEU, 2002: 52)

The National Association for the Care and Resettlement of Offenders (NACRO) has defined the paradox of all the work put in with offenders coming to nought when the criminal record is mentioned:

> ...for all the resettlement work now being done in prisons, prisoners still face enormous difficulties finding employment after release. Not only do they often have a poor education record and little work experience, but they also carry the stigma of a criminal record.
>
> (NACRO, 2005: 16)

The job applicant with a criminal record had three choices. If they declared the record they risked not getting the job. If they stayed silent they also risked not getting the job because the silence would be interpreted as something to hide. Or they could fail to disclose and risk being found out later and run the risk of being dismissed for misrepresentation.

In the past there have even been allegations that the government has tried to turn a blind eye to this paradox and deliberately played down the link between offending and employment. In 1996 a Home Office funded report of a 'National Audit of Offender Employment Policies and Practice' appeared to have been censored from an earlier draft version. The report came at the same time as the Police Bill – later the Police Act 1997 – was going through Parliament, which would introduce widespread screening of job applicants by reference to their criminal records and ministers reportedly did 'not want to be seen to be supporting research that suggests unemployed ex-criminals will re-offend' (Bennetto, 1996b; for more on the Police Act 1997: see Chapter 7).

Others have seen the problem as simply one of competing rights between employers and the wider public on the one hand and ex-offenders on the other. Employers have the right to protect their property and capital from damage and employees have the right to a safe workplace; customers have the right to safe products and services. Employers may even be vicariously liable for an ex-offender's behaviour in the workplace and have to live with the American idea of the 'negligent hiring doctrine'. Ex-offenders have only what rights they can claim for help in 'going straight' and trying to rehabilitate themselves (Sullivan, 1998; Lam and Harcourt, 2003).

Attempts have been made in most Western countries over the last 30 years to help ex-offenders into work by having mechanisms to delete or extinguish an old criminal record. The social process of resettlement coupled with the formal deletion of a criminal record to help live down one's past seemed to offer a positive way forward.

The deletion of a criminal record is not always automatic and for some offenders it may never take place. Different countries vary their systems of criminal record deletion. A conviction record may only be completely expunged in the case of a pardon, a conviction being 'quashed on appeal' or otherwise permanently 'purged'. Sometimes the record may be kept by the police or other record-keeping authority for possible future use in judicial proceedings even if, for all other purposes, the person concerned may consider it non-existent; this may be referred to as the record being 'sealed' or 'spent' for non-judicial/policing purposes.

Records may be excluded in various ways:

(a) Automatically
When the offender has gone through a prescribed period of time without re-offending or has reached a given age. This takes place in Austria, Belgium, Denmark, France, the United Kingdom and other European countries.

(b) by Judicial Decision
On application, a judicial hearing may exclude old conviction records; in practice the court may want evidence similar to (a) above, in that a given time period without re-offending will have to have elapsed. This takes place in Italy, Luxembourg, Portugal and other countries.

(c) by Administrative Decision
On application to a chief of police or relevant ministerial department; again in practice the official may want evidence of a given time period passing without re-offending. This takes place in Cyprus, Iceland and Norway.

These various forms of rehabilitation by record deletion may not be exclusive of one another but may exist as a combination within any one country. The United Kingdom has had an automatic system in place since 1974, based on deliberations from those times.

The Gardiner Report

In the early 1970s, in a social climate more conducive to helping ex-offenders, a group of UK penal policy campaign groups got together to consider what legislative changes could be made to help people with criminal records live down their past. The organisations Justice, NACRO and the Howard League for Penal Reform convened a working party under the Chairmanship of Lord Gardiner to examine the possibilities. Their report was called 'Living it Down: The Problem of Old Convictions' and it is often referred to as simply the Gardiner Report (Gardiner Report, 1972).

The Gardiner Report argued that if there was evidence that an offender was still 'going straight' after a given period of time, that good progress should not be impeded by the revelation of the old conviction record. It was in society's interests, as well as the individual's, that people be helped to live down their former behaviour and to that extent the law should help them. The report cited evidence of an estimated one million individuals in England and Wales who had a criminal record that was 10 years or more old (ibid: para. 16).

A number of case studies were also cited whereby people had been unable to get employment even though eminently suitable for the positions in question. People wanting to go into public life had similar difficulties. The situation was particularly acute for those who had committed their offences as young people or had only ever committed one offence. What was needed was a formal way of expunging these old convictions so that they did not handicap a person in the future.

The report had to agree on what actually constituted a sufficient conviction-free period of time before a criminal record became expunged or 'spent'. It decided to do this by reference to the severity of the sentence imposed at the time rather than the type of offence. The formula presented was:

A. non-custodial sentence – 5 years.
B. custodial sentence of up to 6 months – 7 years.
C. custodial sentence of 6 months to 2 years – 10 years.

Any sentence of over 2 years was deemed sufficient to fall outside the proposed scheme; in other words one's record would never be expunged.

The report had also to grapple with the understanding that a criminal record needed to remain intact in the interests of justice, for any future criminal proceedings. Within the criminal courts the concept of a 'spent' conviction was not going to be applicable. It was only a valid concept to the wider world of employment, insurance, public life, and so on, where rehabilitation was affected.

One further dilemma was the simple fact that a criminal court appearance was always a public affair, where justice could be seen to be done. If the press and public had all the details of the conviction at the point of it being made, how could a veil of confidentiality descend upon it at a later date? If the press reported an old conviction that had become 'spent', what redress did an individual have if the press were only reporting the truth? The values of freedom of expression would come into head-on conflict with the rights of the ex-offender.

The Rehabilitation of Offenders Act 1974

The UK's Rehabilitation of Offenders Act 1974 was implemented from 1 July 1975. It effectively allowed certain criminal records to be regarded as 'spent' after a given period of time. Offenders were allowed to 'legally lie' about the existence of the record for purposes of employment, insurance, and so on. The records themselves were never actually deleted or erased but would remain on police files should they ever be needed again in court; the act did not apply to future court appearances. Anyone with official access to criminal records who disclosed them inappropriately was guilty of an offence under the act.

(a) The Rehabilitation Periods

The act applied only to offenders receiving a custodial sentence of 30 months or less; anything longer and the act did not come into play. For sentences falling below the 30-months criteria, the act allowed the criminal record to be considered 'spent' after a given period of time, calculated according to the severity of the sentence. The time periods were halved for juvenile offenders (see Table 5.1).

The time period was referred to as the 'rehabilitation period' and the person concerned as the 'rehabilitated person' once they had completed the requisite time without further offending. A 'rehabilitated person' could regard the record as 'spent' and therefore effectively as never having happened – as long as they were not back in court.

(b) The Exempted Positions and Jobs

From the start a number of employment and other positions were exempted from the act. This meant that although the criminal record might theoretically be considered 'spent' because all the criteria of the act were met, the job applicant had still to declare them because of the nature of the work.

Many organisations and employers lobbied the Home Office to have their particular case included in the list of exemptions. The list of those who did actually get exemptions was finally agreed on and it gradually grew over the years. The exemption status was granted through a

Table 5.1   Rehabilitation periods for adults under the Rehabilitation of Offenders Act 1974

Sentence	Rehabilitation Period
Prison Sentence more than 30 months	Conviction never 'spent'
Prison Sentence of over 6 months but not more than 30 months	10 years
Prison Sentence of 6 months or less	7 years
Community Orders, Fines	5 years
Absolute Discharge	6 months
Hospital Order	5 years or 2 years after the order ceases to have effect, whichever is the latest

Rehabilitation of Offenders Act 1974 as amended

series of statutory instruments and primary acts and broadly covered those working with children and vulnerable adults, certain professions, including those in law, health and pharmacy, senior managers in banking and financial services and jobs where national security might be at risk (see Table 5.2)

The numbers granted 'exemptions' was greater than those who could request police disclosures of records to verify any declared criminal convictions (see Chapter 6).

It was one thing being able to tell a job applicant that they could not consider any convictions as 'spent' because it was an 'exempted' position. It was another to be able to *check* any declaration with the police with any vetting process. A gap had opened up between the 'exemptions' and the police check. By 1991 the Home Office reported 49 'exempted' positions had been created, of which only 23 could be verified with a police check. The Home Office concluded 'that exceptions under the Rehabilitation of Offenders Act have in a sense been granted as an alternative to vetting' (Home Office, 1991: para. 181).

Some years later the full list of all those organisations who had lobbied for 'exemption' status in the 1970s was revealed (see Hansard, March 27 1990, PQ (written) no. 141).

(c) Further Criminal Proceedings

The 1974 Act was not applicable within the criminal court should the offender ever find themselves back there. In the interests of justice the idea of the 'spent' conviction was not possible (1974 Act, s. 7(2)(a)). A Practice Direction from the Lord Chief Justice, however, did try to introduce the spirit of the act into Crown Court proceedings. After a

Table 5.2 Exceptions to the Rehabilitation of Offenders Act 1974

Professions
1. Medical practitioner
2. Barrister (in England and Wales), advocate (in Scotland), solicitor
3. Chartered accountant, certified accountant
4. Dentist, dental hygienist, dental auxiliary
5. Veterinary surgeon
6. Nurse, midwife
7. Ophthalmic optician, dispensing optician
8. Pharmaceutical chemist
9. Registered teacher (in Scotland)
10. Any profession to which the *Health Professions Order 2001* applies and which is undertaken following registration under that order
11. Registered osteopath
12. Registered chiropractor
13. Chartered psychologist
14. Actuary
15. Registered foreign lawyer
16. Legal executive
17. Receiver appointed by the Court of Protection.

Offices, Employments and Work
1. Judicial appointments.
2. The Director of Public Prosecutions and any office or employment in the Crown Prosecution Service.
3. Procurators fiscal and district court prosecutors, and any employment in the office of a procurator fiscal or district court prosecutor or in the Crown Office.
4. Designated officers for magistrates' courts, for justices of the peace or for local justices' clerks and their assistants.
5. Clerks (including deputy and assistant clerks) and officers of the High Court of Justiciary, the Court of Session and the district court, sheriff clerks (including sheriff clerks depute) and their clerks and assistants.
6. Constables, persons appointed as police cadets to undergo training with a view to becoming constables and persons employed for the purposes of, or to assist the constables of, a police force established under any enactment: naval, military and air force police.
7. Any employment which is concerned with the administration of, or is otherwise normally carried out wholly or partly within the precincts of, a prison, remand centre, young offender institution, and members of boards of visitors (now known as independent monitoring boards) appointed under section 6 of the or of visiting committees appointed under section 7 of the *Prisons (Scotland) Act 1952*.
8. Traffic wardens appointed under section 81 of the *Road Traffic Regulation Act 1967* or section 9 of the *Police (Scotland) Act 1967*.
9. Probation officers appointed under Schedule 3 of the *Powers of Criminal Courts Act 1973*.
10. Any employment or other work which is concerned with the provision of care services to vulnerable adults and which is of such a kind as to enable the holder of that employment or the person engaged in that work to have

access to vulnerable adults in receipt of such services in the course of his normal duties.

11. Any employment or other work which is concerned with the provision of health services and which is of such a kind as to enable the holder of that employment or the person engaged in that work to have access to persons in receipt of such services in the course of his normal duties.

12. Any work which is (a) work in a regulated position (as defined by Criminal Justice and Court Services Act 2000, s. 36); or (b) work in a further education institution where the normal duties of that work involve regular contact with persons aged under 18.

13. Any employment in the Royal Society for the Prevention of Cruelty to Animals where the person employed or working, as part of his duties, may carry out the killing of animals.

14. Any office or employment in the Serious Fraud Office.

15. Any office or employment in the Serious Organised Crime Agency.

16. Any office or employment in Her Majesty's Customs and Excise.

17. Any employment which is concerned with the monitoring, for the purposes of child protection, or communications by means of the Internet.

18. Any employment or other work which is normally carried out in premises approved under section 9 of the *Criminal Justice and Court Services Act 2000*.

19. Any employment or other work which is normally carried out in a hospital used only for the provision of high security psychiatric services.

Regulated Occupations

1. Firearms dealer.

2. Any occupation in respect of which an application to the Gaming Board for Great Britain for a licence, certificate or registration is required by or under any enactment.

3. Director, controller or manager of an insurer.

4. Dealer in securities.

5. Manager or trustee under a unit trust scheme.

6. Any occupation which is concerned with: (a) the management of a place in respect of which the approval of the Secretary of State is required by section 1 of the *Abortion Act 1967*, or (b) in England and Wales, carrying on a nursing home in respect of which registration is required by section 187 of the *Public Health Act 1936* or section 14 of the *Mental Health Act 1959*; or (c) in Scotland carrying on a nursing home in respect of which registration is required under section 1 of the *Nursing Homes Registration (Scotland) Act 1938* or a private hospital in respect of which registration is required under section 15 of the *Mental Health (Scotland) Act 1960*.

7. Any occupation which is concerned with carrying on an establishment in respect of which registration is required by section 37 of the *National Assistance Act 1948* or section 61 of the *Social Work (Scotland) Act 1968*.

8. Any occupation in respect of which the holder, as occupier or premises on which explosives are kept, is required by any Order in Council made under section 43 of the *Explosives Act 1875* to obtain from the police or a court of summary jurisdiction a certificate as to his fitness to keep the explosives.

Table 5.2 (Continued)

Excepted Licences, Certificates and Permits
1. Firearm certificates and shot gun certificates issued under the *Firearms Act 1968*, and permits issued under section 7(1), 9(2) or 13(1) (c) of that Act.
2. Licences issued under section 25 of the *Children and Young Persons Act 1933* (which relates to persons under the age of 18 going abroad for the purpose of performing or being exhibited for profit).
3. Certificates issued by the police or a court of summary jurisdiction under any Order in Council made under section 43 of the *Explosives Act 1875* as to the fitness of a person to keep explosives for private use.
4. Taxi driver licences.
5. Licences granted under section 8 of the *Private Security Industry Act 2001*.

Sources: see The Rehabilitation of Offenders Act 1974 (Exceptions) Order SI 1975 no. 1023. The Rehabilitation of Offenders Act 1974 (Exceptions) Amendment Orders SI 1986 no. 1249 and no. 2268; SI 2001 no. 1192 and no. 3516; SI 2002 no. 441. Banking Acts 1979 and 1987. Financial Services Act 1986. National Lottery Act 1993. Financial Services and Markets Act 2000

guilty verdict and the provision of the criminal record for purposes of sentence, the Practice Direction recommended that 'spent' convictions be marked on the record and not referred to without the authority of the judge, and only in the interests of justice (Home Office, 1975b).

The act in practice

The act was implemented from 1 July 1975 complete with its 'exceptions' and the fact that it would not apply to future criminal court proceedings apart from within the guidance of the Lord Chief Justice's Practice Direction. Within a few years its significance was spelt out in the courts:

> The effect of this Act is that a spent conviction is to be wiped out all together from the knowledge of anyone. Even police officers or court officers cannot disclose it to anyone. If they do they may be liable for a punishment themselves . . . so you can see how strong this Act is in wiping everything out.
>
> (*Reynolds* v. *Phoenix Assurance*, 1978, 2 Lloyds Rep. 22 at 24)

One unintended consequence of the act was that it drew attention to criminal records and employment in a more direct way than had been the case in the past. Some research found that questions about convictions on application forms for work started to increase *after* the act had been implemented. Employers became more aware and whereas before they had been indifferent, they now wanted to know if applicants had a record, whether or not they were 'exempted' or the record could be verified (Breed, 1987: 52).

Evidence also emerged of the extent of employers' ignorance of the details of the act. A common mistake was to believe that applicants could not statutorily be employed until after the rehabilitation period had been completed (ibid). In general:

> ...a majority of employers have little or no knowledge of the workings of the Rehabilitation of Offenders Act. Of those that have some knowledge of the Act, many claimed to have acquired the information by accident or from general knowledge rather than official sources.
>
> (Apex Trust, 1989: 19)

The 1986 decision to include childcare workers into the 'exemptions' under the act had raised further awareness of criminal records and the part they could play in recruitment. Within a few years hundreds of thousands of applicants for this sort of work were having to declare their records and have them verified by a police check (see Chapter 6). Local authorities suddenly found themselves having access to information never previously available to them and a standardised paragraph started to be added to the letters sending out application forms and job specifications to applicants:

> ...the work for which you are applying involves substantial opportunity for access to children. It is therefore exempt from the Rehabilitation of Offenders Act 1974. You are therefore required to declare any pending prosecutions or convictions you may have, even if they would otherwise be regarded as 'spent' under this Act.
>
> (this form of wording was advised in Home Office, 1988b: Annex C and Home Office, 1993b: Annex E)

Critics started to argue that the number of exceptions to the act was debilitating the original idea of the legislation. The Home Office said it had no plans to review the act but it did intend to look at the number of exceptions in relation to the disclosure of records to employers (Hansard HC Debates, 10 November 1992, col. 80WA). This appears to be a recognition of the gap opening up between the number of exempted positions and the fewer number of those entitled to check with the police (see above; Home Office, 1991: para. 181).

The debate on exemptions now got subsumed into the discussions on a new regime for disclosing criminal records that would culminate in the Police Act 1997 and the CRB (see Chapters 6 and 7); a review of the 1974 Act was getting more urgent (Penal Affairs Consortium, 1999).

In the meantime other particular criticisms continued to be made. The rehabilitation periods were criticised as being unduly long and therefore meaningless to some offenders. The government's own Better Regulation Task Force looking at all aspects of 'Fit Person Criteria' found:

> ...the Act...sets out a complex array of rehabilitation periods to determine when different types of conviction are spent. These periods seem to have arisen more from political expediency than any rational justification.
>
> (Haskins Report, 1999: para. 4.3.3)

The task force recommended the government consider reviewing the act.

In 1999 the government did look at altering one aspect of the act. It had been realised that police cautions (for adults) and reprimands and final warnings (for juveniles) were not covered by the act. This meant they could never be considered 'spent' even though they were included now as part of one's criminal record. As they involved no court appearance or conviction – and therefore covered the less serious offences – it was anomalous that they remained open to any employer. The proposal was made to include them into the act (Home Office, 1999b) but at the time of writing (March 2007) this was still awaited.

More recent research by Fletcher and colleagues revealed a continuing ignorance of the act amongst employers and estimated less than 50 per cent of them really understood its complexities. The researchers posed an example to the employers:

> John is 24 and has three convictions. The first, a fine, was received on 1 January 1997. The second was a probation order received on 1 January 1999 and the third was a suspended one-year prison sentence which he received on 1 January 2000.

Only 12 per cent of the employers felt confident about working out when the criminal record would become spent (Fletcher *et al.*, 2001: 10).

The research also found a lack of application by employers when it came to assessing the risk an ex-offender might pose in a given job. At worst there was no assessment made at all and some people with convictions for sexual offences were turned down because of the employer's anger about these sort of crimes rather than any risks of re-offending (ibid: 23).

Breaking the Circle

In 2001 the government announced its intention to review the Rehabilitation of Offenders Act. Home Secretary Jack Straw said he had heard the criticisms and believed 'the time is now right for a fundamental review' (Hansard HC Debates, 25 April 2001, cols. 281–282W).

The completed review was published in July 2002 under the title 'Breaking the Circle'. The circle in question was that created when:

- over a quarter of the working age population has a previous conviction;
- the annual cost of crime is £60 billion;
- employment can reduce re-offending by between a third and a half;
- but a criminal record can seriously diminish employment opportunities.

(Home Office, 2002b: 2)

The review proposed scrapping the existing 'rehabilitation periods' and introducing new time periods – to be known as 'disclosure periods' – based on the length of sentence plus a so-called 'buffer' period. The 'disclosure period' terminology fell into line with the language of the CRB.

The disclosure period made up of the length of the sentence plus the 'buffer' period would mean a 'buffer' period of 1 year following a non-custodial sentence, a 2-year 'buffer' following a custodial sentence of less than 4 years, and a 4-year 'buffer' following a custodial sentence of 4 years or more. For young offenders there would be no 'buffer' period added to non-custodial sentences, a 'buffer' period of 1 year for custodial sentences of less than 24 months and 2 years following a custodial sentence for 24 months or more (Home Office, 2002b).

The report's other main recommendations included:

- a continuation of the exemptions system for certain posts and professions;
- a new judicial discretion to impose longer disclosure periods if the sentencer believed there is a particular risk of significant harm;

- clearer guidance to offenders;
- a voluntary Code of Practice for employers;
- a continuation of the scheme not applying to the courts;
- a 'clean sheet' be given to all young offenders reaching 18, if their offences had been minor and infrequent.

(ibid)

The response to 'Breaking the Circle'

The Home Office published a summary of the responses it received to 'Breaking the Circle'; some 60 organisations and individuals commented on the report. There was overall agreement with the proposals with some differences of opinion on individual points (Home Office, 2003b).

Most respondents agreed with the idea of 'buffer' periods and the way they should be added to sentence length to make up 'disclosure periods'. The idea of halving the 'disclosure periods' for young offenders was also accepted. There was some disagreement, however, on the actual length of the 'buffer' periods, especially when added on to a custodial sentence (ibid: 9–10).

The need to continue to have 'exemptions' to the act was agreed on, as was the need to explain clearly to offenders the workings of the act and to have a voluntary Code of Practice for employers. The idea that there should be a new judicial discretion at the point of sentencing to allow for longer disclosure periods for certain offenders considered a particular risk was also generally accepted, except by NACRO and the Criminal Bar Association, who thought this was unnecessary.

The proposal for a 'clean sheet' at 18 for all young offenders where the offences were minor received little support, but the government agreed to revisit the idea at a later date. The Republic of Ireland introduced exactly such legislation for its young offenders in its Children Act 2001 s. 258, even though it has no Rehabilitation of Offender legislation for adults.

Conclusions

The Rehabilitation of Offenders Act 1974 comes from a time when the climate for ex-offenders was not as cold as it is today. The aim was to allow offenders to regard their criminal record as 'spent' and to help them live down their past in order to get on with the rest of their lives.

The provisions of the act have been criticised for being difficult to follow and ever more weakened in their effect. One critic has said the act 'has been repeatedly and relentlessly amended... so as to be almost impossible to be read intelligibly' (Samuels, 2002). A review of the act was completed in 2002 but as yet new legislation is still awaited.

6
Criminal Records and Employment Screening

The widening use of criminal records both within and beyond the criminal justice system has been outlined in Chapter 4. The largest category of use, however, is now that of using the records for employment screening purposes and for registration with professional bodies. This chapter looks at that category. The number of people screened in this way has grown inexorably over the last 20 years and the work has led to the development of the CRB which came online in 2002 (see Chapter 7).

As early as the 1750s the link had been made between known offenders and employment. Henry Fielding's 'Register Clerk' at his Bow Street Magistrates Court (see Chapter 2) recorded the names of convicted offenders and in 1749 the compiled register was used to form the Universal Register Office 'as a labour exchange where employers might examine prospective servants and study their character references' (Linebaugh, 1991: 252).

Later, when policing became more organised, the police inevitably became knowledgeable about recidivists even before the compilation of the Habitual Criminals Register in 1869. Employers were not slow to see the value of that information:

> In 1857 the Chief Constable of Bedford gave confidential information to a local employer about one of his workmen (and)...in 1863 the Chief Constable of Lincolnshire protested that his men were 'constantly receiving letters from private enquiry offices seeking information as to the character, respectability, and money value of persons residing in the towns and villages'.
>
> (Emsley, 1991: 107)

We might surmise that employer demand for such information continued after the Habitual Criminals Act 1869 and the Prevention of Crimes Act 1871 established the embryonic national collection of criminal records.

For the best part of the twentieth century the Home Office regularly produced guidance to the police in the form of the 'Consolidated Circular to the Police on Crime and Kindred Matters'; the circular was discontinued only in the late 1980s. The edition dated 1 January 1925 (pp. 14–15) contained guidance on the movement of criminal record information between the police and employers or professional regulatory bodies.

Two categories of disclosure were identified:

- Notifiable occupations – where the police had knowledge of an arrest or conviction of someone from a given occupation and could pass this on to an employer or professional body of their own volition.
- Requested disclosure – where designated bodies, employers or licensing authorities were entitled to request 'character' information from the police, including criminal record histories.

Such disclosures in the 1920s were relatively few in number but they did seek to protect vulnerable members of the public and endorsed the idea that this information exchange was all about positions of trust.

Notifiable occupations

The biggest category of police disclosure of arrest and conviction records were those committed by people from a 'notifiable occupation'. Employers might well be aware of their employees being in court, but equally they might not. In the case of some employers or regulatory bodies there was an understanding that the police would take it upon themselves to report the person concerned if they worked in certain occupations and the police held information that questioned their suitability to continue in those professions or office. In 1955 this understanding covered the following professions and occupations:

- registered medical practitioners
- registered dentists
- certified midwives
- nurses
- teachers
- magistrates
- driver of a public service vehicle
- holders of air crew licences

- solicitors
- residential care workers with children
- youth leaders
- minister of any religious denomination.

(Home Office, 1955: Appendix, paras. 1–5)

Another four professions were added in 1973:

- barristers
- civil servants
- staff of the UK Atomic Energy Authority
- Staff of the Civil Aviation Authority.

(Home Office, 1973: Schedule 1)

And another three in 1986:

- prison officers
- British Telecom staff
- British Nuclear Fuels staff.

(Home Office, 1986a: Schedule 2)

The category of residential care workers with children (agreed in the 1955 Circular) was extended in 1986 to other 'field' workers with children, including social workers and probation officers (Home Office, 1986a: Annex A, Schedule 2). Professions that appear to have been deleted from the 1973 list included staff of the Civil Aviation Authority, public service vehicle drivers, ministers of any religious denomination and holders of air-crew licences.

The 'notifiable occupations' scheme has not always worked as smoothly as it should. Sometimes the police have not established a person's occupation and sometimes – even when they have – they have not notified the appropriate authority or employer (Home Office, 2004d: paras. 75 and 144).

In 2006 the list of 'notifiable occupations' was revised and re-issued yet again, this time in two categories. Category 1 was those occupations where employees and regulatory bodies would be notified automatically and Category 2 would be at the discretion of the police. Category 1 saw the re-inclusion of Civil Aviation Authority Staff, and the addition of ambulance drivers, taxi drivers and personnel from all the armed services. Category 2 contained casino and lottery workers, post office workers, pharmacists, psychologists and osteopaths (see Tables 6.1 and 6.2; Home Office, 2006a).

Table 6.1 Notifiable Occupations (Automatic)

Persons who provide education at any school or further education institution, specifically	– Teachers – Student Teachers – Teaching Assistants – Ancillary staff in any type of school or Further Education institute – Proprietors of Independent Schools – Care workers in Special or residential schools – Youth Workers in the Youth Service
Persons employed in the care of children in	– Community Homes – Children's Homes – Probation Hostels – Nursery Nurses – Social Workers – Probation Officers
All persons employed in the care of adults in	– Care Homes – Their own home (where the person needs personal care due to incapacity) – Ancillary staff in any type of care home or employed in the care sector – Adult Placement Schemes – Hospitals, Clinics, Medical Agencies or NHS bodies – Care workers – Nurses employed in the care sector – Care managers – Registered Medical Practitioners – Medical Students – Nurses – Midwives – Health Visitors – Barristers – Bar Students – Pupil Barristers – Solicitors – Trainee Solicitors – Enrolled Students – Managing Clerks – Solicitors' Employees

Table 6.1 (Continued)

	– Civil Servants (this includes Government Executive Agency staff, e.g. Job Centre Plus, Criminal Records Bureau
All Staff and Contractors of	– The United Kingdom Atomic Energy Authority (UKAEA) – BNFL, also so known as the British Nuclear Group (BNG) – Urenco – UK Nirex – British Energy – Amersham (GE Healthcare) – Ascot Research Reactor
	– Taxi drivers – Police officers – Police staff
All Personnel in the	– Royal Navy – Queen Alexandra's Royal Navy Nursing Service (QARNNS) – Royal Navy Reservists (where known)
All Personnel in the	– Army – Royal Marines – Queen Alexander's Royal Auxiliary Nursing Corps (QARANC) – Army Reservists (where known) – Territorial Army (where known) – Royal Marines Reserve (where known)
All Personnel in the	– Royal Air Force (RAF) – Royal Air Force Reservists (RAAF) – Princess Mary's Royal Air Force Nursing Service (PMRAFNS) – Airline Pilots – Aircraft maintenance Engineers – Aircraft Engineers – Licensed Aircraft Engineers – Air Traffic Controllers – Assistant Air Traffic Controllers
	– Magistrates
	– Nursery Manager – Nursery owner

- Person in charge of a Nursery
- Nursery Supervisor
- Crèche manager
- Playgroup leader
- Holiday play scheme leader (manager)
- Child minder

- Paramedics
- Other ambulance staff (Emergency Care Practitioners; Technicians; Care assistants)

- Pharmacists

- Secure Training Centre staff
- Escort Custody Officers

Source: Home Office, Circular 6/2006, 'The Notifiable Occupations Scheme', Appendix A, Category 1

Table 6.2 Notifiable Occupations (Discretionary)

Casino Staff	– Casino Dealers
	– Casino Croupiers
	– Casino Cashiers
	– Casino Inspectors/Pit bosses
	– Casino Security officers
	– Casino Supervisors
	– Casino Managers
	– Casino Executives
	– Directors of Casino Companies
Bingo Staff	– Directors of Bingo Companies
	– Bingo Managers
Gaming machine staff	– Sellers/Suppliers of Gaming Machines
Lottery Staff	– Lottery Promoters
	– Directors of External Lottery Manager companies
	– All Royal Mail employees
	– Arts Therapists
	– Biomedical Scientists
	– Chiropodists/Podiatrists
	– Clinical Scientists
	– Dieticians
	– Occupational Therapists
	– Department Practitioners
	– Orthoptists

Table 6.2 (Continued)

	– Prosthetists/Orthotists
	– Physiotherapists
	– Radiographers
	– Speech and Language Therapists
	– Pharmacy Technicians
	– Pre-registration Pharmacy Students
	– Chartered Psychologists
	– Chartered Clinical Psychologists
	– Chartered Counselling Psychologists
	– Chartered Educational Psychologists
	– Chartered Forensic Psychologists
	– Chartered Health Psychologists
	– Chartered Occupational Psychologists
	– Chartered Neurophysiologists
	– Chartered Sport and Exercise Psychologists
	– Optometrists (Ophthalmic opticians)
	– Dispensing Opticians
	– Registered student optometrists
	– Registered student dispensing opticians
	– Osteopaths
	– All registered Dentists
	– All enrolled dental hygienists
	– All enrolled dental therapists
	– All dental students and student dental hygienists and dental therapists
	– Chiropractor
	– Chiropractic practitioner
	– Chiropractitioner
	– Chiropractic Physician/Doctor of Chiropractice
	– Door Supervisors (Bouncers)
	– Vehicle immobilisers (Wheel-Clampers)
	– All Security Guards (static and patrol)
	– Store Detectives
	– Dog Handlers
	– CCTV operators

>   –   Key holders
>   –   Passenger Carrying Vehicle (PCV)
>   drivers (Bus Drivers)
>   –   Veterinary Surgeons
>   –   Veterinary Practitioners
>   –   BT employees
>   –   Farriers

Source: Home Office, Circular 6/2006, 'The Notifiable Occupations Scheme', Appendix 2, Category 2

Requested disclosure

Reports on people in 'notifiable occupations' take place as and when they happen. More systematic screening involved employers, regulatory bodies or licence approving bodies having the right to *request* police-held records at the point of recruitment or ratifying a licence application. The early circulars suggest this was quite a limited right available to only a few employers:

- The Admiralty (for their own police)
- The War Office (for their own police)
- The Air Ministry (for their own police)
- Head Post Masters (for post office workers).

(Home Office, 1955: Appendix, para. 6)

This list was added to over the years by new laws putting criminal record disclosure on a statutory footing. Requests could be made on dealers in securities (Prevention of Fraud (Investments) Act 1958, s. 5), workers in casinos and other gambling establishments (Gaming Act 1968: Schedule 5, para. 3) and drivers of heavy goods vehicles or public service vehicles (Transport Act 1968, s. 35(1) and s. 36(3)).

In 1973 the Home Office re-produced the full list with the addition of three further categories 'which (do) not have a specific statutory authority':

- prospective adoptive or foster parents
- applicants for criminal injuries compensation
- applicants to join the police.

(Home Office, 1973: Schedule 2)

In approving foster parents, local authorities had a statutory duty to see if the applicants had 'been convicted of any offence which would render it undesirable that the child should associate with him' (Boarding Out of Children Regulations 1955 no. 1377 Regulation 17(1)(b)) even if there was no statutory duty on the police to provide it.

In a statement to the Commons the then Home Secretary Robert Carr, re-affirmed the underlying principle to all these arrangements:

> ... the supply of police information will continue to be governed by the general principle that no information is given to anyone, however responsible, unless there are weighty considerations of public interest which justify departure from the general rule.
>
> (Hansard HC Debates, 14 June 1973, cols. 1680–1682)

There was little debate on the mix of statutory and non-statutory (circular) authorisations for disclosure that had now arisen. Circulars received no public debate in any democratic forum and – in the 1960s and 1970s – were hardly known to the public. They might even have served a purpose in drawing a partial veil of secrecy over this disclosure work. James Rule reports a conversation in 1971 with senior Home Office civil servants who played down the degree of criminal records going to employers and other non-police agencies, and who 'were anything but forthcoming on these topics'. Rule reproduced sections of the circular in his book to illustrate that what statements those civil servants did give him were 'seriously inaccurate' (Rule, 1973: 79–80).

In the Commons, the Home Secretary only added to the ambivalence that surrounded circulars:

> I am not sure that I can accede to the request to publish circulars of certain kinds that are issued to the police, although I shall look into the matter.
>
> (Hansard HC Debates, 14 June 1973, col. 1681)

The compromise was to put them into the House of Commons library which was 'open' to MPs but not necessarily anyone else.

In 1984 the Council of Europe in one of its formal recommendations held that criminal record disclosures should be authorised under legislation only (Council of Europe, 1984: 1(2)). In the United Kingdom the preferred method remained that of the circular and the biggest new category of disclosures was that now agreed on childcare workers in the widest sense of that word.

'To devise a system'

The 'discovery' of child sexual abuse had proceeded apace at the start of the 1980s as a new generation of paediatricians and social workers tried to raise general awareness and levels of child-protection understanding (Parton, 1985). The case of Colin Evans was taken as the trigger-event that prompted the extension of criminal record disclosure to the pre-employment screening of childcare workers. In terms of the volume of requests and subsequent demands on the police to meet those requests, criminal record disclosure work would now take a quantum leap forward.

Evans had been convicted of the murder of 4-year-old Maria Payne in 1984. Evans was well known to the Thames Valley Police and had a history of sex offences against children that went back to 1966. After the trial it was revealed that he had been working voluntarily with children, and staff at the local social services department were aware of this. Although Evans had not met his victim through his voluntary work, questions started to be asked as to how this could happen (Boseley, 1984). Colin Evans was imprisoned for life, and the home secretary announced a review of the arrangements for disclosing the criminal records of those seeking work with children.

The only formal arrangements that existed at this time for child-care workers were those in the 'notifiable occupations' category, which included residential care workers with children and youth leaders. Foster parents and adoptive parents were covered but they were not really employees. In truth it could be argued that this was not really a review of the arrangements because there were no such arrangements to review. At some point a decision had already been made to add local authorities to the list of those who could request a criminal record disclosure to assist their recruitment and selection decisions. The terms of reference of the review reveal quite clearly that this was all about the means to arrange these disclosures, not whether it should or should not be done:

> ...to devise a system under which information about the unsuitability by reason of criminal background of people seeking positions where they will have substantial opportunities for access to children can be communicated to those bodies which are responsible for engaging such people.
>
> (Home Office/DHSS, 1985: para. 1.2)

The bureaucratic imperative 'to devise a system' took precedence over any debate as to whether these disclosures were going to be helpful or not, or over any ethical questions of information privacy, rehabilitation or re-settlement of offenders.

The review recommended a new local system of requests to local police forces, with the police disclosing criminal records and the job applicant having to consent to the disclosure. A centralised national system was ruled out as too expensive and too slow. On receipt of any criminal records local employers would assess their relevance and make the appointment decision. The review estimated that about 100,000 requests per annum might be generated and 'should impose little additional work for the police'; 'in smaller (police) forces, the extra work involved may be capable of being absorbed, but in others an extra part-time post may be justified' (ibid: para. 6:21).

The 1986 circulars and the disclosure of records on childcare workers

In July 1986 two Home Office circulars appeared, outlining the new arrangements. 'Police Reports of Convictions and Related Information' (Home Office, 1986a) went to the police as the providers of criminal records and 'Protection of Children: Disclosure of Criminal Background of those with Access to Children' (Home Office, 1986b) went to local authorities as the employers and 'requesters' of records.

Why the new arrangements were still to be based on administrative circulars rather than any statutory basis was left unanswered. Job applicants had to consent to a check with the police on any criminal records. Local authorities were to appoint senior nominated officers as the link-point to their local force and as the person who would formally request disclosure. The circulars tried to define the positions that would need these disclosures and the nature of 'substantial opportunities for access' to children, and offered guidance on what constituted a relevant conviction. It also stated that 'the police will...require to be indemnified by the local services concerned against any liability incurred as a result of provision of information in response to requests made' (Home Office, 1986b: para. 23).

This requirement for indemnity was not new and had been a condition of disclosures going back to 1955 (Home Office, 1955: para. 9). In effect it was a safeguard against the police being sued for providing incorrect information. In the past, indemnity had been held by the Home Office, now all local authorities were being asked to provide it in the following words:

> ...this authority undertakes to indemnify the police against any liability or civil claim which may be incurred by a police authority or any individual serving or former police officer or serving or former member of civil staff as a result of the provision by the police to the authority of reports of convictions or cautions.
>
> (Home Office, 1986a: para. 5, 1986b: para. 23)

Some critics argued that they should not have to cover in this way for police inaccuracies or incompetence in producing information. In the London Borough of Tower Hamlets the authority's solicitor said indemnity 'was absolutely ludicrous...he had never heard about anyone being indemnified against their own negligence' ('Social work jobs at risk over police row', *New Statesman and Society*, 22 July 1988). Most local authorities simply agreed to the indemnity. In London the Metropolitan Police reportedly told councils 'that if they failed to sign the indemnity they would get no service' (Hyder, 1988; see also Thomas and Hebenton, 1991).

This somewhat stark 'take it or leave it' attitude also applied to the consent that the job applicant was required to give for a police check. Although in theory this was a free consent, under no duress, and the applicant did not have to give it, everyone knew that failure to give consent would mean the application was destined to go no further and the job would be lost. The term 'Hobson's choice' could be applied to this 'free' consent.

In 1988 a second Home Office circular appeared for local authorities, elaborating on the 1986 version. It contained more advice on what 'substantial access' meant, guidance on agency and contractual workers, on students completing practice placements and more detail on the senior nominated officers' role. This circular also referred to the possibility of non – criminal record information being disclosed by the police, which it referred to as 'other relevant information' (Home Office, 1988b: para. 17). Although there had been no reference to this category of 'soft' information in the 1986 circular to local authorities, it had been mentioned in the complementary circular to the police as 'information outside the scope of this circular which gives cause for serious concern' (Home Office, 1986a: para. 7).

The 1988 circular repeated word for word the advice of the 1986 circular on how to judge the relevance of an old offence (Home Office, 1986b: paras. 15–16; Home Office, 1988b: paras. 17–18). The police were always going to give out the full criminal record if one existed and it was for employers to make the appointment decision. The guiding factors were listed as:

(a) the nature of the conviction
(b) the nature of the appointment
(c) the date of the offence (e.g. was it very old)
(d) the frequency of any pattern of offending.

On this basis the employer made his or her decision. The idea that the *police* could decide on relevance by disclosing only relevant offences agreed in advance on a particular post had been considered but not pursued and 'such sharing of responsibility for the employment decision is entirely unsatisfactory: responsibility must always rest squarely with the employer' (Home Office, 1991: para. 147).

As the disclosure of criminal records to local authorities for pre-employment screening – or the 'police check' as it was referred to – became embedded in the mindset of local authorities, new circulars saw disclosures now extended to health service employees working with children (Home Office, 1988c) and to time-limited pilot schemes in the voluntary sector where there was access to children (Home Office, 1989). The numbers of people having their criminal records disclosed for vetting purposes started to rise, and the beginnings of a countervailing critique began to be heard.

Criticisms of criminal record checks

As long as criminal records had been used only within the criminal justice system by police and judicial processes any problems or difficulties arising in their use could be contained and dealt with within the system. The more that records were going to be passed outside to non-criminal justice agencies the more any such problems or difficulties were going to be a matter of public discourse.

The criticisms were at first muted in the belief that vetting was more important than the rights of applicants with criminal records ('Vetting: needs of service outweigh civil liberties', *Social Services Insight*, 26 July 1986–2 August 1986: p. 5). It was later suggested that the introduction of checks had 'raised hardly a ripple of public or professional debate' (Unell, 1992: 18).

In the late 1980s a number of organisations representing ex-offenders started to raise questions about criminal record disclosures (Apex Trust, 1989, 1990) and to publish damage-limitation advice for the people they worked with (NACRO, 1990). The National Council for Civil Liberties produced a dossier of cases wherein people with criminal records believed they were getting a raw deal:

> ...the Home Office disregarded the implications for civil liberties when it set up the system in 1986 and has failed to monitor its implementation. The arrangements are too sweeping in scope.
>
> (NCCL, 1988)

The 'relevance' of old convictions was a cause for particular concern as it became clear that employers varied in their interpretation of 'relevance'. In Kent the Social Services Department went so far as to suggest jobs should be refused to anyone with *any* offence in order to take no chances (Brindle, 1989). For someone with a criminal record it became impossible to know in advance if their record was going to be 'relevant' or not.

In the voluntary sector a new Police Checks Monitoring Group was formed from a consortium of organisations to oversee developments that were now viewed with concern (PCMG, 1988). The pilot schemes set up in the voluntary sector were later evaluated for the Volunteer Centre UK, and the degree of caution exercised in decision making based on criminal records was further revealed. Agencies were found to be working to the 'What if?' principle, which resulted in 'the safety of the child often appear(ing) to be confused with the safety of the organisation' (Unell, 1992: 104–105).

Other more understated criticisms were targeted at the secondary discrimination that different racial groups might experience from criminal record checks. If black people were over represented in the criminal justice system, as research was now suggesting (Hood, 1992), it followed that exclusion from possible employment was also going to be a more likely experience.

In 1992 the opening up of the European Union's border to allow free movement in search of employment also raised the question of vetting workers from overseas. Other countries might be less inclined than the British to allow the disclosure of criminal records in this way and even if they did, the mechanisms to get their criminal records to employers in the United Kingdom were hardly well established.

A more pressing matter for those having to carry out criminal record disclosures was the sheer volume of requests now coming in. In 1987 the number of requests had been 343,901 but by 1989 it had risen to 508,942 (House of Commons, 1990a: Minutes of Evidence p. 2, para. 7).

In the year ending March 1993 around 665,000 childcare checks were made, an increase of 23 per cent on the previous year (Home Office, 1993c: para. 23), and way in excess of the original 1985 estimate of 100,000 a year (Home Office/DHSS, 1985: para. 6.21).

The whole process of criminal record disclosure was taking on a bureaucratic life of its own. Having issued its circulars, the Home Office could only look on from afar as over 100 local authorities and 43 police forces in England and Wales entered into their own local arrangements. The numbers of requests rose and, like Topsy, disclosures just 'growed and growed', and the workload on the police grew proportionately. Delays in getting police checks done had become a familiar complaint (Platt, 1988).

The Home Office were particularly worried that the definition of substantial access to children was being stretched too far. Staff with only marginal contact with children were having criminal record checks carried out on them. The Home Office would lament that 'there is evidence that the system is being misused to obtain checks on individuals whose access (to children) is more limited' and:

> ... at a time of heightened awareness of child abuse, organisations are understandably concerned to protect against the possibility of child abuse by their staff and ... police checks are perceived as a reliable means of doing so, especially as they are free at the point of use.
>
> (Home Office, 1993c: 28)

This heightened awareness of child abuse also affected the interpretation of 'relevance' and led to more cautious decision making. This was added to by the implementation of the 1989 Children Act as from October 1991, and a generation of child-protection workers having to re-learn procedures and language. At the same time notorious cases still made the headlines. In November 1991 the sentencing of Frank Beck for abusing children in Leicestershire children's homes over a period of 13 years added to the general climate of chill ('Head of Children's Homes jailed for life, five times', *The Independent*, 30 November 1991).

The Beck affair prompted a number of inquiry reports into how he could have been appointed and remained undetected. In particular, the Warner Report (1992) led to far more attention being paid to interviews, selection and screening of residential childcare workers (see Hebenton and Thomas, 1994, for a critique). Norman Warner, who wrote the report, had been the director of social services for Kent in 1989 when that department had taken the very cautious line on interpreting criminal records (see above).

'Other relevant information'

Apart from criminal record information, it was agreed at this time that the police could pass on other forms of non-conviction information to local authorities. As already noted, this was described as 'information outside the scope of this circular which gives cause for serious concern' (Home Office, 1986a: para. 7) and included 'cases recorded as undetected where no proceedings were taken' (ibid: para. 8). This non-conviction information was also described as 'soft' information and could include such items as investigations which had not led to a charge, the convening of discussions or a conference to consider unresolved child-protection matters, or even an acquittal where perhaps the case had been lost on a 'minor' technicality or poor evidence from a child. In the widest sense it meant police 'intelligence' held on file.

Again, as noted above, this category of information was not referred to in the 1986 circular guidance to local authorities (Home Office, 1986b) and is to be found only in the circular that went to the police. This situation was remedied by the 1988 version of the circular which referred to 'other relevant information' defined as 'factual information which the police would be prepared to present as evidence in court, or details of acquittals or decisions not to prosecute where the circumstances of the case would give cause for concern' (Home Office, 1988b: para. 17). Whether or not local authorities were actually receiving 'other relevant information' for the 2 years 1986–1988 is uncertain.

Throughout the 1990s the disclosure of 'other relevant information' and the uses made of it in recruitment and selection decision would be 'low visibility' activities between local authorities and the police (Home Office, 1993c: para. 16). This position changed dramatically following the conviction of Ian Huntley for two child murders in Soham, Cambridgeshire, in 2003. 'Other relevant information' was held on Huntley but not disclosed, which could have prevented him getting work giving access to children; the subsequent Bichard Inquiry would put a spotlight on these previously dark corners (see Chapter 7).

Other databases

In the early 1980s two separate databases existed independently of the new childcare screening arrangements. 'List 99' was a list of people considered unsuitable to work in schools or educational environments and the Consultancy Service was a list of those unsuitable to work with children in social work or residential care settings; both lists were kept centrally by their respective government departments – the, then, Department for Education and Science and the Department of Health and Social Security. Individuals could be listed even without a criminal record.

The origins of 'List 99' can be traced back to 1926 and its name is said to be taken from the room number of the office that first held it. The 'List' has evolved over the years, expanding to include all workers in schools – not just teachers – and workers in further education (1982), and expanding again to cover independent schools in 1994. In January 2006 there were 4045 names on 'List 99' (Hansard HC Debates, 19 January 2006, col. 967).

The secretary of state can bar a person from working in education on four grounds:

- misconduct;
- unsuitability to work with children;
- inclusion on the Protection of Children Act (POCA) List (see below) or;
- on medical grounds.

An individual is automatically added to the 'List 99' and barred if they commit an offence against a child whilst working in an educational setting; the full list of offences is set out in Schedule 2 of the Education (Prohibition from Teaching or Working with Children) Regulations 2003 (SI 2003/1184). They are also automatically added to the list and barred if they have been included on the POCA List (see below) or been made the subject of a Disqualification Order (Criminal Justice and Courts Services Act 2000, Part II as amended), which prevents a person working with children.

The secretary of state has discretion to add people to the 'List 99' and bar them from working in education settings when they are deemed unsuitable to work with children. Prior to 2000 the secretary of state had discretion to partially ban individuals from working and this way a residual 210 of the 4045 on 'List 99' are partially banned (Hansard HC Debates, 19 January 2006, col. 967). Following a media onslaught on Secretary of State Ruth Kelly in January 2006 (see, e.g. 'Minister Approved Paedophile to Teach PE', *Daily Mail*, 9 January 2006; 'Kelly let more sex offenders work in schools', *Daily Telegraph*, 12 January 2006; 'How many perverts are in our schools?', *Daily Express*, 12 January 2006) plans were announced to take away this ministerial discretion.

A new Independent Barring Board (IBB) was to be introduced made up of about 10 members and with a staff of 100; the IBB would take decisions off the secretary of state and was expected to be making about 20,000 decisions a year (Hansard HL Debates, 24 May 2006, col. 828). The IBB was to be introduced as part of the Vetting and Barring Scheme to be established by the Safeguarding Vulnerable Groups Bill published in March 2006. An interim period would take these decisions away from the politicians until such time as the bill became law (DfES, 2006a; Hansard HC Debates, 19 January 2006, col. 969). The Safeguarding Vulnerable Groups Act received its Royal Assent in November 2006 (see also DfES, 2006b).

The Consultancy Service held a similar list to 'List 99' for people considered unsuitable to work with children in social-care settings. The Consultancy Service Index, as it was known, was a non-statutory advisory system that did not ban anyone, but was available for any employer to consult as part of their selection procedures. In 1961 the Home Office – then responsible for childcare services – had 'admitted' maintaining the index as part of its general responsibility for children in care (Utting Report, 1997: para. 14.21); it later moved to the Department of Health.

How often local authorities actually consulted the index is less certain. In 1984 it was reportedly consulted 12,500 times and some 18 positive identifications made; in 1985 the figure had risen to 20,000 inquiries (Home Office/DHSS, 1985: para. 3.11). The total number of names held in 1985 was 3000 (ibid: para. 3.8), and this had risen to 6000 by 1989 (Hansard HC Debates, 20 October 1989, col. 4982PQ).

By the mid-1990s local authorities were consulting the index about 55,000 times a year (Hansard HC Debates, 28 October 1996, col. 41). This was a more than doubling of the number of inquiries 10 years earlier but still paled into insignificance against the numbers now being the subject of police checks. This had passed the 600,000 a year barrier (Home Office, 1993c: para. 23) and illustrated the nature of the imbalance between police checks and checks on the Consultancy Service Index. In truth the index did not figure very high on the local authority agenda.

The Protection of Children Act 1999 transformed the Consultancy Service index into the statutory Protection of Children Act List or POCA List. Inclusion on the new list now meant an effective ban on working with children (DoH, 2000). By this time a new database listing those unsuitable to work with vulnerable adults – the Protection of Vulnerable Adults or POVA list – had joined the POCA list and List 99 as a source of information for vetting (see Chapter 7).

The demand for yet more criminal record disclosures

As the disclosures for criminal records on childcare workers grew in volume, other employers and organisations started to demand their own right of access to the records. If there was a new heightened awareness of child abuse, so too there was a new awareness of 'risk' generally, criminal records in particular, and the need to protect the public. A government White Paper, at the time, on crime and penal measures was significantly titled 'Crime, Justice and *Protecting* the Public' (Home Office, 1990b; emphasis added). Pre-employment screening by using criminal records was now seen as a prime way of achieving 'protection'.

The body charged with deciding who could have access to criminal records was not the Home Office but the police through an ACPO Standing Sub-Committee on Disclosure. The sub-committee met 'at regular intervals to review policy and to consider requests for new proposals for vetting made by outside bodies', and 'in all instances the decisions – both on policy and individual disclosure – are ones for chief officers, and Ministers have no powers to intervene' (Home Office, 1993c: para. 11). The requests started to mount up.

In 1991 disclosures were agreed on proprietors and officers in charge of old peoples' homes and nursing homes (DoH, 1991), and following a campaign led by the Association of District Councils, applicants for licenses to be taxi drivers were now to have their criminal records disclosed following new provisions in the Road Traffic Act 1991 (s. 47) (Department of Transport, 1992).

Not everyone was successful in their bid to get access to criminal records. Amongst those requests turned down by the ACPO Sub-Committee were:

> firefighters
> patients seeking human fertilisation and embryology treatment
> court security officers
> persons caring for vulnerable adults
> RSPCA staff
> nurses and health visitors (with adults)
> licensed insolvency practitioners
> personnel deployed by employment agencies
> school governors
> trustees of charities
> private security industry staff
> and others.
>
> (see Home Office, 1993c: Annex D)

The example of patients seeking human fertilisation and embryology treatment provides an interesting case study. Although this does not involve an employment position, the newly formed Human Fertilisation and Embryology Authority (HFEA) in 1990 wanted to screen all applicants for this treatment. The law required treatment centres to ensure 'the welfare of any child who may be born as a result of the treatment' (Human Fertilisation and Embryology Act 1990, s. 13(5)) and one way to do this was to check criminal records.

In the late 1980s – before the act was passed – a woman in Manchester had been refused treatment and been told it was for medical reasons. She was not happy with this explanation and sought a judicial review of the decision taken at the hospital. It transpired that the real reason was that doctors thought her lifestyle, including convictions for soliciting and prostitution, made her unsuitable to be a parent (Singh, 1988).

To avoid any similar incidents and to meet with the new law, the HFEA now stated that it wished:

> ... to avoid treatment being provided where there is reason to suppose there is a risk of harm to the child, for example, where people have been convicted of offences against children (e.g. those listed in Schedule 1 to the Children and Young Persons Act 1933).
>
> (HFEA, 1991a: para. 3.18)

The HFEA was aware that disclosure would be dependent on the outcome of further consultations with ACPO. The ACPO did not agree to their request, and the subsequent HFEA Code of Practice, although still making reference to 'evidence of a previous relevant conviction', could only say that treatment centres should make such 'inquiries of any relevant individual, authority or agency as it can' (HFEA, 1991b: para. 3.21).

The HFEA subsequently maintained this position but re-visited the idea of having formal access to criminal records in 2005 when the Human Fertilisation and Embryology Act 1990 was due for review; the complexity of the situation was also recognised and the HFEA Chair agreed that potential parents could find the assessment difficult. Not least, 'they sometimes point out that those able to conceive naturally do not receive any assessment like this' ('IVF couples could face criminal records checks', *Daily Telegraph*, 31 August 2005).

What case studies like this did illustrate was the high level of demand for criminal record disclosures now being made. Some of them fell outside of the general stated reasons for disclosure – national security, protection of vulnerable people and the need to ensure probity in the administration of the law – but the demand was also resisted because it 'could have imposed resource burdens on the police...which would have jeopardised its service to other recipients of police information' (Home Office, 1993c: Annex D). It might also be surmised that this level of demand and the growing culture of disclosure may have contributed to the number of improper disclosures and leaks from the PNC discussed in Chapter 3.

Enforced subject access

A further indication of the growing demand for criminal records for employment screening involved the data protection laws. The 1984 Data Protection Act contained 'subject access provisions' whereby individuals had a right of access to any information held about them on computer; organisations holding this information had to provide it on request from the individual concerned. This was seen as not only an individual's right but as part of the enforcement mechanisms available to monitor the act.

In the late 1980s as the Data Protection Act became more familiar, employers who had no direct access to criminal records saw that they could use the 'subject access provisions' to get individuals to do their own 'do-it-yourself' criminal record disclosure. A job applicant could be asked to go to the police and request a printout of any criminal record, or a document indicating there was no record. An individual was not obliged to do this, but inevitably risked losing the job if he or she did not. The term 'enforced subject access' came into being.

The then data protection registrar was immediately critical of what he saw as a misuse of the 1984 Act and questioned whether Parliament intended the 'subject access provisions' to be used in this way. In 1989 he produced a Guidance Note outlining why this was a misuse of the act and what its limitations were, including the fact that – at this time – cautions and minor offences might be held manually rather than on computer so employers would not be getting the full picture. Overall the registrar argued that if employers needed criminal record checks they should be formally arranged and with the approval of the ACPO Sub-Committee on Disclosure; in the meantime he saw it as something that 'has become a significant issue' (DPR, 1989).

The registrar raised the problem in his annual reports and in evidence to the House of Commons Home Affairs Committee (House of Commons, 1990a: Minutes of Evidence pp. 26–27). He suggested that the practice be made a criminal offence, although the Home Office was not persuaded (Home Office, 1991: para. 177). In 1995 the police were still describing it as 'a significant issue' (ACPO, 1995: para. 2.7.2.6).

The Data Protection Act 1998 s. 56 does make 'enforced subject-access' for recruitment or employment purposes a criminal offence but the section is only due to be implemented when the CRB introduces its Basic Disclosure provisions. Basic Disclosure will obviate the need for 'enforced subject-access', but its introduction was postponed indefinitely in February 2003 following technical operating difficulties (for more on this see Chapter 7). In the meantime the use of 'enforced subject-access' continues and according to the Information Commissioners Office, 'the overwhelming majority of the 200,000 odd police subject access requests per year are currently enforced' (The Chief Constables of West Yorkshire, South Yorkshire and North Wales Police and the Information Commissioner, Information Tribunal, 2005: at para. 82).

The 1990 Home Affairs Committee report

The Home Affairs Committee that examined criminal records in 1990 has already been referred to (see Chapter 3). Here we need to consider the committee's comments on arrangements for using criminal records for employment and other vetting purposes, which they believed did 'not provide a satisfactory mechanism for making records available' (House of Commons, 1990a: para. 21).

The committee was particularly critical of the idea that chief constables were effectively steering these policies in terms of who could and could not have access to records. They could do this in terms of the categories of disclosures determined by the ACPO Sub-Committee, and as individual chief constables and data protection users (later re-named 'controllers') they could disclose to any individual organisation they chose:

> *... the fact that 51 police forces might permit access in a haphazard and unaccountable manner has worrying implications for the liberty of the individual*
>
> . (ibid: para. 21; emphasis in original)

The committee recommended a new agency should be responsible for both holding criminal records and providing them for vetting purposes and that that agency in turn should be overseen by a board that would advise on access to records and other relevant matters. New laws should lay down the principles governing criminal record disclosure and only recordable offences should be disclosed (ibid: para. 41); by implication 'other relevant information' should not be disclosed.

When the Home Office responded to the Home Affairs Committee report it was not persuaded of the need to establish a new agency independent of the police to hold and disclose criminal records. It also did not like the idea of just disclosing recordable offences and, on the contrary, thought that other information, including police cautions, could be 'crucial' to the assessment of a person's suitability for some work (Home Office, 1990a: 6–7).

The Home Office Scrutiny Report revisited

Most of the Home Office's 1991 Scrutiny Report that followed the Home Affairs Committee report refers to general maintenance problems with the national collection of criminal records. Parts of it, however, address questions of vetting and possible future developments, and the trend to ever higher numbers of requests was yet again confirmed:

> ...the main change which has increased the burden on the police...has been the extension of vetting in 1986 to those in the public sector, such as teachers, social workers and health workers, whose job would give them 'substantial opportunity for access to children'...it represented a very large increase in the number of persons vetted.
>
> (Home Office, 1991: paras. 115–116)

An additional cause of the increase was identified as employers covering themselves against possible litigation for having failed in a duty of care in not requesting a disclosure:

> ...it suggests in effect that employers should safeguard themselves against the risk of later challenges in the courts by going through the motions of seeking vetting even in respect of posts where under current policy it is clearly unavailable.
>
> (ibid: para. 185)

As we saw in Chapter 5, such an interpretation of the law was known in America as the 'negligent hiring doctrine'; here it was accused of helping create 'a sustained incremental pressure to widen vetting' regardless of what employers actually wanted to do (ibid: para. 186).

One proposal to cope with the demand was the idea of a two-tier system of childcare vetting. At one level was a full disclosure as at present, the other just disclosed what was on the PNC (ibid: para. 145). The Home Office went so far as to produce a draft circular in 1992 outlining how such an arrangement might work but employers felt they were being short-changed and said it was a 'victory for common sense' when the idea was dropped; it was alleged that had the proposals been acted upon 'Youngsters would have been put at serious risk' ('Two-tier vetting axed', *Community Care*, 18 March 1993: 4; Home Office, 1993c: Annex C, para. 11).

On other matters, the Scrutiny Report was not as convinced as the Home Affairs Committee that chief constables were taking their own decisions and believed there were genuine efforts at convergence and consistency even if there were 'confused or uncomfortably shared accountability' questions (ibid: para. 119). It re-visited the Home Affairs Committee's idea of a new central agency, possibly named the National Criminal Records Agency, and it wanted this to be a self-funding body with sole charge of the records and disclosing to the police, employers and others and *charging* for its service (ibid: para. 100); the part of the agency disclosing to employers would be a discrete entity known as the Vetting Agency (ibid: para. 168). All of this was to be a long-term project premised on the idea that all criminal records would be computerised as soon as possible.

The 1993 circular

In October 1993 the Home Office produced a further circular on criminal record disclosure for childcare purposes (Home Office, 1993b). This was to be its final guidance on the arrangements until the system changed completely and went over to a statutory system in 2002.

The October 1993 circular was the third in the 7 years since childcare 'police checks' had started in 1986. In essence it was much the same as the others (Home Office, 1986b, 1988b), albeit with greater elaboration to try and pin down concepts such as 'substantial access to children' to perhaps reign in the massive amount of requests now coming into the police and the accompanying burden these demands were placing on them. A new paragraph, for example, was inserted amplifying the role of the local authority, senior nominated officer:

...it is the responsibility of the senior nominated officer to make sure that the guidelines given in this circular are properly observed. Failure to do so may be an unwarranted infringement on the civil liberties of individuals, and result in abuse and overloading of the system. This in turn imposes unnecessary strain on police resources and is likely to lead to delays in the processing of all checks in the relevant force area.

(Home Office, 1993b: para. 21; emphasis in original)

It was almost as though the Home Office was metaphorically stamping its foot in frustration at the uncontrollable growth in disclosures that had been released across the country and which it was impotent to do anything about.

Conclusions

The use of criminal records to vet people for certain forms of employment started slowly. It moved on to a larger scale with the introduction of 'police checks' on childcare workers in 1986. The arrangements for the police disclosure of criminal records to specific employers – mainly local authorities and health authorities – were of a local nature and based upon Home Office circulars rather than any statutory basis. The police were allowed to also disclose any non-conviction information they might hold on someone.

The numbers of people being vetted in this way started to rise inexorably and with a consequent rise in the workload for the police. In 1985 the estimated volume of disclosures that would be required for childcare workers was put at 100,000 a year; by 1993 it was running at over 600,000 a year. On top of this, the police were being pressed by other employers to open up disclosures to them so that they could carry out similar checks. As an interim measure, employers not granted access started asking job applicants to use the subject access provisions of the Data Protection Act as a form of DIY police check.

Criticisms of these localised arrangements came from a number of directions. Employers found them slow to come through. Job applicants found employers to vary in their implementation and not give a fair chance to ex-offenders trying to 'go straight' and put their lives together. The police disliked the workload put on them. Questions started to be asked about the possibility of changing the system.

7
The Criminal Records Bureau

A month before issuing its third and final 1993 circular on disclosure arrangements, the Home Office started a complete review of all aspects of criminal record disclosure for purposes of pre-employment screening. Over the next 10 years the 1993 review would lead us to the Police Act 1997 and ultimately the CRB, which spluttered into life in 2002. The whole exercise would take criminal record disclosures to a new level with localised arrangements being replaced by a national agency, and a service free at the point of delivery, turned into a multi-million pound industry with its own monthly customer newsletter called *Disclosure News*.

The 1993–1996 review

The Home Office launched its review of police checks in England and Wales for employment screening purposes in 1993. The stated reasons for the review were the rising numbers of requests and the consequent burden on the police in terms of costs and resources. Other reasons were the perceived inconsistencies in the arrangements and the civil liberties questions. There seems little doubt that the latter reasons were less of a priority than the main problem of high volume and costs (Home Office, 1993c).

The review Consultation Paper estimated the number of checks made in the year ending 31 March 1993 at over 900,000, which was an increase of 30 per cent on the year before; childcare checks were responsible for 665,000 of this total. The average cost for each check was said to be £11.83 for a straight check on the PNC and £14.67 if a check was also needed on local records. This all amounted to an annual cost to the police in England and Wales of £14 million (ibid: paras. 23–26).

The Consultation Paper went on to look at what it called 'pressures for change', which in reality were pressures for yet more disclosures. One of the noted inconsistencies was that of childcare workers in the private sector and parts of the voluntary sector not having access to police checks. Further pressure came from those wanting checks extended to workers with vulnerable adults such as elderly people, those wanting more checks on 'fit and proper persons' for licensing and other contexts and those wanting more vetting as a crime prevention measure (ibid: para. 28). The ACPO and the Home Office were noted to have agreed to an embargo on opening up any new categories of disclosure after December 1991 pending computerisation of the national collection of records but that had still not stopped taxi drivers being added in from April 1992 (ibid: para. 35).

Civil liberty questions raised included the problem of local authorities ignoring the circular guidance to obtain checks on individuals who did not need checking (ibid: Annex C, paras. 6 and 10), and the police passing of 'other relevant information' to local authorities by telephone without the knowledge of the applicant (ibid: para. 21). The Scrutiny Report had also referred to this practice of telephoning 'other relevant information' through and described it as 'a well established unofficial practice – and all the more dangerous for that' (Home Office, 1991: para. 155).

The Consultation Paper asked for responses to 12 questions from the starting point of whether or not criminal records should in principle be restricted. Questions were asked on the desirability of releasing 'other relevant information' and if so, how should that be defined, and the desirability of releasing minor conviction details. In general it asked for comments on the broad criteria for authorising criminal record checks and whether different levels of checks were needed (see Home Office, 1993c: 2 for the complete list of questions).

The major questions revolved around the need for an overall new form of vetting, possibly through a centralised private agency allowed to charge for the cost of each check; this was certainly the proposal that made the headlines (see, e.g. Travis, 1993). Added to this was the question of bringing employment screening out of the *demi-monde* of circulars and into the daylight of a statutory legal context.

'On the Record'

The 1996 White Paper 'On the Record' collated the responses to the 1993 review exercise and laid out the government's further thinking.

The 3-year wait seemed quite a long one in the terms with which such consultations are usually carried out. During these 3 years a number of stories appeared in the press about the government's plans for 'privatising' the criminal record collection.

In December 1994 the *Daily Express* ran the headline 'Bosses to buy crime files on job-hunters'. Billed as an 'exclusive' by their Home Affairs correspondent, it gave no source for its story but linked the idea to the vetting of personal security personnel (or 'bouncers') then being considered by a House of Commons Select Committee. Unnamed 'Ministers' were said to 'believe' that a new private agency could take over the disclosure of criminal records and be financed by the private security industry. The suggested name of this new commercial agency was to be the Criminal Inquiries Agency or CIA (sic) (Hooley, 1994).

A few weeks later in January *The Guardian*'s Home Affairs editor ran a similar story, under the headline 'Ministers plan police record sales agency'. Once again unnamed 'Ministers' were said to 'believe' that 'a commercial agency, financed by the security industry, should be set up to handle individual inquiries about job applicants'. The pressure group Liberty were said to strongly oppose the idea of passing 'highly confidential information to a private, unregulated, profit-based company' (Travis, 1995).

A third story appeared in February, just weeks after *The Guardian*'s report. This time the Home Affairs correspondent for the *Sunday Times* had been given access to a 'restricted document' prepared for Home Secretary Michael Howard, proposing the partial privatisation of 'a huge section of the Home Office' including the criminal record collection. The story was now disconnected from its associations with the private security industry and was portrayed as an exercise saving costs and involving large international companies as the only way to keep pace with rapid changes in information technology. Shadow Home Affairs spokesman Jack Straw described it as 'wholly wrong' and said 'the public are completely opposed to the privatisation of such services' (Leppard, 1995).

What the public really thought of the idea at this time has never been properly researched. One theory about these three newspaper stories is that they were based on deliberate government briefings to sound-out public opinion as measured through any general reaction coming back through the media. If that was the case then the exercise only confirmed a general indifference amongst the general public and no great reaction to the idea in one direction or the other, and ironically it was the police themselves who showed most concern. A Home Office minister reassured them. Speaking at a conference:

> Mr. Maclean dismissed reports in the press that the Government planned to sell off criminal records on the PNC to the private sector as 'completely wrong'.
>
> (quoted in 'Minister refutes PNC "sell off" claim', *PNN Net News*, 8 April 1995)

The White Paper 'On the Record' was published in June 1996, proposing the new central agency to take over the disclosure of criminal records held by the police. The old localised arrangements would end and there would be a fixed charge made for every police check carried out by, what was now called, the Criminal Record Agency (CRA). The fact that criminal records were disclosures made for different purposes was reflected in the proposal that there would be a three-level hierarchy of disclosures. This seemed to be a re-emergence of the ill-fated 1992 two-tier system proposal (see Chapter 6). The most comprehensive were to be called Enhanced Criminal Record Checks, followed by the interim level of Full Criminal Record Checks and finally there would be a Criminal Conviction Certificate. The first two would have automatic exemptions from the Rehabilitation of Offenders Act 1974 built in, but the last one would honour the act and its concept of 'spent' convictions (Home Office, 1996b).

The Criminal Record Agency was to be a Next Steps Agency with access through civil servants to the criminal records held on Phoenix on the PNC. The White Paper believed this meant the 'proposals do not envisage the privatisation of this area of work' (ibid: para. 15). Employers would have to register with the CRA as *bone fide* bodies, in order to receive 'Enhanced' and 'Full' checks and the expectation was that this would only be available to employers needing 200 or more checks a year (ibid: para. 37); for certificates the onus would be on individuals to apply, pay the fee and produce for employers if requested.

The proposal to have a Criminal Conviction Certificate came as something of a surprise. The Consultation Paper had made no hint of the need for such a disclosure which would effectively mean *any* employer could ask for such a certificate for *any* job. Although this might obviate the need for 'enforced subject access', it was a clear departure from the principle laid out in 1973 (see Chapter 6) and in the Consultation Paper that criminal record information should normally remain confidential unless disclosure was justified by the general public interest (Home Office,

1993c: paras. 60–62). Suddenly the criminal record collection was wide open to any employer. The Penal Affairs Consortium pointed out that this meant employers could receive 'an enormous amount of information about past offences with no relevance to the job for which someone is applying' (Mills, 1996). In Parliament Tony Benn M. P. argued 'we will create a new class of unemployable people with convictions' (Hansard HC Debates, 12 February 1997, col. 393).

The rhetoric up to now had been that the new arrangements would help protect children and vulnerable adults. The home secretary now played down this dimension and spoke of 'positions of trust' and the need to help 'people wishing to live or work abroad who need to produce evidence that they have no criminal record' (Home Office, 1996c). The position of the emigrant worker had never been considered in the 1993 Consultation Paper or the 1996 White Paper. This was either an attempt to cover the regulation of the 'bouncers' who presumably needed something other than enhanced or full checks, or even some far-sighted attempt at social engineering to link criminality with economic opportunity in order to increase the deterrence factor and reduce crime.

The White Paper revealed that the Consultation Paper had prompted some 180 responses and in summary there was no objection to the idea of charges for all these disclosures as long as they were kept to a minimum and the service provided was fast and efficient. The responses also confirmed that there was still an unmet demand for access to the national collection of criminal records. As to the idea of there being a centralised agency taking over, the response was mixed (Home Office, 1996b: para. 9).

The Police Act 1997

'On the Record' was enacted through Part V of the Police Act 1997 as one of the last acts of the Conservative administration; it received its Royal Assent on 21 March 1997. The act confirmed the White Paper's three levels of disclosure which were now termed:

- Enhanced Criminal Record Certificates (s. 115);
- Criminal Record Certificates (s. 113); and
- Criminal Conviction Certificates (s. 112).

The Criminal Conviction Certificate withheld 'spent' convictions and cautions which the two higher levels did not. The Enhanced Criminal Record Certificate also allowed for the disclosure of any non-conviction information thought relevant by the police; such information had to be disclosed by the local chief constable (s. 119(2)), but could be withheld, if necessary, from the job applicant if it might, for example, interfere with an ongoing police investigation (s. 115(7) and (8)). This information was comparable to 'other relevant information' available under the existing arrangements; now it was to be known as 'approved' or 'additional information'.

The Enhanced Criminal Record Certificate and the Criminal Record Certificate were to be disclosed only to employers who were registered to receive them. Registration took two forms:

- Registered bodies – employers who were entitled to ask 'exempted' questions of job applicants, that is, exempted under the Rehabilitation of Offenders Act 1974 (Police Act 1997, s. 120).

  In this way the Police Act 1997 sought to close the anomalous gap that had been identified between those who could ask 'exempted' questions under the 1974 Act and those who were entitled to request a check of records from the police (see Chapter 5; Home Office, 1991: paras. 180–182). Registration was to be with the new central agency.
- Umbrella bodies – would act for smaller employers who had occasional need to check on individuals 'exempted' under the Rehabilitation of Offenders Act. They would also register with the new central agency.

The registered body and the umbrella body would both be charged for their initial registration and for each disclosure of criminal records; the umbrella body was entitled to add on an extra administrative charge for the smaller employers using its services. The original idea in the White Paper that only those requesting 200 or more disclosures a year should register had been dropped (Home Office, 1996b: para. 37); registration was now permissible with just the one criterion being met – the right to ask the 'exempted question'. Within the respective bodies a named person – the Lead Counter signatory – would sign the application forms for disclosure. The registered bodies and the umbrella bodies would now become the customer network of the central agency.

The Police Act itself made no reference to the central agency that would be required on the assumption that it would be part of the Home Office; Scotland was to have its own arrangements through the SCRO (s. 121).

Various offences could be committed in all these processes, including the giving of false statements and false identities to obtain a certificate as well as actually altering or counterfeiting a certificate (s. 123). 'Registered persons' or 'Registered bodies' also committed an offence if they made an unauthorised disclosure of criminal record information (s. 124), and failure to comply with a statutory code of practice to be produced by the Home Office (s. 122) could lead to 'de-registration' from the system (s. 124).

The Criminal Records Bureau – planning

The formal announcement of the centralised agency came in December 1998. The new agency was now called the CRB and was to be a self-financing agency under the management of the UK Passport Agency (Hansard HC Debates, 14 December 1998, col. 356); the Passport Agency would later be re-named as the Passport and Records Agency and later still as the Identity and Passport Service. An accompanying press release moved the emphasis back towards a strengthening of 'child protection safeguards' and Home Secretary Jack Straw was clear that 'dangerous people need to be stopped from working with children and young people (and) the creation of a Criminal Records Bureau is an important step towards achieving this'. The CRB was to be located on Merseyside, where it would create an estimated 1200 new jobs (Home Office, 1998b). The press release said little about the much wider vetting to be introduced in the form of the Criminal Conviction Certificate (later re-named as the Basic Disclosure) and it was left to some sectors of the press to point this out (Travis, 1998).

The Home Office considered bids for the CRB contract throughout 1999 and at the same time had to field 'a large number of representations from voluntary organisations' requesting that they should be exempt from paying for each check; the government was unmoved, believing 'it will not be practicable to provide any free checks from the Criminal Records Bureau for volunteers' (Hansard HC Debates, 5 July 1999, col. 324).

The CRB announced that the Capita Group plc had been selected as the preferred bidder to work in partnership with it in July 2000. Capita would be the private sector partner in the public – private partnership to operate the bureau with a contract worth £400 million over 10 years. Charles Clarke for the Home Office once again emphasised the CRB's role in protecting children and young people:

> ..it is especially important that employers and voluntary organisa-
> tions should be able to access information about criminal convictions

when checking the suitability of those who will be working with children, young people and vulnerable adults.

(Home Office, 2000c)

The deal was that Capita would provide all the essential information, technology infrastructure and business processes and be working in partnership with the CRB, the police and others.

An implementation team took on the work of making the CRB operational within the framework of the Police Act 1997. A Code of Practice was produced for 'registered persons' as required, covering matters relating to fair use of information and its appropriate handling, and the sanction of de-regulation re-iterated for improper breaches of information confidentiality (CRB, 2001).

Throughout the first half of 2001 the CRB went on the road to create awareness of its existence and service. Some 23 'registered body roadshows' were held between January and June, attended by 5000 participants (NAO, 2004: para. 3.12). At these 'roadshows' it became apparent that the terminology was changing again and the hierarchy of disclosures was now referred to as the CRB's Disclosure 'products':

- Enhanced Disclosure;
- Standard Disclosure; and
- Basic Disclosure.

The Home Office explained that:

> The CRB's service will operate under the 'brand name' Disclosure. This has been arrived at on the advice of marketing specialists. Most applicants for the CRB's service will have no criminal convictions, and no other information recorded against them ... it has been considered preferable to avoid the use of the word 'criminal', and to adopt Disclosure as a term which, while capturing the essence of the service, appears less judgemental.
>
> (House of Commons, 2001a: Appendix 1, para. 27)

As the planning continued, the fees were announced to the House of Commons. The voluntary sector – who were originally told they were going to have to pay for the checks – were now told they would get them for free (Hansard HC Debates, 5 February 2001, col. 433WA) and the statutory and private sector were going to be charged £12 for each

Enhanced and Standard Disclosure they requested (Hansard HC Debates, 2 April 2001, col. 69W). Other obstacles, however, did now start to emerge that would delay the agreed implementation date. Enhanced and Standard Disclosures were due to start in July 2001 but a new date of March 2002 was agreed. Service level agreements were drawn up between the CRB and the police as operators of the PNC, as well as with all the local forces who were going to provide – and be paid to provide – non-conviction information. Some rapid re-thinking also had to take place when the 'roadshows' revealed that most applications for Disclosure were going to be paper-based and not telephoned or e-mailed in, as had been expected (Hansard HC Debates, 12 March 2003, col. 307W).

A 'one-stop shop'

The 1996 White Paper 'On the Record' had proposed that the CRB would have access to more than just the criminal records on the PNC. It would also be able to give employers the non-conviction information held by individual police forces which had been referred to as 'other relevant information' and it would also have access to the two databases – 'List 99' and 'The Consultancy Service' – held by the relevant secretaries of state on people considered unsuitable to work with children (Home Office, 1996b: para. 16; see also Chapter 6). Employers, as registered bodies, would no longer have to make different requests to different agencies but could obtain it all through the CRB. The Utting Report, established in the wake of yet more reports of abuse in children's homes, said the new system should act as 'a one-stop shop for enquirers' (Utting Report, 1997: para. 14.12).

As we have seen, the Police Act 1997 ensured that 'approved' or 'additional' non-conviction information held by the police would be made available.

'Approved information' was information that the police were willing to share with the job applicant and it went to them as well as to the employer or registered body. It might, for example, be information about a pending prosecution or an earlier acquittal. Whatever it is, the law requires that it 'might be relevant' to the current job application (s. 115(7)).

'Additional information' is similar in nature and must also be relevant to the job application (s. 115(8)). The difference is that 'additional information' is more sensitive and has to be treated with a greater degree of confidentiality. The information goes to the employer or responsible body only and *not* to the applicant. The rationale for this differentiation is that 'additional information' is likely to interfere with current police activities concerned with the 'prevention or detection' of crime.

The two categories of information are only available as part of the CRB's Enhanced Disclosure package, and a request is made to local forces where the applicant has lived to see if any such information exists. When the CRB took on its responsibilities, funding was made available to local forces to ensure this information was readily accessed and made available to the CRB (Home Office, 2003a: para. 8). 'Approved' and 'Additional' information would later come under the microscope of the Bichard Report (see below).

The CRB would also have access to the other databases holding information on people unsuitable to work with children. 'List 99' and the 'Consultancy Service Index' (see Chapter 6) were now re-constituted and strengthened and a third list added to them, comprised of people unsuitable to work with adults. The CRB would have direct access to all three lists.

The Protection of Children Act 1999 re-named the Department of Health's 'Consultancy Service Index' as the Protection of Children Act List or POCA List, and put it on a statutory footing. Individuals had a right of appeal against inclusion on the list and amendments were made to the Police Act 1997 to ensure that the CRB would be able to access the list (Home Office, 1999c; DoH, 2000).

'List 99' had been on a statutory basis (Education Reform Act 1988, s. 218) and was now made the subject of new regulations (Education (Restriction of Employment) Regulations 2000, SI 2000 no. 2419). There is a right of appeal against inclusion. Formally, 'List 99' is known as the Department of Employment List or 'the 1988 List' but most people still call it 'List 99' (DfES, 2006a: paras. 1.6–1.7).

The third list that the CRB would have access to concerned those unsuitable to work with adults in various care settings. The Care Standards Act 2000 (Part VII) placed a duty on the secretary of state for health to keep such a list (s. 81) which would become known as the Protection of Vulnerable Adults List or POVA List; the Police Act 1997 was amended to give the CRB access, and the POVA List became available from June 2004 (DoH, 2004).

All three lists were maintained by the DfES Safeguarding Children Operations Unit in Darlington. Their expertise in managing the POCA List and 'List 99' was felt necessary to start the POVA List off (see Figure 7.1).

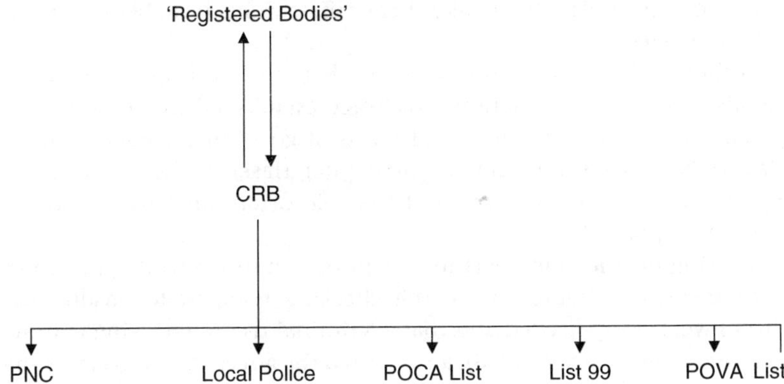

Figure 7.1 The 'one-stop shop'

Continuing criticisms of criminal record checks

The critics of criminal record checks continued to be heard in the 1990s and not least just before the implementation of the CRB. Some of these criticisms had been heard before, such as the continuing delays experienced by those wanting access to records (Utting Report, 1997: paras. 14.9–14.11) and the undesirable practice of allowing people to start work with children before the check had been completed (e.g. SSI, 1999: Chapter 11). Other critics also emerged, taking a more in-depth look at what was going on in the checking process.

Joanne Smith followed up the criticism already made that employment decisions were not always based fairly and proportionately on the relevance of the criminal record disclosed. Her research involved visiting 118 local authority social services departments in England and Wales to look at the decision making on the employment of social workers: who made the decisions and what factors they would take into account. The decision makers were provided with ten hypothetical candidates with nine of them having criminal records. They were then given the option of asking for further information to help them make their decisions. The inconsistency and variation in decision making was noted, including the six authorities prepared to take on someone with a record for indecent exposure once they knew the record was 20 years old and had resulted from urinating in a public place (Smith, 1999).

Smith's conclusions were that if this was a balancing act between the rights of children and the rights of adults (ex-offenders) then the arrangements in place 'prevent either of these rights from being consistently respected' (ibid).

Further criticism of criminal record checks came from the government's own Better Regulation Task Force established to advise on the effectiveness and credibility of all forms of government regulation. In May 1999 under the Chair of Christopher Haskins, they produced a report on 'fit person criteria' and the role of criminal record checks (Haskins Report, 1999).

Focusing on the employers in receipt of criminal records, the report recommended a tightening of the checking regimes, to ensure that checks were really needed and that a 'criminal record checking culture' was not being created (ibid: 8), and wanted the government to give more advice on how records played their part in recruitment decisions. The inconsistent decision making revealed by Smith was noted with 'wide discretion and varying interpretations caus(ing) geographical inconsistencies' (ibid: para. 4.34). At its worst the report believed this could lead to potential offenders working their way round the country in order to find the weakest barrier into various employments; something they were told was already happening in the case of mini-cab drivers seeking licences (ibid).

In anticipation of the CRB the Better Regulation Task Force report wanted more guidance from the government for employers, and also suggested that the number of checks be reduced to a minimum in order to reduce costs; one way to do this would be to make checks 'portable' between employers rather than a need to re-check all the time. The report also suggested that negotiations with other countries be entered into to cover the vetting of overseas workers, and that the Rehabilitation of Offenders Act 1974 be completely reviewed.

In response Charles Clarke for the government described the report as 'an illuminating analysis of a crucially important and highly sensitive subject' and stated the government's view that 'the limitations of relying on criminal record checks cannot be over-emphasised too strongly' (Better Regulation Commission, 24 September 1999; Response to Fit Person Review at www.brc.gov.uk/government_responses/fitpersonresponse.asp). Nearly all of the report's recommendations were accepted.

Other critics of the looming CRB pointed out the potential for 'social exclusions' that its implementation would bring. The Better Regulation Task Force report had referred to 'real concerns over the potential for negative effects such as social exclusion and the creation of barriers to employment' (Haskins Report, 1999: 27). The campaign group Liberty now described it as a recipe for disaster and the extension of disclosures by means of Criminal Conviction Certificates on anyone for any job probably breached the European Convention on Human Rights (Parratt, 1999). Fletcher and colleagues came to the same conclusion that it would be these certificates that would 'heighten discrimination against offenders in the labour market' (Fletcher *et al.*, 2001: 40; see also Bell, 2000).

Finally – and at a more pragmatic level – questions were raised as to whether the CRB would actually be able to function at all in meeting the needs of employers across the country. In particular, was the time scale for preparation too short, and were the continuing problems of data quality (see Chapter 3) going to prove problematic?

The House of Commons Home Affairs Committee took on these questions and looked again at the criminal records data quality reports that had created concerns (Russell, 1998; HMIC, 2000a). The Committee thought it unacceptable that one undesirable person slipped through or one blameless person was misrepresented:

> The Home Office must ensure that improvements are made to the quality of data stored on the Police National Computer. The Criminal Records Bureau should closely monitor the number of complaints it receives that certificates are incorrect in the first year of operation.
>
> (House of Commons, 2001a: para. 50)

On the wider front it recommended that the CRB take its time and 'get it right' even if this meant delaying the July 2001 start date (ibid: paras. 44 and 51).

The government replied that it recognised the issues raised but thought delay was unnecessary. The reply pointed out that Phoenix was 'multi-functional' and held lots of information over and above the criminal record, such as personal characteristics and modus operandi, and that 'inaccuracies or omissions are far more likely to arise in these areas than in relation to conviction data', which was the data the CRB would be using (House of Commons, 2001b: para. 11). The government agreed that complaints should be monitored and the appeals machinery should deal with disputes promptly (ibid: para. 12). The CRB's July 2001 start date was put back to March 2002.

The Criminal Records Bureau – implementation

The Criminal Records Bureau went live on 11 March 2002. A last-minute Gateway Review by the Office of Government Commerce produced a number of concerns about the functionality of the information technology, the need for more staff training and a new business case to be drawn up to reflect the delayed start, but on balance it was felt best to proceed. As with the original D-Day the 'troops' were in place and the momentum considerable; a decision had to be made and there was 'now no turning back' (NAO, 2004: paras. 3.15–3.16).

In the background were the political considerations of 'confusion and bad publicity that would result from delay' and the pragmatic consideration that the police had now simply stopped accepting vetting applications – as planned – under the old localised arrangements (ibid: para. 3.16). In the first month 2765 Disclosure application requests were made and 21 issued. In the first 6 months 523,979 applications were received and 256,641 Disclosures issued. The gap between applications requested each month and numbers of Disclosures issued was slowly widening (Hansard HC Debates, 21 January 2003, col. 292W).

By May there were rumblings of discontent that the CRB was being overwhelmed by the number of applications coming in. Supply teacher agencies were complaining that the promised 90 per cent of responses within 3 weeks were not being met. The CRB retorted that up to 50 per cent of applications were incorrectly completed, and Education Secretary Estelle Morris and Home Secretary David Blunkett were reported to be holding emergency meetings to demand answers. By the end of May the Department for Education and Skills had pulled out of the arrangements and decided to vet using 'List 99' alone (Curtis, 2002).

The CRB had prepared itself for call-centre work with telephone-based and online applications. Now 78 per cent of its applications were coming in on paper just as the 'roadshow' seminars had predicted (Hansard HC Debates, 12 March 2003, col. 305W). On top of this the sheer demand for criminal record information was greater than expected and not least because of the need to vet new teachers before the start of term in September.

As the summer of 2002 progressed, the CRB put a Service Improvement Plan in place. This included:

- training for registered bodies to improve the quality of application form completion;
- recruitment of extra staff;
- temporary seconding of 220 Passport Agency staff to CRB;
- outsourcing of data entry from application forms to Hays plc, who passed the work to their facilities in Chennai, India.

(NAO, 2004: para. 5.1)

In August 2002 the murder of the school children Jessica Chapman and Holly Wells in Soham, Cambridgeshire, became a focus of intense media attention. When the arrested suspect – Ian Huntley – was found to have been working as a caretaker at Soham Village College, the question of vetting was inevitably raised. The Department for Education and Skills now dropped its 'List 99' vetting and went back to awaiting full Enhanced Disclosure.

More confusion was caused when the National Care Standards Commission announced that it would not implement its deadline of 1 August 2002 whereby all care-home workers and managers should have been checked. Providers of services and managers in the care-home sector were still required to obtain a CRB check and would be alright as long as they 'make every effort to organise their CRB checks as quickly as possible' (NCSC, 2002).

Any 'confusion and bad publicity' that might have resulted from a delay in starting operations in March 2002 were now coming home to roost. Television news pictures of children unable to start term on time made for uncomfortable images for the government. In September they decided to send in a troubleshooting Independent Review Team (IRT) to find out what was going wrong. The IRT provided a report for the home secretary in December 2002, and in the meantime CRB checks on a further 700,000 staff working with vulnerable adults were postponed indefinitely (Hansard HL Debates, 1 November 2002, col. 48WA).

The Independent Review Team

The Independent Review Team took 3 months to produce their report for the home secretary, and made a total of 10 recommendations for the future:

1. A complete review was needed of all the roles involved in the screening process from Registered Bodies, through to the CRB, Capita and local police forces;
2. The role of Registered Bodies needed more recognition and upgrading, especially with regard to identity checks, and quality of applications; the number of Registered Bodies needed reducing;
3. Registered Bodies needed to go over to electronic applications;
4. The difference between Enhanced and Standard Disclosures needed clarifying;
5. PNC records needed flagging when police intelligence existed;

6. Basic Disclosures had to be put on hold; and when they were introduced, should go through Registered Bodies;
7. New technology was needed for many of these recommendations and therefore a new revised contract with Capita was necessary;
8. Identification of applicants might be improved with the introduction of fingerprinting;
9. The status of the CRB needed revising; and
10. other legal changes would be needed to implement some of these recommendations.

(IRT, 2002)

The Home Office tried to put a brave face on the IRT report for which they were duly 'grateful'; they were also 'grateful for the patience shown by the CRB's customers during what has undoubtedly been a difficult period' (Home Office, 2003c). Other observers were more blunt:

> ... the grim news that the Criminal Records Bureau system is drastically inadequate and has been poorly managed has a weary, sad inevitability about it ... (and) sounds like a cracked record that has been played many times down the years.

(Bentley, 2003)

All the recommendations were accepted by Home Secretary David Blunkett, who made a written ministerial statement (Hansard HC Debates, 27 February 2003, cols. 32–36WS). The Basic Disclosures (rec. 6) were put on indefinite hold and arrangements to re-classify the CRB as a free-standing agency no longer a part of the Passports and Records Agency were started (rec. 9).

Pilot schemes were initiated on intelligence flagging (rec. 5) and on the use of electronic applications by registered bodies (rec. 3). A Consultation Paper was published looking at the proposed changes in general (Home Office, 2003d) and a specific Consultation Paper came later on the proposal to introduce fingerprinting as a form of identification by registered bodies (rec. 8) (Home Office, 2003e).

Three of the IRT recommendations (1, 2 and 4) were going to need legislative changes and these were effectively made by the Criminal Justice Act 2003 s. 328 and Schedule 35, which amended the Police Act 1997, with new sections 120ZA, 120AA, 120AB and 122A. The registered bodies were singled out for particular attention, after the IRT suggested there were too many of them and as 'customers' they were too distant from the CRB.

In 2002 there were 8200 registered bodies but research carried out for the IRT found that 1936 of them had never submitted an application for a Disclosure (Home Office, 2003d: para. 16). The original idea to have a close network of customers developing degrees of expertise with a high volume of applications – at least 200 a year – had never materialised (see above). Instead anyone entitled to ask the 'exempted questions' under the Rehabilitation of Offenders Act 1974 could apply to be a registered body even if they made only a few applications a year.

Further CRB research in 2004 revealed a total of 13,600 registered bodies creating a network of customers that was 'disparate and unwieldy' (CRB, 2005a: para. 8.1). Even worse was the lack of compliance by many of them in following the CRB Code of Practice, with some 34 per cent 'assessed as posing a risk to the integrity of the Disclosure service' (ibid). In other words, approximately 4500 registered bodies were taking an 'inconsistent and variable approach' in their applications and in their handling of criminal records disclosed to them.

The sort of problems now being revealed were reported in the CRB's monthly newsletter *Disclosure News*:

- Application forms coming in damaged or defaced (*Disclosure News*, 25; April 2005).
- Incomplete forms (*Disclosure News*, 14; May 2004).
- Inappropriate signatories (*Disclosure News*, 28; July 2005).
- Using out of date forms (*Disclosure News*, 35; February 2006).
- Trying to pass off workers as volunteers (to avoid payment) (*Disclosure News*, 29; August 2005).
- Illegal use of the CRB logo (*Disclosure News*, 28; July 2005).
- Forms being forged (*Disclosure News*, 25; April 2005).
- Insufficient confidentiality being accorded to records (*Disclosure News*, 17; August 2005).

Mostly, these problems led to forms being sent back to registered bodies and delays building up in the processing. More seriously, some 80 cases had had to be referred to the police in 2004 (*Disclosure News*, 25; April 2005). It all seemed reminiscent of the old regime and the Home Office's metaphorical foot stamping 12 years earlier in 1993, when confronted by increasing numbers of disclosures and abuse of the system (Home Office, 1993c: para. 21; see Chapter 6).

A new regulatory framework

The CRB now tried to rein in the registered bodies and bring them to heel. Draft regulations were drawn up and put out for consultation (CRB, 2005b), containing new criteria for being able to become a registered body. The draft regulations placed new and increased responsibilities on any registered body to ensure:

- forms were completed accurately;
- forms were only submitted on 'eligible persons';
- identities were confirmed (and staff given training to help that confirmation);
- the CRB Code of Practice was complied with;
- a minimum 100 applications were made in a 12-month period;
- the CRB could request any information regarding compliance; and
- any future electronic interfaces were compatible with the CRB.

In addition, the Home Office was given new powers to 'de-register' bodies, and to request payments by monthly accounts rather than just as accompaniment to a disclosure request (CRB, 2005b).

Following the consultation exercise with registered bodies, most of these proposals appeared in the Police Act 1997 (Criminal Records) (Registration) Regulations 2006 (SI 2006 no. 750), which came into force on 6 April 2006. The regulations repeated the old requirements of declarations regarding being able to ask the 'exempted' questions, the need to name authorised persons as lead and counter signatories, and the need to pay a £300 registration fee. Most of the new demands placed on registered bodies were to be found in the Regulation 7.

This regulation confirmed that in future all registered bodies needed to be making 100 or more applications a year (Regulation 7(c)) even though 62 per cent of respondents in the consultation exercise had declared themselves unhappy with the idea (CRB, 2005b: 23–25). The CRB quickly began a process of de-registration, starting with all those registered bodies who had made either no applications at all in the previous 12 months or had only made less than 10. They were given 21 days to appeal against the decision, but otherwise were simply referred to umbrella bodies for a continuing service (*Disclosure News*, 37; April 2006).

Other new demands included a statutory duty to ensure forms were fully completed and identifications fully carried out (Regulation 7(e) and 7(f)). An earlier consultation that had proposed fingerprinting for some applicants was not followed through (Home Office, 2003e). There was a new duty to follow the CRB Code of Practice (Regulation 7(h)) and new duties placed on umbrella bodies.

Umbrella bodies had been introduced as bodies that would help out the smaller employers who needed to do occasional checks but not on a large scale. Umbrella bodies could register with the CRB and act for any number of smaller employers and organisations. They could also add on any administrative fee they liked to the disclosure charge and make their own 'profits' from criminal records. Some were criticised for adding on 'disproportionate' amounts (Home Office, 2003d: paras. 21–23).

Some voluntary organisations in England and Wales felt they were being abused by umbrella bodies and suggested that the government should sponsor its own umbrella body to avoid this happening (see, e.g. NCVYS, 2003). In Scotland and Wales the devolved governments had already done this. An organisation called the Central Registered Body for Scotland had been established by the Scottish Executive to provide disclosures for volunteers (see www.crbs.org.uk/) and in Wales a similar service was provided by the Criminal Records Unit of the Wales Council for Voluntary Action based in Colwyn Bay (see www.wcva.org.uk/).

The Home Office has not been persuaded to introduce anything similar in England and the chosen way of bringing high-charging umbrella bodies to heel has been that of using market forces. Regulation 7(d) now requires all umbrella bodies to deposit their charges with the CRB so that they can be published on the CRB website. The idea is that those seeking an umbrella body in their area can compare the prices and make an informed decision on where to take their business.

To ensure compliance with the new demands of Regulation 7, the regulations provided for new powers of entry for compliance teams and new powers to request documentation (Regulation 8). The secretary of state got new powers to de-register anyone not complying with Regulations 7 and 8 (Regulation 9).

Whether or not this new regulatory framework was going to result in a more cohesive and 'intelligent' customer network remained to be seen (see also Thomas, 2006). In May 2006 over 14,750 different organisations made up the registered body network (CRB, 2006a: 10).

Political repercussions

Most of the problems associated with the registered bodies and the new regulatory framework required to pull them into shape were contained at a local level within Home Office, CRB and registered body circles. It was the financial part of the deals being drawn up that concerned those at a higher political level.

The Independent Review Team's Recommendation 7 had required the Home Office to re-negotiate its contract with Capita. It was this aspect of the CRB functioning that concerned many observers and would later attract the attention of the National Audit Office and the House of Commons Public Accounts Committee:

> ...we must look closely at the role played by a handful of major government IT suppliers that dominate the sector...safe in the knowledge that they are too enmeshed in the cogs of government to be dropped. Despite the millions of pounds of tax payers' money that has been wasted...they continue to pick up lucrative deals.
>
> (Bentley, 2003; see also Cohen, 2002)

Capita repeated its argument that the service changes had thrown them and would later explain that 'the job we were eventually asked to deliver was a very different one than the one we tendered for' (House of Commons, 2004: Evidence p. 11). The critical miscalculation was the registered bodies preferred use of paper applications rather than using the CRB call centre or electronic means of application. The CRB had had to transfer staff from their call centre to process the paper applications at the eleventh hour, and of those applications as many as 50 per cent had multiple errors (NAO, 2004: paras. 3.13 and 4.12). In retrospect the Home Office accepted that 'there should have been much more extensive consultation much earlier' (House of Commons, 2004: Evidence p. 10).

In a robust exchange with Richard Bacon MP on the House of Commons Public Accounts Committee, the Chief Executive of the CRB, Vince Gaskell, explained why the taxpayer had had to find another £150 million:

> *Mr. Bacon*: What is the total amount of money you are expecting to be paid over the lifetime of this contract?
>
> *Mr. Gaskell*: Over the lifetime of this project we now expect that figure to be approximately £400 million.
>
> *Mr. Bacon*: So it has gone from £250 million to £400 million?
>
> *Mr. Gaskell*: That is correct.
>
> *Mr. Bacon*: For a slower service that is delivered a year late and it provides less than it did originally. That is right is it not, it is being delivered late?

Mr. Gaskell: The figure is correct yes.

Mr. Bacon: Is it right that it is being delivered late?

Mr. Gaskell: Yes.

Mr. Bacon: Is it right that it is delivering less now than it was originally proposed to deliver?

Mr. Gaskell: That is also correct.

Mr. Bacon: But it is costing £150 million more.

Mr. Gaskell: Yes.

(ibid: Evidence p. 5)

The cost of Disclosures now increased and the new laws recommended by the IRT were put into place.

The commodification of criminal records

The most radical change that the Police Act 1997 and the CRB had brought about in the policies of criminal record disclosure had been that of charging for the service. Criminal records became a saleable product; employers and others have become customers who make up the market. Under the old localised arrangements the Home Office would try to contain the demands being put on the police for disclosures and one argument for fees was that it might also contain demand. Now the CRB actively tried to build up its market and seek out new customers for its product. The aim was for the CRB to be self-funding by 2005–2006.

Early estimates of charges were optimistic. In April 2000 Home Office Minister of State Charles Clarke said the charges would be 'between £5 and £10 depending on the type of certificate' (H. C. Debates, 8 May 2001: col. 301W). The first charges to be announced were set at £12 for both Enhanced and Standard Disclosures; the government said it 'was determined that fees should be kept as low as possible' (H. C. Debates, 2 April 2001: col. 69W). Registered bodies also had an initial £300 registration fee to pay.

The voluntary sector had long foreseen financial problems if they had to pay anything like these sort of fees and had lobbied hard to be able to get free Disclosures. A number of voluntary organisations collectively briefed MPs at Westminster in June 1999; one of them estimated an additional £750,000 a year, every year, would hhave to be found (Scout Association, 1999).

The arguments continued and eventually the government had relented and agreed to free checks to the voluntary sector (Hansard HC Debates, 5 February 2001, col. 433WA).

Table 7.1   Fees for CRB disclosures

	Enhanced Disclosures	Standard Disclosures
March 2002	£12	£12
1 July 2003[1]	£29	£24
1 April 2004[2]	£33	£28
6 April 2006[3]	£36	£31

[1] announced Hansard HC Debates, 5 June 2003, cols. 27–29WS
[2] announced Hansard HC Debates, December 2004, cols. 49–50WS
[3] announced by CRB (CRB, 2006b)

Everyone else was going to have to pay £12 for their Enhanced or Standard Disclosures (Hansard HC Debates, 2 April 2001, col. 69W). In 2003 the fees doubled after the IRT report had recommended Capita's contract needed re-negotiating to the 'changed and evolving circumstances' (IRT, 2002: rec. 7; see above). Over the next few years the fees would rise again on two occasions (see Table 7.1).

An underlying financial concern for the CRB was the fact that only two out of three of their products were being sold. The Basic Disclosures had been put on indefinite hold in February 2003 until such time as the two higher levels were performing to standard. The IRT had also recommended that Basic Disclosures – when they ever did materialise – be channelled through registered bodies in order to improve identification validation, use the existing communications channels established and protect employers from possible fraud should applicants have direct contact with the CRB (IRT, 2002: rec. 6; Home Office, 2003f: paras. 18–20).

The proposal to route Basic Disclosures through registered bodies has never gone any further. The proposal did run counter to the IRT's ideas to reduce the number of registered bodies and make them a closer customer network for the CRB. If implemented, more registered bodies rather than less might be needed (Home Office, 2003f: paras. 19(v) and 22). Basic Disclosures were seen as the real lucrative market with their anticipated high volume; early estimates had put this market as high as 5 million a year which was to be the key to future developments:

The CRB's aim of broadening its product portfolio lies, in part, in the development and delivery of a Basic Level Disclosure Service. Indeed, the delivery of a product that will permit Basic Level Disclosures is now a pressing consideration for the CRB...the increase in volume attributable to a Basics service will contribute towards the CRB's aim of becoming a self-funding organisation, both through increased fee revenue and by securing economies of scale from our cost base. The CRB's profile will also be raised as a result of enabling the general public to access the Basic's service.

(CRB, 2004: 17–18)

The CRB still hoped to go live with its Basic service in 2005; the only damper was news coming from Scotland that the initial estimates of a sizeable Basic Disclosure market were over optimistic. New research commissioned by the CRB now put the market much lower at 500,000 disclosures per annum (ibid: Annex 4). If the Basic Disclosures did raise the CRB's profile, however, it would help in other parts of the market:

...there are a number of sectors where current demand for the Disclosure service is noticeably lower than expected. By increasing the general level of awareness of our service and the importance of Disclosure checks, we will ensure the latent demand is generated from these organisations who should be making greater use of the CRB.

(ibid: 13)

Another 'new product range' was the idea of the periodic updating of checks (ibid: 10). The CRB believed 'a carefully planned and well implemented renewals policy will contribute to our strategic aim of developing capacity by increasing the breadth and depth of our service' (ibid: 13). Such a policy would seem to override the existing 'Notifiable Occupations Scheme' and move away from recommendations of the 1999 Haskins report that checks should be as minimal as possible, and portable between employers, let alone be requested repeatedly by the same employer (Haskins Report, 1999: 19 and 23–24); at the time the government had accepted these recommendations, while pointing out that it would be for organisations to make these decisions unless they were prescribed by law (Better Regulation Commission, 24 September 1999: Response to Fit Person Review – http://www.brc.gov. uk/government_responses/fitpersonresponse.asp).

At the start of 2007 the CRB announced that it would not be increasing fees that year because it had now achieved its self-funding status, and had done so without the need for the Basic Disclosures – always held to be the key to self-funding (CRB, 2007a).

The Bichard Report

After the trial and conviction of Ian Huntley for the murder of Holly Wells and Jessica Chapman, both aged 10, it emerged that Huntley had been known to the police over several years for allegations of sexual offences involving young girls. None of these allegations had ever been prosecuted in court and Huntley therefore had no criminal record for sexual offences. The fact remained, however, that the police still held information on him that might have suggested a predatory pattern of behaviour, and that vetting arrangements had not stopped him getting work as a caretaker in proximity to children and young people (Morris, 2003). Sir Michael Bichard was asked to conduct an inquiry into the issues that arose (Bichard Report, 2004).

The Bichard inquiry looked at the period preceding the advent of the CRB when police checks were carried out through local arrangements (see Chapter 6). The report's recommendations, however, had clear implications for the CRB and the screening arrangements that now existed.

The report also had implications for the police and their general handling of information and intelligence which Bichard wanted to see put on a national scale. The ramifications of the Bichard Report were considerable and the report had its own Bichard Implementation Programme Board within the Home Office which produced regular reports to indicate implementation progress (Home Office, 2004e, 2005h, 2006b).

As noted in Chapter 3, Bichard made recommendations concerning the quality of police data collation and the need for its governance by statutory codes. The Inquiry Report now also recommended a new discrete register be started on all those who want to work with children or vulnerable adults (rec. 19); the register would be held by a central body having access to criminal records through the CRB to help decision making on inclusion or de-registration. This recommendation was carried forward in the Safeguarding Vulnerable Groups Act 2006 introducing a new Vetting and Barring Scheme for teachers and childcare workers, to be administered by the CRB (DfES, 2006b).

Bichard made numerous recommendations on vetting, some of which repeated recommendations of the 2002 IRT Report on the CRB. Emphasis was placed on accurate identification (Bichard Report, 2004: rec. 22–24) and the need for fingerprinting (rec. 25) and address verification (rec. 26). It was also suggested (rec. 31) that the CRB have access to yet more non-conviction databases including those held by H. M. Customs and Excise, NCIS, the National Crime Squad, British Transport Police and the

Scottish and Northern Ireland equivalents of the Protection of Children Act list and the Protection of Vulnerable Adults list; all this new access was duly enabled by the Serious Organised Crime and Police Act 2005, ss. 163–168.

Bichard had further suggestions for what had been referred to as 'other relevant information' (or police intelligence) that might be disclosed to employers. 'Other relevant information' was now referred to by the CRB as 'approved' or 'additional' information (see above).

What exactly constitutes 'approved' or 'additional' information is not always an easy decision to make. In the Huntley case it may have been straightforward but at other times it was not. As though to illustrate the dilemmas – just as the Bichard Inquiry started its deliberations – the Court of Appeal ruled on a case where they thought such information was improperly disclosed.

The case involved a man investigated and charged with acts of indecent exposure but then never taken to court or prosecuted. The information remained on file and was eventually given to the CRB as 'approved information' when the man concerned was the subject of an Enhanced Disclosure. The CRB passed it on to the employer who withdrew the offer of a job that had been made. The court criticised the police decision to disclose, which it felt had been made with insufficient scrutiny (*R (X)* v. *Chief Constable of the West Midlands Police* [2004] EWHC 61 (Admin) QBD).

Bichard was clear that police intelligence was important and needed to play its full part in employment-vetting arrangements. He also recommended that it be made available between forces on a national level. Until such a system was in place an interim arrangement that effectively allowed the CRB to know when various forces held information was suggested as the way forward. This police local cross-check system (PLX) had already been piloted in the Metropolitan Police, Staffordshire Police and West Midlands Police for the CRB and Bichard now called for it to 'be given urgent priority' (Bichard Report, 2004: paras. 4.32–4.33).

The PLX System – or I-PLX if its Interim status is added to the acronym – was a free-standing database that enabled the CRB to identify the police force that held the intelligence. It did not hold any intelligence itself and did not link to the PNC because 'initial studies indicated that flagging the PNC would not be the most effective way forward' (Home Office, 2004d: para. 137). The PLX system was formally launched on 2 March 2005 (Home Office, 2005i).

The Home Office produced detailed guidance to chief officers of police on just how decisions on 'approved' and 'additional' information should be taken. Using the letter of the law as a starting point that disclosure had to be 'relevant for the purpose described', the guidance set out nine key principles on who should make the decision and how they should make it:

1. the decision was an important one and should be made by a senior officer at Assistant Chief Constable level or higher;
2. the decision needed to be fully recorded and open to later scrutiny;
3. the decision should be based on credible and clear information;
4. information needed to be judged on its individual merits;
5. information needed to be reasonably current and 'old information should not be included solely on the basis "once an offender always an offender" ';
6. information needed to be relevant for the purpose for which disclosure is sought;
7. information should be presented in a meaningful way and its relevance made clear;
8. information had to be self-contained, i.e. coming primarily from the police and not other agencies;
9. information about third parties should be marked as 'approved'.

(Home Office, 2005j: paras. 14–41)

This level of detailed guidance was in marked contrast to anything that had gone before, and doubtless reflected the concerns of Bichard and cases like *X* v. *Chief Constable of the West Midlands Police*.

The Bichard Report makes reference to the Home Office funded IMPACT Programme (Intelligence Management, Prioritisation, Analysis, Co-ordination and Tasking) as the new information sharing environment to take forward its recommendations on intelligence. The IMPACT Programme now lent its name to a new police national database, known as INI (Impact Nominal Index) launched in February 2006. The INI was another free-standing database that allowed the police – as opposed to just the CRB – to know which other forces held intelligence on individuals. In its initial stage it only operated for force Child Abuse Investigation Units, but with the intention for it being rolled out more widely at a later date (Home Office, 2006b: para. 3.8).

Meanwhile work continued to give the police the capacity to have direct access to intelligence held by other forces. Direct access would take the police beyond the INI, which was just an index as to where information was held. A pilot scheme already existed between a consortium of forces known as the Cross-Regional Information Sharing Project (CRISP) and this now formed the basis for developing a fully fledged national data sharing system (Home Office, 2006b: para. 3.18) which in turn would become part of the proposed National Police Database.

The overseas worker

One last concern of the Bichard Report was that of the overseas worker coming to the United Kingdom. The report recommended proposals be brought forward as early as possible to improve the checking of people from overseas who want to work with children and vulnerable adults (rec. 30).

Under the old system of checking (pre-2002) the Home Office was clear that normally 'the police cannot make enquiries about the antecedents of people from other countries' (Home Office, 1993b: para. 47). The best that could be offered was a guide to what might be available from other European countries (ibid: Annex G; see also Loucks *et al.*, 1998).

The CRB did create an Overseas Information Service which gave advice on what might be expected of other countries but had no direct lines of communication to receive criminal record information from them. In follow-up progress reports to Bichard, the Home Office could report progress on the development of embryonic exchange initiatives with other European countries and Australia (Home Office, 2005h: paras. 4.31–4.32), and it was anticipated that 'Australian conviction data should be available for testing purposes from early 2007' (Home Office, 2006b: para. 4.41; see also CRB, 2006a: 9).

The CRB was conscious that some countries did not have good criminal record repository systems and that this was always going to be a problem when individuals came from those countries to work in the United Kingdom. Countries identified included India, Zimbabwe, South Africa and the Philippines, whose record systems were considered 'of insufficient quality or unreliable' (Home Office, 2006b: para. 4.42). The CRB was proceeding with discussions with these countries about 'how to establish some useful level of data exchange' (ibid).

In the meantime a continuing mystery has been the case of people from the Republic of Ireland coming to the United Kingdom for work, taking advantage of the open border arrangements that existed within the Common Travel Area between the two countries. In 1993 the Home Office had reported that the republic had 'no arrangements for disclosure to prospective UK employers' and not even any within the republic itself save on prospective adoptive and foster parents (Home Office, 1993c: Annex G). Yet thousands of Irish people must have been coming to the United Kingdom and many of them working with children since the introduction of the 1986 childcare checking regimes; in 2004 the Garda added to the mystery by stating that it had been responding to requests from UK police since 1987 (Garda Siochana, 2004: para. 2.1.1).

Some UK police forces did admit to making informal inquiries with the Irish Garda Siochana. An officer in the Devon and Cornwall police revealed in 1990 how she did this out of 'expediency' and found 'the response time from the Garda Siochana is good' (Cannings, 1990: 224–225); this officer – Della Canning – later became chief constable of North Yorkshire. How this squared with the Data Protection Acts of both countries is uncertain.

Other new initiatives for exchanging criminal records between European countries are looked at in the next chapter.

Criticisms of the CRB in practice

The CRB has made a total of 8,990,597 disclosures on applicants for work between its inception in March 2002 and May 2006; of this total some 1,063,852 were Standard Disclosures and 7,926,745 were Enhanced Disclosures (Hansard HC Debates, 9 May 2006, col. 198W).

The CRB itself has estimated that about 5 per cent of its disclosures contain criminal record information and/or 'approved' or 'additional' information from the police; this would make for a total of 4–500,000 (CRB, 2006a: 4). A reported 20,000 people have been prevented from obtaining employment because disclosures have been interpreted as making them 'unsuitable' (CRB, 2005c).

From a different angle these figures mean over 7 million (95 per cent) disclosures have been just blank sheets of paper sent to registered bodies, and if only 20,000 people have been 'blocked' from gaining employment when up to 500,000 disclosures have contained records, then some 480,000 disclosures are deemed irrelevant and presumably only confirming what applicants have self-declared on their job application forms. The CRB would point out that the very existence of disclosure arrangements 'acts as a deterrent against those potential employees who would be considered inappropriate to be placed in a position of trust' (CRB, 2006a: 4).

Whether or not this all represents value for money is hard to assess. Just how do you measure whether children and vulnerable adults are better safeguarded now than they were before 2002? Certainly the amounts of money involved are considerable and on an anecdotal basis are even now detracting from direct patient care in some hospitals and residential care facilities (see, e.g. Hayes, 2003).

The Manifesto Club have also pointed to the financial burden now being imposed by what they call 'the CRB industry' or 'the child protection industry' and how that 'industry' is taking up a growing part of the budget of organisations that work with children (Manifesto Club, 2006: 13). The report from the Manifesto Club takes the criticisms even wider to demonstrate what they call 'out of control' arrangements that fuel mistrust and makes children suspicious of all adults. They cite volunteers put off by the idea of vetting, and organisations covering their backs rather than making honest assessments. They quote Eileen Munro of the London School of Economics:

> …people prefer a mechanical process like a CRB check because there is no judgement involved and so no risk of making a mistake for which they might be blamed.

> (ibid: 4)

More specific criticisms have been made by the campaign group NACRO, based on evidence they receive from their 'Resettlement *Plus* Helpline'. This helpline is for enquiries from prisoners, ex-offenders and others about a range of issues including criminal record disclosures. About 20,000 enquiries a year are made and NACRO estimates that almost two-thirds (63 per cent) of them are about disclosures (NACRO, 2006: 28). On the basis of the evidence they have, NACRO has grouped the criticisms into five areas (see generally NACRO, 2006: part 1).

1. Checking posts not exempt from the Rehabilitation of Offenders Act
Some employers were found to be 'routinely' misusing their access to the CRB by requesting checks on posts that should not be checked because there is no exemption from the 1974 Rehabilitation of Offenders Act. NACRO cites research by Suff showing as many as 11 per cent of employers are doing this (Suff, 2005) and thereby, in effect, rendering their requests for disclosure as illegal.

2. Running Enhanced checks instead of Standard checks
NACRO believes it has evidence that employers are 'routinely' requesting Enhanced Disclosures that they are not entitled to. The high number of Enhanced as opposed to Standard Disclosures has been noted above and NACRO states unequivocally that this is 'because the disclosure service is being misused' (NACRO, 2006: 9). Although the Police Act 1997 (s. 115)

defines the difference, the natural caution of employers directs them to request the higher level Enhanced Disclosures, despite the fact that the job falls outside the definitions – and despite it costing more.

The Enhanced Disclosure also enables the employer to have non-conviction information ('approved' and 'additional') which NACRO believes can be more damaging to an applicant than straight criminal record information:

> ... employers take the line that if the police have taken the trouble to disclose this sort of information, then the police must believe both the information to be true and that the subject represents a danger.
>
> (ibid: 10)

3. Failing to observe the Code of Practice

NACRO finds the code is 'frequently breached by employers', leading to inevitable discrimination. A significant number (20 per cent) have no written policy on the recruitment of ex-offenders and many do not make the code available to applicants as they are required to. Some managers do not know of the code's existence themselves.

4. Refusing to employ people or dismissing them

In particular this was evidence of discrimination when the criminal record bore no relation to the job in question and no specific risk assessment had even been attempted.

5. Social and economic costs

NACRO looked more closely at the presumed deterrent effect of disclosure arrangements. It found that this deterrent effect did undoubtedly exist, but wondered if it was also deterring some people who were eminently suitable, and were not applying because they thought they would not be treated fairly.

NACRO calculated that if a third of men have a criminal record by the time they are in their early thirties and a significant proportion of women now have records, this would mean around 25 per cent of the work force have the potential to have a record. But if only 5 per cent of disclosures are revealing a record (see above), what is happening to the other 20 per cent, other than deterrence, discrimination and social exclusion?

One other area of concern not reported by NACRO has been that of the inaccurate criminal record. This was the re-emergence of the data quality question when applicants were attributed with criminal records they did not have, and by default, presumably those who did have previous conviction histories, had no record attached to their name.

In 2003 a Parliamentary question revealed that 400 people had been mistakenly attributed with criminal records but Hilary Benn, minister for the Home Office, was quick to minimise the numbers as being only 0.03 per cent of the total of disclosures made at that time (Hansard HC Debates, 19 March 2003, col. 824W). The same 'tiny percentage' was cited again when a radio station revealed another 193 mistakes in 2004 ('Innocent labelled criminals in error', *The Guardian*, 17 April 2004) and again in 2006 when a Sunday newspaper put the figure at 1500 ('Branded as Criminals', *Mail on Sunday*, 21 May 2006). The other defence was that a lot of the mistakes were made because forms were being completed inaccurately. The *Mail on Sunday* believed that:

> ...despite its refusal to accept the blame for the latest blunder, the Home Office has quietly made a string of compensation payments to the people it has wrongly branded criminals.
>
> (ibid)

Conclusions

The Home Office started a review of the localised criminal record checks arrangements in 1993 and followed it up with a White Paper in 1996. The main changes being proposed were that criminal record disclosures be put on a statutory footing, be centralised at one point of contact and that a new non-police agency be created to co-ordinate requests from employers. It was further recommended that the agency be able to charge for each disclosure and in so doing become a self-funding agency.

The resultant Police Act 1997 put these proposals on the statute book and work commenced on creating the new Criminal Record Bureau as a public – private partnership to be based in Liverpool. The CRB would disclose criminal records on three levels – Enhanced, Standard and Basic – and those entitled to receive the first two would have to register with the CRB.

The CRB made a hesitant start to its operations in March 2002. The prime difficulty proved to be a different expectation between the CRB and its registered customers for Enhanced and Standard Disclosures. The CRB had thought requests would be coming in electronically; the customers preferred old-fashioned paper applications. Some unhealthy media headlines and a growing backlog led to emergency re-thinking and a troubleshooting Independent Review Team was sent in to the CRB to rescue the situation. In due course a new regulatory framework came into force in 2006. In the meantime Basic Disclosures had been put on hold and recriminations bounced between the Home Office, the CRB and politicians about the lengthy delays, the need for changes and the growing costs.

An additional critic was heard in the 2004 Bichard Report in the aftermath of the Soham murders. The Bichard Inquiry was looking at events that preceded the CRB starting up in 2002 but its recommendations included some that affected the current system. In particular it was concerned with the matter of non-conviction or 'other relevant information' that the police could disclose, and proposed various ways of improving this aspect of the new centralised arrangements. Bichard was also concerned with the position of overseas workers and how they should be vetted.

8
An International Perspective

Individual countries have always jealously guarded their right to devise and implement their own criminal justice and penal policies. What went on in one nation state was regarded as their business and no one else's. In today's age of faster communications and population movements such degrees of sovereignty become challenged, and not least when those communications and movements involve criminal activity that transcends national frontiers. The police of different jurisdictions need to co-operate and that co-operation includes the exchange of information and the exchange of criminal records.

Here we explore some of the different ways individual nation states have chosen to construct and maintain their national repositories of criminal records before looking at how they might exchange these records – and other police-held information – across international borders. Such exchanges may take place on an ad hoc basis between neighbouring countries across what are known as 'common travel areas' or through such specific arrangements as exist for the policing of the Channel Tunnel between England and France. Exchanges may also be formalised between police forces through more considered arrangements, sometimes referred to as 'transnational policing networks'. The better known of these networks include Interpol and Europol. This chapter ends with the recent developments in Europe for the specific exchanges of criminal records.

National criminal record repositories

Most Western industrialised countries now have their own national collections of criminal records. Here we briefly look at how this has been done by some European countries, the United States of America and Canada.

Europe

The European Union Member States have variously located their national criminal record repositories with the police, ministries of justice, ministries of the interior or the national prosecutor's office. The breakdown for the 25 States (in 2006) is twelve with a ministry of justice (Belgium, Czech Republic, Finland, France, Germany, Greece, Italy, Netherlands, Poland, Portugal, Slovenia and Spain), seven with the police (Austria, Cyprus, Denmark, Ireland, Malta, Sweden and the UK) and four with a ministry of the interior (Estonia, Hungary, Latvia and Lithuania). Two Member States have their records held by prosecuting authorities (Luxembourg and Slovakia). Those countries that have the ministry of justice controlling records often, in practice, give the records to the police or courts to have physical control of them, with the ministry regulating their use.

In the Republic of Ireland, for example, the national collection of criminal records is kept by the police service – An Garda Siochana. When the republic was formed in 1922, it took over the collection of records maintained under the statutory authority of the British Habitual Criminals Act 1869 and Prevention of Crimes Act 1871. The records were entrusted to the newly created ministry of justice but passed to the Garda in 1929, when they were referred to as the Dublin Criminal Register.

As the national repository the Dublin Criminal Register ran parallel to a localised set of records kept by the police just for the Dublin area. In 1972 the two offices were amalgamated into the present Garda Criminal Records Office (GCRO). The records are now computerised and available to 200 police stations throughout the republic ('Garda poised to enter high-tech revolution', *The Irish Times*, 21 September 1996); the computerised system is known as PULSE (Police Using Leading Systems Effectively).

The Swedish national collection of criminal records (*Person-och belastnings registret*) is held by the National Police Board on a computerised database governed by the Police Register Act (*Svensk Författningssamling*, 1965: 94) and the Criminal Register Act (*Svensk Författningssamling*, 1963: 197).

The Belgian collection is held in computerised form by the ministry of justice and the Danish collection (*Det Centrale Kriminalregister*) held by the police under the guidance of the ministry of justice. The Austrian collection (*Strafregister*) is held jointly by police and ministry of justice with police access being through the EKIS (*Elektronische Kriminalpolizei-liche Informationssystem*) computer system (for more details on all EU systems, see European Commission, 2005a: Annex 1).

United States of America

The assembling of a national criminal record system in twentieth-century America had to contend with the sheer size of the country and the historical factor of immigrants trying to leave behind their past in Europe and the old world:

> ...a part of the American promise to immigrants was freedom of movement and the ability to start a life over in a new town and place without the entanglements of one's past.
>
> (Laudon, 1986: 33)

Federal prisons made a start on record keeping with a system based at Leavenworth penitentiary in Kansas (Powers, 1987: 153). An independent system was started by the American members of the International Association of Chiefs of Police who formed their National Bureau of Criminal Identification in 1896. Both systems were merged by the department of justice's Bureau of Investigation in 1923; the bureau was formally re-named as the Federal Bureau of Investigation (FBI) in 1935.

The history of the United States of America in the 1920s and 1930s was one riven by economic depression, prohibition and organised crime. A national criminal history record was now promoted by the FBI as a tangible mechanism to help deal with the threats posed by crime:

> ...criminal history record systems were preferred by professional groups and the federal government as one technologically sophistic-ated way of coping with this new insecurity.
>
> (Laudon, 1986: 35)

Records started to be collated at a local level, state level and federal level. Communication between the various systems was limited and the expansion uneven and haphazard. Thirty-two states had their own criminal record repositories by 1940, but even through to the late 1950s 'there was no coherent managerial philosophy or set of practices at federal and state levels which guided the management of criminal justice information' (ibid: 37). As a result 'records were inaccurate, incomplete and ambiguous' (ibid: 38).

The developing information technologies of the 1960s stimulated new thinking about criminal records, as did the increasing number of middle-class people who found themselves getting records. The latter phenomenon has been attributed to the post-war baby boomers coming through to adulthood, and white-collar workers finding themselves in conflict with the law over adolescent crimes, political protests (esp. Vietnam and civil rights), traffic-related offences and soft-drug use.

The US Attorney General approved FBI proposals in 1965 to computerise all national police information systems – including the national collection of criminal records – and the emergent National Crime Information Center (NCIC) started in 1967. Unlike the development of the United Kingdoms's PNC, the FBI was to experience a strong countervailing force against having such a centralised database of criminal records.

The Law Enforcement Assistance Administration (LEAA) had been formed in 1968 specifically to promote crime reduction initiatives at state level and lower. The LEAA wanted a de-centralised state level system of criminal records rather than the FBI's centralised arrangement. The scene was set for 'a fierce bureaucratic battle between the LEAA and the FBI' (Gordon, 1990: 56).

In 1968 the LEAA had helped create Project SEARCH, based in California, to act as a 'think tank' for all the states, on questions of criminal record systems. Project SEARCH (Systems for Electronic Analysis and Retrieval of Criminal History Records) now argued for a system based on local state records that could be accessed through a 'message-switching' arrangement (ibid: 56–57).

The FBI's idea for a centralised repository won the day and criminal records were added to the NCIC in 1970. But the states were reluctant to play their part and input records to the centre, and by 1977 only 11 of the 50 states were co-operating and only a million records were on the database. The FBI looked again at the 'message-switching' idea and came up with the Interstate Identification Index or 'Triple I' that used state repositories that could be accessed on a national scale (ibid: 59).

Project SEARCH was wound up in 1979 (Zenk, 1979) but SEARCH – The National Consortium for Justice Information and Statistics – continues as a 'think tank' on criminal records to this day (see www.search.org). The 'Triple I' system came on line in 1983, and by 1993 26 states were participating in it; by May 2003, 45 states were participating. Many of the states had joined at the prompting of the department of justice's National Criminal History Improvement Program that started in 1995 to improve the data quality and integrity of criminal record collections (BJS, 2005; see also BJS, 2003).

The NCIC itself was upgraded with a new information system from July 1999 and is now known as NCIC, 2000. The new system serves 80,000 criminal justice agencies and 700,000 law enforcement officers and gives access to over 39 million records of different kinds organised in 17 databases (FBI, 1999). It is hosted by the FBI's Criminal Justice Information Services division based at Clarksburg, Virginia, and facilitates 4.8 million transactions a day (FBI, 2006).

Canada

Canada follows the model of America with criminal records on the more serious offences held at a national level and the less serious stored only at state level. The Royal Canadian Mounted Police hold the national collection at the Canadian Police Information Centre (CPIC) based in Ottawa. CIPC is a computerised system for officers across the country and it is also interfaced with the United States' NCIC.

The CPIC was developed in the mid-1960s from meetings between the federal attorney general and state level attorneys general. It was given a budgetary approval in 1967 and became operational on 1 July 1972. The CPIC holds a number of different files but from a criminal records point of view, just three are of significance:

- the full criminal record;
- a criminal record synopsis; and
- a criminal name index.

The criminal name index holds only names with an indication that a record may exist; the full criminal record holds conviction history, jurisdiction, acquittals, absolute and conditional discharges, and the synopsis holds only personal details and the conviction history (Flaherty, 1989: 284–291).

The international exchange of police information

The police of any two countries have always been able to communicate and exchange information in the interests of crime reduction and the investigation and prosecution of criminals. Sometimes these communications have been politicised through governmental channels for purposes of 'extradition' or similar activities. More often they have been lower level activities between police officers on the ground and especially at points of frontier crossing. As early as 1898 the police forces of various European countries met in Rome to discuss co-operation to combat terrorism; a meeting now attributed as the beginnings of Interpol (Jensen, 1981: see below).

Common travel areas

Some neighbouring countries have such historical and cultural affinities that they develop arrangements to facilitate travelling and migration between themselves. These arrangements form 'common travel areas' which then extend themselves into common 'policing' arrangements. In Europe the two main 'common travel areas' are between the United Kingdom and the Republic of Ireland and between the Nordic states of Sweden, Denmark, Norway and Finland.

The 'common travel area' between the United Kingdom and Ireland emerged in 1923 after the establishment of the Irish Free State. It was an agreement to allow free movement between the two countries with minimal need for controls, and has subsequently been formalised through the United Kingdom's 1971 Immigration Act and 1972 Immigration (Control of Entry Through Republic of Ireland) Order (SI 1972/1610). The UK government has described the 'common travel area' as 'an important part of our immigration control arrangements, recognising geographical proximity and shared close interests' (Hansard HC Debates, 13 January 1998, col. 165WA); the area also includes the Isle of Man and the Channel Islands.

The UK police and the Irish Garda Siochana have developed their own close working arrangements which include a necessary exchange of information as appropriate. This was formally recognised in the 1985 Anglo-Irish Agreement (Article 9) and its successor the Good Friday Agreement (1998: paras. 28–29).

The Nordic 'common travel area' was created in 1954 as a Passport Union area between Finland, Denmark, Sweden and Norway, and confirmed in a convention a few years later (UN, 1959). Nordic citizens can travel across their frontiers without presenting passports and non-Nordic citizens need present them only on entering the Nordic area. The area covered includes the Faroe Islands, Greenland and the Aland Islands, making a total population covered of 23 million people.

The Passport Union does allow the exclusion of a person from within the Nordic States:

> ...who has previously been sentenced to imprisonment and may be expected to commit a criminal offence in a Nordic State (or)...who figures in the lists of expelled (*utvisad*) aliens maintained by any of the contracting parties.
>
> (UN, 1959: Article 6(e) and (f))

The police of the Nordic 'common travel area' inevitably work together. This has led to some problems when Norway chose not to join the European Union. The other three police forces became party to various international policing arrangements that had to have special arrangements built in to accommodate Norway (see below).

The Channel Tunnel

A unique exercise in international police co-operation resulted from the completion of the Channel Tunnel between England and France in the early 1990s. The original Treaty of Canterbury in 1986, that started the whole process, had always envisaged the need for a protocol to cover the exercise of policing, immigration and customs control (Treaty of Canterbury, 1986: Article 4(2)).

The Kent Constabulary had established a Cross Channel Intelligence Conference with their French colleagues in the Pas de Calais as far back as 1969 and in preparation for the opening of the 'fixed-link' now created their own European Liaison Unit (Gallagher, 1992). The actual protocol on policing the Tunnel was signed in November 1991 and made public in January 1992. Amongst many things the protocol required the respective police to work closely together and 'to the fullest possible extent co-operate, assist one another and co-ordinate their activities in discharging their duties' (Protocol France no. 1, 1992: Article 3); this was to include 'the exchange of information which may be of use in the performance of their duties' (ibid, Article 3(e)).

The 1959 Council of Europe Convention

On a wider, more multi-layered scale, conventions between countries have exhorted the police to exchange information. Sometimes this has not specifically referred to criminal records and it has had to be surmised that records would inevitably be included in such information. In February 2007 some 32 countries were recorded as having formal arrangements to exchange criminal records with the UK (Table 8.1).

In 1959 the Council of Europe agreed a convention on police co-operation amongst its Member States that formalised positions on who to contact and how, as well as matters relating to extradition and formal procedures. In and amongst the convention were specific references to the exchange of criminal records:

> ...a requested Party shall communicate extracts from and information relating to judicial records, requested from it by the judicial authorities of a Contracting Party and needed in a criminal matter, to

Table 8.1 Countries having bilateral arrangements with the UK for the exchange of criminal records

---

Antigua and Barbuda
Argentina
Australia
Bahamas
Bahrain
Barbados
Bolivia
Canada
Chile
Columbia
Ecuador
Granada
Hong Kong SAR
India
Ireland
Italy
Malaysia
Mexico
Netherlands
Nigeria
Panama
Paraguay
Romania
Saudi Arabia
Spain
Sweden
Thailand
Trinidad and Tobago
Ukraine
Uruguay
USA

Source: Hansard HC Debates, 7 February 2007, col. 971W

the same extent that these may be made available to its own judicial authorities in like case.

(Council of Europe, 1959: Article 13)

and

...each Contracting Party shall inform any other Party of all criminal convictions and subsequent measures in respect of nationals of the latter Party, entered in the judicial records. Ministries of Justice shall communicate such information to one another at least once a year.

(ibid: Article 22)

Article 13 was discretionary, but Article 22 was mandatory. In other words when any country convicted a person from another country within the Council of Europe arrangements, they were obligated to notify the country of the person's origin. These were known as 'Article 22 notifications', and each country had to designate a 'central authority' to act as the receiving body for such notifications.

The United Kingdom seems to have been fairly unimpressed by the 1959 Convention. While many Council of Europe Member States ratified it in the 1960s and 1970s, the United Kingdom only got round to doing so in 1990 as the prospect of a frontier-free Europe started to loom (Spencer, 1990: 94–95); it was implemented by the Criminal Justice (International Cooperation) Act 1990.

From 1991 onwards the United Kingdom started receiving 'Article 22 notifications' with the Home Office acting as the designated 'central authority'. The Home Office in turn sent them on to the police through the NIB within the Metropolitan Police Service for inclusion on the PNC. There were problems with lack of information and lack of fingerprints and sometimes problems of translation (Amroliwala, 2007: paras. 2.3–2.4).

This arrangement broke down after 1995 when the NIB became the NIS and Phoenix came online, allowing forces across the country to update the PNC. From this point on the overseas records started to pile up at the Home Office with no one paying much attention to them. They were regarded as more of a statistical return rather than anything that might be useful for operational policing purposes; they were not part of any ongoing police investigations and the very fact that Article 22 of the 1959 Convention required them to be sent only 'once a year' only confirmed their limited status and that this was just a bureaucratic process (ibid: paras. 2.7 and 3.5). The existence of this stockpile at the Home Office would cause a political row when it came to light in January 2007 (see below).

In the meantime, the non-ratification of the convention did not stop the United Kingdom from sending the names of those with criminal records to Italy in 1990 to help the policing of football supporters at the World Cup finals that year, but the information was passed at a political level rather than policing:

In order to strengthen the arrangements for World Cup security, the Home Secretary forwarded to the Italian Minister of the Interior the names of certain convicted football hooligans, with his recommendation that the Italian authorities consider excluding them from the country during the World Cup.

(House of Commons, 1990b: 11)

On the ground, British police in Italy liaised directly with their Italian counterparts using a portable computer 'providing text and photographs on suspected or convicted hooligans' (ibid); the legality of these arrangements was questioned at the time (Broadbent and Vincenzi, 1990) but subsequent developments have only built on these beginnings for subsequent World Cups in France (1998) and Germany (2006) as well as European Championships in Sweden (1992), Belgium (2000) and Portugal (2004). The European Union has now produced a handbook to guide all Member States involved in football matches with each other. It looks at all aspects of crowd control and public order policing and requires States to have a designated National Football Information Point to act as the co-ordinating point for the exchange of information; information that might include personal information on individuals (Council of the European Union Decision, 2002/348/JHA; Council of the European Union, 2006: 8).

The 2000 European Union Convention

The European Union (and its predecessors the Common Market and the European Community) had traditionally not got itself involved in matters of policing and criminal justice, which were considered outside of its spheres of activity and 'competence'. Some inter-governmental meetings did take place in the 1970s and 1980s under the auspices of the TREVI Group (see below) but it was only with the signing of the treaty on European Union in Maastricht in December 1991 that the European Union started to fully play its hand on policing and criminal justice.

The Maastricht Treaty saw the architecture of the European Union now being built on three pillars. The first pillar covering the traditional concerns of the Union on economic and business matters, the second pillar covering a community, foreign and security policy and the new third pillar covering justice and home affairs matters, including policing, criminal activity and security. With increasing economic integration in

Europe, justice and home affairs matters have moved up the European Union's agenda.

By the mid-1990s the European Union decided it was time to produce its own convention on police co-operation in Europe to complement – and supersede – the 1959 Council of Europe version. A draft of this convention appeared in 1996 but was put on hold when the decision was made to appoint a special committee to look at organised crime in Europe and how best to respond to it. This committee was referred to as the 'High Level Group' and duly reported in early 1997 with an action plan adopted by the EU Justice and Home Affairs Council in April. The Action Plan took the draft convention in new directions, concerning operational activities of such bodies as Europol (see below) and recommended the establishment of a European network for judicial co-operation. It re-iterated the conventional wisdom that information exchange could be achieved more rapidly between central contact points in each country (Official Journal 251/1-18, 15 August 1997: esp. para. 19).

A final version of the Convention on Mutual Assistance in Criminal Matters between the Member States of the European Union was agreed on 29 May 2000 (Official Journal C197/01, 12 July 2000; it is also reproduced in House of Lords, 2000: Appendix 2). The convention emphasised the need for information exchange, whether formally requested or offered by one country to another spontaneously (Articles 6 and 7). It was incorporated into UK law by the Crime (International Co-operation) Act 2003.

The EU Convention is not as specific as the 1959 Council of Europe Convention in naming criminal records as a form of information that might be requested and exchanged. We are again left to assume that this is a form of information that might be included.

Transnational policing networks

The process of policing across national boundaries inevitably leads to a variety of agencies and institutions formalising arrangements for communications and the exchange of information. These arrangements may broadly be described as 'transnational policing networks'. The different agencies and laws governing their activities can lead to disparate results that do not always run smoothly (Hebenton and Thomas, 1998).

Here we consider the biggest 'transnational policing networks' that have been created for Europe and, indeed, the whole world.

Interpol

Interpol – the International Criminal Police Organisation – is probably the best known formalised transnational policing network for the exchange of information between police forces. With 184 member countries Interpol has been recognised by the United Nations since 1971 as an 'inter-governmental organisation'.

The origins of Interpol have been traced back to an international meeting in Rome in 1898 to discuss questions of terrorism (Jensen, 1981) but its more formal beginnings emanate from a later meeting in Monaco in 1914, and its first office was opened in Vienna in 1923. Interpol has never been an operational police force but an organisation that facilitates co-operation between forces of different jurisdictions. Since 1946 its headquarters, General Secretariat, have been in France, moving from Paris to Lyon in 1989, and each Member State has its own National Central Bureau (NCB) linked to Lyon; arrangements also cater for sub-regional bureaux (Anderson, 1989; Bresler, 1992; Hebenton and Thomas, 1995: 64ff).

For many years Interpol had a poor reputation amongst national police forces, being variously described as a 'post office' that simply passed information from A to B and did so very slowly, or as an organisation you might – as a police officer – be seconded to as a form of exile or 'punishment'. When the Home Affairs Select Committee looked at international police co-operation, they found 'Interpol's performance was subject to considerable criticism in evidence and in the course of our visits' (House of Commons, 1990c: vol. 1, para. 69).

Interpol has improved its reputation with the advent of information technology to speed up its information exchange. In 1987 it replaced its largely manual record system and introduced a computerised Criminal Information System. This enabled an improvement in the storing and retrieval of information, faster response times to NCBs and direct access to Interpol's officers, who in turn started to develop their own Analytical Criminal Intelligence Unit. A new Automated Search Facility (ASF) was started to search a database containing images, photographs and fingerprints and exchange them with NCBs. Following its move to Lyon in 1989, Interpol now had:

> ...one of the most sophisticated automated search and image transmission systems in the world. It enables rapid, reliable and secure exchange of information. NCBs will have access to an enormous store of data.
>
> (Benyon *et al.*, 1993: 226)

Today Interpol fulfils its stated aim 'to ensure and promote the widest possible mutual assistance between all criminal police authorities' (Article 2 of Interpol's Constitution cited in House of Commons, 1990c: vol. 2, p. 3) through three core priorities:

- an international communications network for police in member countries;
- a set of operational databases and data services; and
- various types of operational police support.

Interpol has five main databases for use by its member police forces:

- a nominals database;
- stolen travel documents database;
- stolen vehicle database;
- DNA database; and
- fingerprints database.

The nominals database holds details of some 166,000 international criminals of which 33,000 are described as 'fugitives'. The number of searches has risen significantly in recent years and by around 270 per cent between 2000 and 2004. Germany, for example, made 511 requests of the database in 2004, leading to 310 arrests in 40 different countries (Kersten, 2005).

Communication between Interpol HQ in Lyon and its constituent NCBs has been further enhanced with the introduction of a secure network known as I24/7. This global police communications network can transmit messages, images, files and general information and by February 2005 some 75 per cent of the Interpol community was connected to the system, with 100 per cent expected to be online by the end of that year:

> ... the Interpol network therefore offers the unique possibility of building up a genuine, planetary network in terms of secure communications and access to essential police service and information for investigations – among which the databases are at the forefront.
>
> (ibid)

The Schengen Information System (SIS)

The Schengen Agreement was signed in 1985 between the five European countries – Belgium, the Netherlands, Luxembourg, France and Germany. The aim was to enable the free movement of people between these countries with no border checks. The Schengen Agreement later became the Schengen Convention (1990) and was fully implemented on 26 March 1995. By this time other countries had joined, including Italy (1990), Spain and Portugal (1991), Greece (1992) and Austria (1995); Denmark, Finland and Sweden joined in 1996. In its early days the Schengen arrangements fell outside of EU competence and the area of free movement being created was sometimes referred to as 'Schengenland'; the Treaty of Amsterdam brought it into EU competence in 1997. Schengen itself is a small town in Luxembourg where the 1985 Agreement was signed.

In order to facilitate the area of free movement, states joining the Schengen arrangements had to agree to a series of compensatory measures being put into place. These included such things as a common definition of the rules for crossing external borders into 'Schengenland' and uniform controls at these borders, the requirement for all non-EU nationals moving from one country to another to make a declaration, and separate channels in airports for those travelling within the Schengen area and those arriving from outside. These compensatory measures are known as the Schengen *acquis*, and countries unable to agree the Schengen *acquis* could not join.

The SIS is a critical component of the Schengen *acquis*, as a compensatory measure for open borders. Border controls provide 'squeeze' points to check people's movement; with no borders these checks needed to be done in a different way. The contracting parties to Schengen believe that closer co-operation between their police forces is essential to reconciling freedom of movement with a degree of security. The SIS enables forces to share information on known criminals and other 'undesirable aliens' moving through Schengenland, and consists of a 'hub and spokes' system between a central computerised database in Strasbourg and national SIS offices in each country that signs and implements the Schengen Convention. The SIS has been described as a 'spectacular novelty' (Schutte, 1991) and as 'one of the most innovative features' of the Schengen Convention (O'Keefe, 1992); its Orwellian overtones have been noted (Baldwin-Edwards and Hebenton, 1994).

Although not directly concerned with storing criminal records it is clear that the SIS does transmit information on people wanted for arrest and extradition, court appearances and 'aliens' convicted of serious offences or an offence carrying a custodial sentence of 1 year (Schengen Convention, 1990: Articles 93–100). The aim is to provide 'alerts' to the police in the countries where the person might be. At the outset the Home Office was clear that it had no plans to link the SIS to the United Kingdom's PNC (Hansard HC Debates, 18 February 1992, col. 93).

The national SIS offices of the SIS are referred to as SIRENE Bureaux (Supplementary Information Request at the National Entry). The bureaux are not directly referred to in the Schengen Convention but clearly play a critical role in inputting new data and being available to talk more informally to each other and, as the name suggests, to pass on 'supplementary information', once a name has been given.

Oversight of the SIS for data protection purposes is undertaken by its own Joint Supervisory Authority (JSA). Relations between the JSA and those operating the SIS have not always been good. In its second Annual Report the JSA complained that it had to 'fight for recognition of its rights and independence from the Schengen decision-making bodies' (JSA, 1998: Chapter 1). The role of the SIRENE Bureaux as a possible way of getting round data protection laws has been noted (see also House of Lords, 1999: paras. 9–12; and generally Justice, 2000).

The United Kingdom and the Republic of Ireland have never fully accepted the Schengen Convention. Arguments have been premised on the island nature of the two countries and the difficulties of opening borders. Channels of information between the United Kingdom and European police forces were seen as sufficient without the need for access to the SIS (Lambert, 1993). This position changed in 1997 when the Treaty of Amsterdam incorporated the Schengen Convention into the European Union legal framework and at the same time allowed Member States to sign-up for parts of the convention.

The UK government now decided that although it wanted to maintain its national frontier controls, it did want to get involved with the Schengen arrangements. In particular it wanted to participate in police co-operation, customs and criminal justice co-operation, including the Schengen Information System (Hansard HC Debates, 12 March 1999, cols. 380–382; see also NCIS, 1999; Home Office, 1999d). The Republic of Ireland followed suit and both countries' applications were accepted in 2000 and 2002, respectively (Council Decision 2000/365/EC, 29 May 2000 and Council Decision 2002/192/EC, 28 February 2002).

As the European Union moved towards enlargement from 15 Member States to 25 in May 2004 and to 27 in January 2007, the new accession countries were expected to make applications to join the Schengen Convention and the *acquis* was re-published in a catalogue form for their consideration (Council of the European Union, 2002). Other non-EU countries had already joined, with Iceland and Norway being admitted in 2001 and Switzerland in 2004. If all the new countries now joined, some 30 states would potentially be accessing the SIS and negotiations started on upgrading it to a second-generation SIS II (EC Com (2005) 230 final). The contract was awarded to the Hewlett Packard company:

> SIS II will provide information on wanted persons as well as stolen vehicles, ID documents and banknotes through a database accessed by national police authorities of all participating member states. Once it is fully functional in 2007, SIS will be much more flexible than the current system and will also be able to store photographic images and fingerprints.
>
> (Hewlett Packard, 2005)

The work was also to include the development of the European Union's Visa Information System (VIS) (see below). Critics bemoaned the lack of transparency and accountability that seemingly attended all these developments (see, e.g. 'EU Schengen Information System II – *fait accompli?'*, *Statewatch*, 15 January 2005: 17–20).

The European Police Office (Europol)

Not long after the British joined the European Union (or European Community as it was then called) in 1974, they were instrumental in starting a forum to discuss police co-operation in Europe. The TREVI group was set up in 1976 in the wake of various terrorist activities, including 'sky-jackings' and the hostage taking of Israeli competitors at the Munich Olympic Games. Interpol had been reluctant to take on terrorism at this time and the need for an alternative initiative was recognised (Bresler, 1992: 161; Hebenton and Thomas, 1995: 75ff).

The TREVI was shrouded in mystery for many years and the official explanation was always that it fell – as an inter-governmental meeting – outside the 'competence' of the European Union. Even as an acronym there is uncertainty as to what it stands for. The UK police were advised of its existence and structure in a Home Office circular dated 2 September 1977 (Circular 153/77) but this circular has never been made public. When references to TREVI started to emerge in public, the very secrecy of the group prompted allegations of it being 'positively dangerous and undemocratic' (House of Commons, 1990c: 60) and one observer suggested 'the extent of public information about TREVI seems to be in inverse proportion to the importance attached to it by governments and police officers' (Cullen, 1992: 71).

A TREVI Programme of Action was published in the name of EC Interior Ministers following a meeting in Dublin in 1990. Chapter 2 of the programme considered the need for a common information system 'to collect data and descriptions of persons and objects for purposes within the scope of this document' (Programme of Action, 1990: para. 15.1). It was also revealed that the TREVI group had its own 'rapid and protected communications system' which had been agreed on in 1986 (ibid: para. 2.4).

The TREVI group emerged blinking into the political daylight following the signing of the Maastricht Treaty on Political Union in 1991, and the creation of the EU 'third pillar' on justice and home affairs. The K4 Committee – taking its name from the relevant article of the Maastricht Treaty – now took on the task of creating the European Police Office – or Europol. A temporary home was found for Europol in Strasbourg, but before long they had moved into permanent premises in The Hague in offices vacated for them by the Dutch police. The K4 Committee now had to write an acceptable Europol Convention, which was eventually signed in July 1995.

Europol essentially links all the police forces of the European Union together to tackle serious organised crime through its headquarters in The Hague in another 'hub and spokes' arrangement. As with the SIS, each country provides its own Europol National Unit (ENU) as single points of contact and in turn seconds officers to work in The Hague. Europol was charged with tackling 'terrorism, unlawful drug trafficking and other serious forms of international crime where there are factual indications that an organised criminal structure is involved' (EU Council, 1995: Article 2). As the 1990 Programme of Action had foretold, information exchange would be at the heart of its activities:

'Europol shall have the following principal tasks:

1. to facilitate the exchange of information between the Member States;
2. to obtain, collate and analyse information and intelligence;

3. to notify the competent authorities of the Member States without delay via the national units…of information concerning them and of any connections identified between criminal offences'.

(ibid: Article 3)

Europol formally came online on 1 July 1999.

The Europol mandate initially restricted Europol to dealing with serious and organised crime and thus differentiated it from Interpol, which will look at any crime – or volume crime – and not just the serious and organised. Suggestions have now been made that Europol should move towards dealing with volume crime.

Europol now provides analytical support to investigations within any of the 27 Member States by means of Analysis Work Files (AWFs). An AWF can be initiated by Europol or by a Member State as long as the following criteria are met and the subject matter is:

- a mandated crime area;
- affecting two or more Member States;
- involving organised crime; and
- is in line with Europol work programmes and priorities.

(Europol, 2006: para. 2.8)

The Europol Computer System (TECS) supports this work and the Europol Information System (EIS) came online in October 2005 to link Europol to all its Member States' national units; the EIS:

…gives Member States the ability to store and share basic types of criminal data such as 'offence', 'person', 'means of communication', 'means of transportation' etc.

(ibid: para. 3.1)

Some 180,920 operational messages passed through Europol and the Europol National Units in 2005 (ibid: 1).

Other Transnational Policing Networks

Interpol, the SIS and Europol are the three biggest Transnational Policing Networks, but they are not the only ones. In Europe there are arrangements for exchanging information of various kinds through the different mechanisms of the European Union: Eurodac, VIS, the Customs Information System (CIS) and various other bilateral and multi-lateral arrangements.

- Eurodac

In order to tighten up its external borders and to better police asylum seekers and possible illegal immigrants, the European Union has developed its Eurodac system. Eurodac was conceived as a necessary measure to facilitate implementation of the 1990 Dublin Convention which sought to regulate the applications for asylum lodged anywhere in Europe (FCO, 1991). The aim was to reduce the number of multiple-applications for asylum and to deter so-called 'asylum shopping' whereby applications might be lodged in different countries.

The Dublin Convention enabled Member States to communicate information between each other in order to help determine asylum requests (ibid: Article 15). Eurodac is primarily an identification system based on electronic fingerprints and does not hold criminal records. Its gestation was long and drawn out, having first been proposed by the Dutch in 1991 (Home Office, 1996d: para. 2) and coming online only in January 2003 from its central base in Brussels (Home Office, 2003g; see also Council of the European Union, 2000).

- Visa Information System

The idea of a system to double check visa applicants coming into the EU from outside has led to the development of the VIS. The concept was first mooted in 2002 and a formal decision to develop it, made in 2004 (Official Journal L213, 15 June 2004: 5–7). The aim was to ensure that applicants were identified correctly and fraudulent and multiple applications were rooted out. The private company Hewlett Packard, in consortium with Seria plc, was awarded the contract to provide the system (Hewlett Packard, 2005). The VIS will allow Member States of the EU to check the personal details of applicants regardless of which country they had applied to and these details would include digitised fingerprints and photographs. Approximately 20 million people apply for visas to enter the EU every year.

The campaigning journal *Statewatch* believes the VIS was somewhat railroaded through the EU political mechanisms and presented as a *fait accompli*. In particular the VIS was to be co-developed with the SIS II and effectively they would become an integrated database. The two systems would share a 'Common technical platform' and a 'centralised architecture' and:

> ...there will be a broad law enforcement access to VIS (including access for the security and intelligence services), providing, in

conjunction with SIS II an EU-wide fingerprint database of wanted persons, suspects and *all* visa entrants.

('EU: Schengen Information System II – *fait accompli?*',
Statewatch, January 2005–February 2005, 15(1): 17–20;
emphasis in original)

The Visa Information System will consist of a centralised database (Central VIS or CS-VIS) and a National Interface (NI-VIS) within each Member State.

- Customs Information System

The Customs Information System (CIS) is another European Union wide database that evolved from the earlier Systems Custom Enforcement Network (SCENT). The CIS central database is in Brussels with terminals available in each of the EU Member States. The system holds details of known and suspected offenders and is governed by its own convention (Official Journal C316, 27.11.1995).

- The Prüm Convention

Seven Member States of the European Union moved towards their own form of international police co-operation through the signing of the Prüm Convention in May 2005. The seven countries were Austria, Belgium, France, Germany, Luxembourg, Spain and the Netherlands and the town of Prüm in Germany, where the agreement was made, gave the convention its name. The aim was to provide an even closer European transnational policing network than anything yet provided by Europol or the Schengen arrangements. Italy declared their intention to join this inter-governmental group in July 2006.

The model of police co-operation envisaged put information exchange at the centre of activities. DNA and fingerprint repositories were to be the main form of identifying and 'matching' individuals, and this would be followed up with the exchange of any other relevant data. The convention spoke of better cross-border co-operation and 'particularly mutual exchange of information' (Article 1(1)) between 'national contact points' (Article 6(1)). Information could be exchanged on request from another country, including 'supplying data from police databases and police records' (Article 27(2)(8)) (Council of the European Union, 2005).

The Madrid bombing of March 2004 and the growing fear of terrorism prompted this move toward the Prüm Convention. Other features of the convention included possible joint operations and the deployment of air marshalls in airliners.

At the time of writing (March 2007) it is unclear whether the Prüm Convention represents the start of something that will become EU-wide or is the start of the fragmentation of EU initiatives. At present there are only seven signatories out of 27 EU Member States. On the other hand the Schengen Convention started out in similar fashion to become EU-wide and for some the Prüm Convention has already been nicknamed 'Schengen III'. The UK Government has said it would 'carefully consider any formal proposals... to transpose the (Prüm) Convention into EU law' (Hansard HL Debates, 29 January 2007, col. 5WA).

Exchanging criminal records in Europe

Whilst conventions and 'transnational policing networks' facilitate the international exchange of police-held information in a general sense, initiatives have now begun in Europe to specifically effect the transfer of criminal records and to ensure that receiving Member States are able to take them into account.

As organised crime had been a motivation for improving international police co-operation in the 1990s, so terrorism would take up the cause after the turn of the century. The terrorist attacks in New York (September 2001), Madrid (March 2004) and London (July 2005) brought countries together in mutual support against this new threat, and gave impetus to information exchange as an important factor in the new policing arrangements. Criminal records were also now recognised as a critical form of information.

On a micro-scale the exchange of information in the form of criminal records was promoted as a child-protection measure and not least after the case of Michel Fourniret came to light. Fourniret was a Frenchman with convictions for offences against children. He was freed from prison in 1987 and in 1992 moved to Belgium and was employed as a caretaker in a village school. The Belgian authorities knew nothing of his background until the 62-year-old was re-arrested in 2003 for new offences.

In October 2004 the European Commission proposed ways in which criminal record information could be more quickly transmitted between the Member States of the European Union (European Commission, 2004). It also recognised that speed of transmission in itself was not going to be sufficient. Countries had first to know exactly which other country held records, before they knew who to request them from, and once in receipt of them, need to understand them and interpret them meaningfully. The commission now produced a more expansive

White Paper on the subject of criminal records and their international exchange (European Commission, 2005a).

What was now proposed was a central European index of names that all Member States would feed into. The central index would not hold the actual records, but would just indicate whether a given individual had a record and where it might be found. The country wanting the record could then request it on a bilateral basis from the country holding it. Each participating Member State would need to create its own Criminal Records European Unit (CREU) as a national central authority, to feed records into the index and request disclosures from other CREUs. After a year of discussion the commission was able to propose a Council Framework Decision on the legislative device for bringing about the new arrangements (European Commission, 2005b).

Before the decision was made on who would organise the central authority in the United Kingdom,the Home Office had already opined that they wanted 'to explore whether this framework can also support the exchange of intelligence and other information which falls short of conviction data' (Home Office, 2006c: para. 4.39).

Once the Council Framework Decision (reference Com (2005) 690 final 2005/0267) had been confirmed in November 2005, EU Member States set about appointing their national central authorities to facilitate this criminal record exchange. In the United Kingdom three organisations bid for the contract to be the central authority – the CRB, SCRO and ACPO. The Home Office awarded the contract to the ACPO and the UK central authority for European criminal record exchange became known as ACRO (ACPO Criminal Record Office). Work started in May 2006 within the Hampshire Constabulary near Winchester with just three staff; Hampshire already acted as host to the ACPO DNA and Fingerprint Retention Project (see Chapter 3) (Hansard HC Debates, 15 May 2006, col. 664W; ACPO, 2007; CRB, 2007b; Council of the European Union, 2007).

One of the first things ACRO found was the backlog of 'Article 22 notifications' that had come in to the Home Office from 1996 onwards containing details of UK nationals who had offended in Europe. These 'notifications' had come in under the umbrella of the Council of Europe 1959 Convention on Mutual Assistance in Criminal Matters (see above). None of them had been put on the PNC.

The existence of these 'notification' files only came to light in January 2007 when the House of Commons Home Affairs Committee was making its own general inquiry into 'Justice and Home Affairs Issues at European Union Level'. The revelation created a political row for Home

Secretary John Reid – already reeling from a number of high-profile criticisms of the Home Office – and a media firestorm. The possibility was raised that some of these 27,500 people could have come back to the United Kingdom and, for example, slipped through CRB vetting to get jobs with children and putting those children at immediate risk. Reid weathered the storm with ministerial statements, the announcement of an enquiry and more funding for the ACRO to employ more staff (Morris, 2007a,b; Hansard HC Debates, 10 January 2007, cols. 285–299 and 16 January 2007, cols. 31–32WS).

The resulting inquiry report shed light on the confused accountability and what lessons could be learnt, and whether or not ministers should have been alerted. Whilst the 'notifications' had been stockpiled on the basis that they were not significant in terms of immediate operational policing concerns, officials were criticised for not picking up on the 'public protection' possibilities that arose and the need for records to be on the PNC and therefore available to the CRB (see Amroliwala, 2007: passim). At the same time an Overseas Crimes Task Force was established in the Home Office to assist ACRO in clearing the backlog, ensure any public protection issues were dealt with and liaise with European colleagues to ensure the data quality of what was being received (ibid: para. 3.28). Nothing was said – at least in public – about the quality or quantity of the information that the United Kingdom itself would be sending to other European countries.

Conclusions

International co-operation between police forces has achieved greater prominence as improved communications and air travel have made the world metaphorically smaller. Individual countries with their own forms of policing – and criminal record collection – have looked at ways of assisting each other and this assistance has mostly been about how to share information for the benefit of all parties.

Police information exchange means the exchange of information above and beyond that of just criminal records, but criminal records, nonetheless, have usually been part of the package. Various formal arrangements have come into being to facilitate the smooth flow of information through such channels as 'transnational policing networks' that include organisations like Europol and the Schengen Information System, and improvements made to old existing channels such as Interpol.

In 2005 the European Union proposed specific arrangements for the transfer of criminal records between the Member States of the EU and for the better recognition of these criminal records by the Member States and their judicial arrangements. The United Kingdom's newly formed ACRO came into being in 2006 to facilitate these arrangements.

A continuing thorn in the side of all these developments in the exchange of criminal records across frontiers has been the vexed question of data protection. Hayes has identified three main problems which inhibit data protection in the police sector:

- the absence of binding international standards;
- the processing of personal data from different sources on an unprecedented scale;
- the unregulated exchange of police data around the world.

(Hayes, 2005)

One attempt to introduce an EU-wide draft resolution on data protection in the police sector was abandoned in 2001, and in 2004 some provisions of the Hague Programme seemed to throw the doors open even wider. The Hague Programme was a schedule of improved police co-operation following the terrorist attacks in Madrid. In and amongst was the so-called 'principle of availability' that suggested police-held information of any kind should be passed to other police forces if it existed as a matter of course. A second attempt at a Council Framework Decision on data protection was adopted by the commission on 4 October 2005 (Com (2005) 475) and a similar adoption made of a decision on the 'principle of availability' made on the same day (Com (2005) 490).

9
Conclusions

Nelson Mandela visited Leeds in April 2001 and was made a Freeman of the city. In his acceptance speech he said he did not deserve it as he was 'a foreigner, an old age pensioner and someone who had a criminal record'. The good burghers of Leeds enjoyed the joke. For many people, however, the existence of a criminal record hanging round their neck is anything but a joke.

The criminal record has developed considerably since its humble beginnings in the Victorian annual publication of an Alphabetical Register of Habitual Criminals. The capacity today to move criminal record information around the country – and around the world – in 'real-time' has contributed to the significance of the criminal record. Those in receipt of criminal records have increased in numbers and the ability to 'live down' your past and let it be 'forgotten' has decreased. The criminal record database has developed from being used only by the criminal justice system and its agencies to one that is now used way beyond the confines of that system. What does it all mean for such concepts as privacy?

Privacy and information privacy

Privacy and the 'private sphere' of life has often been put forward as something to be valued by citizens of any democratic country. Civil society exists separate from any governmental intrusions and in turn the entitlement to be 'left alone' grows into the right to privacy. Privacy of the home, privacy of the family and privacy of your own personal history. The idea is that we actively consent to the opening up of these private areas which we otherwise regard as privileged and deserving of safeguard (Westin, 1967). The Orwellian dystopia of an all-knowing State otherwise hangs over us and Big Brother is watching us.

At one point in twentieth-century history these dystopias were assigned to non-democratic states such as Germany in the 1930s or the Stalinist era of the Union of Soviet Socialist Republics (USSR). Lenin reportedly said of the USSR, 'we recognise nothing private. Our mortality is entirely subordinate to the interests of the class struggle of the proletariat', and the German Nazis declared 'the only person who is still a private individual in Germany is somebody who is asleep' (Lyon, 1994: 185–186; see also Kempner, 1946 for an intriguing account of German databases in the 1930s and their use to 'triangulate' the position of citizens).

The post-war United Nations' Declaration of Human Rights included the right that 'no one shall be subjected to arbitrary interference with his privacy, family, home or correspondence' (UN, 1948: Article 12) and the Council of Europe re-iterated the right 2 years later with its requirement that 'everyone has the right to respect for his private and family life, his home and his correspondence' (Council of Europe, 1950: Article 8). The trouble was that exact definitions of privacy were hard to come by and there were always qualifying conditions that privacy could, for example, always be intruded upon in the interests of crime prevention or detection.

Information privacy was a somewhat more exact matter. Unlike the general idea of privacy, information privacy was more tangible and more easily reduced to particular items of information, data, records or other written forms that related to identifiable individuals. With the arrival of information technology in the 1970s and onwards, the need to give citizens forms of 'data protection' to ensure their information privacy came into being (Wacks, 1989).

In the early days of criminal records collation it was relatively easy to maintain them as confidential repositories open only to the police and courts as and when they needed them. The narrative of this book would suggest that information technology has improved the collection and dissemination of criminal records and their associated means of identifying individuals in a way that makes them instantly available to more and more recipients. The CRB has made 8,990,597 disclosures of criminal records between March 2002 and May 2006 (see Chapter 7). 'Data protection' measures and rehabilitation of offenders laws have been seemingly powerless to prevent this happening because this is all done in the name of safeguarding children and other vulnerable adults and preventing crime. Developments are in hand to make these same records available across international frontiers to other parts of Europe.

Pre-employment screening using criminal records

In Chapters 7 and 8 we noted the growing use of criminal records to vet applicants for work, and the creation of the CRB to facilitate this pre-employment screening. We looked at some of the criticisms of these arrangements, including job refusals seemingly unrelated to the criminal conviction record, employers not following the CRB Code of Practice and problems such as inaccurate records. We considered the variation between employers' selection decisions and the criminal record in front of them and the employer who refuses to appoint simply because he dislikes the sort of offence committed rather than on any relevance to the post in question (see Chapter 5). The whole business of employer decision making based on disclosed criminal records was noted as one of 'low-visibility' and with a lack of redress for the aggrieved applicant.

While some people are correctly refused employment based on an assessment of their criminal record there is the uncomfortable feeling that having a criminal record that blocks you from employment and an income has the potential to become a greater punishment than the original punishment meted out by the court. We might even be creating a form of second-class citizen unable to come back from a period of punishment to lead a normal life. Punishments are normally time-limited but having a criminal record may be a much longer burden to bear.

McWilliams and Pease have put the probation service at the heart of the rehabilitation of offenders. They are clear that rehabilitation is not necessarily the same as reform, but is about restoring and 'regrading' a person back into society who has been 'de-graded' for the duration of his or her punishment.

> ...the attempt to help the offender return to and remain as a full member of society, with the status and obligations which that membership confers, is rehabilitation. If offenders are not rehabilitated in this sense when formal punishment ends, then de facto punishment persists. Rehabilitation serves as a means to limit punishment to the extent pronounced.
>
> (McWilliams and Pease, 1990)

As it is desirable for offenders to see a clear-cut end to their punishment, so too it is desirable for society to give offenders the opportunity to lead normal lives after that punishment. The Court of Appeal has pronounced that 'it is in the public interest that persons should renounce a life of crime and that they should take up honest work and live a proper life' (Meyers [1996] 1 Cr. App. R (S.) at p. 251) and the law empowering courts to pass community sentences involving some kind of community service have always had caveats that such service should, where possible, avoid any times at which the offender might normally be working (e.g. Powers of Criminal Courts (Sentencing) Act 2000, s. 47(2)(b)).

In that context the way in which employers use criminal records and make their vetting decisions is deserving of more attention. Borrowing from the work of von Hirsch and Wasik (1997), who have written about the similar problem of convictions leading to civil disqualifications, the following conceptual framework is offered:

1. Vetting decisions should be premised on how to reduce risk in the workplace. The information contained in the criminal record then becomes just one factor in the risk assessment that is made. The criminal record does not 'speak for itself' but has to be related to the risk posed.
2. Risk-based decisions should focus on the individual and not switch to the interests of the organisation, that is, risk-avoidance posturing which is more about organisation protection than any protection being accorded those who might come into contact with this worker.
3. The special vulnerability of the occupation or activity should be a deciding factor. Workers with children are clearly working with a vulnerable group but some have greater access to children than others.
4. The conviction should be relevant to the risk, again making the risk-assessment central to the decision making.

With these four perspectives in mind, employer decision making should become a fairer process and could be completed within a proper procedural framework rather than in the current low-visibility fashion that these decisions are made. A system to enable decisions to be reviewed would also ensure a degree of transparency where the decisions – in a recordable manner – could be subjected to scrutiny to ensure they are proportionate and relevant to their purpose.

Without such transparency and safeguards we run the risk of creating a second-class citizenship of those with criminal records. A status with the potential to stay with a person for longer than the attendant punishment that brought the record into being.

Surveillance studies

The United Kingdom's criminal record database and its use by law enforcement agencies, and by employers for pre-employment screening, allows the database to be located within the emerging studies of 'surveillance'. Surveillance has been defined as:

> ...any collection and processing of personal data, whether identifiable or not, for the purpose of influencing or managing those whose data have been garnered.
>
> (Lyon, 2001: 2)

A database by itself is not surveillance but it is a supporting mechanism of surveillance – the term 'dataveillance' has been coined. Although we may talk of surveillance as an 'emerging study' it does, of course, have a longer history than at first might appear.

The classic architecture of surveillance was first posited by the philosopher Jeremy Bentham in 1778 in the form of prison design – the panopticon – where the prison officers kept watch over the prisoners. This very concrete application of surveillance took place between the clearly identified observer and the observed, who were contained in one place. In the 1940s George Orwell saw the potential of surveillance technologies based on the panopticon to contain and discipline whole societies in his novel *Nineteen Eighty-Four*. Orwell (1949) and Foucault (1977) identified numerous social institutions working on the principle that populations could be ordered through surveillance.

> The types of surveillance accentuated in the panopticon model typically involve the monitoring of people who reside at a lower point in the social hierarchy...where specific marginalised or dangerous groups are situated under the unidirectional gaze of the powerful who can watch while remaining unseen by their charges.
>
> (Haggerty, 2006)

Today such direct links between observer and observed are more diffuse, and not least because of the rise of what some have called the 'electronic panopticon' (Gordon, 1986). The vertical relationship is further replaced by a more horizontal one. The thousands of employers, for example, now in receipt of criminal records have all the privileges of surveillance over their prospective employees, allowing them to categorise and sort the applicants – on paper – into the employable and non-employable.

The police now move into a position of collating and disseminating information for all sectors of society and no longer just for their own purposes or judicial purposes. The police become generators of information for others to use in risk-assessment exercises in a range of employment and other licensing fields (Ericson and Haggerty, 1997). How these risk assessments are made may vary from agency to agency, depending on who exactly has access to the information held on the database.

In the interests of crime detection and crime prevention the criminal record database aims to make the invisible (offender or potential offender) visible. The additional problem here is that electronic databases only bring up information that is a proxy for a person's actual identity: information that is partial or possibly inaccurate, and information that is out of date and no longer applicable because it makes no allowance for change. Theorists of surveillance talk now of 'data doubles' for this proxy information: information about a given person but not necessarily recognisable as that person. At its worst it mounts an assault on the very sense of 'self':

> ...the data double is more real than the person behind it...the notion of individual biographical truth...is further marginalised by pragmatic institutional choices, where both actuarial calculations and data-matching procedures constantly produce real consequences for individuals represented by their ersatz doubles. The very nature of the data double phenomenon indicates that it both functions as truth and, given its Multiplicity, Versatility and Arbitrary Constitution, also negates the possibility of truth.
>
> (Los, 2006)

In an attempt to tie up data and give it more integrity with an identifiable person there is increasing resource to bodily identifiers such as electronic fingerprints, DNA samples and other biometric sources such as the patterns in the iris of the eye.

Bibliography

ACPO (Association of Chief Police Officers) (1987) Codes of Practice for Police Computer Systems, London.

ACPO (Association of Chief Police Officers) (1995) Code of Practice for Data Protection, London.

ACPO (Association of Chief Police Officers) (1997) Sex Offenders Act 1997, Implementation Guidelines, August. ACPO Crime Committee, London.

ACPO (Association of Chief Police Officers) (2002) Code of Practice for Data Protection, London.

ACPO (Association of Chief Police Officers) (2003) Information Systems Community Security Policy, London.

ACPO (Association of Chief Police Officers) (2006a) Guidance on the Management of Police Information, National Centre for Policing Excellence, Wyboston.

ACPO (Association of Chief Police Officers) (2006b) Retention Guidelines for Nominal Records on the Police National Computer, National Centre for Policy Excellence, Wyboston.

ACPO (Association of Chief Police Officers) (2006c) Data Protection: manual of guidance, October, London.

ACPO (Association of Chief Police Officers) (2007) ACPO Statement on Criminal Convictions abroad (Press Release) 10 January.

Adam, H. L. (1931) CID: behind the scenes at Scotland yard, Sampson Low, Muston and Co. Ltd., London.

Amroliwala, D. (2007) Report of the inquiry into the handling by Home Office officials of notifications, by other European countries, of criminal convictions for UK citizens, February, Home Office, London.

Anderson, M. (1989) Policing the World: Interpol and the politics of international police co-operation, Clarendon Press, Oxford.

Anderson, M. and den Boer, M. (eds.) (1992) European Police Co-operation: proceedings of a seminar, University of Edinburgh, Department of Politics.

Anderson, M. and den Boer, M. (eds.) (1994) Policing Across National Boundaries, Pinter, London.

Apex Trust (1989) Making Rehabilitation Work, London.

Apex Trust (1990) Realising the Potential: the recruitment of people with a criminal record, London.

Audit Commission (1988) Improving the Performance of the Fingerprint Service: police papers no. 2, HMSO, London.

Audit Commission (1993) Helping with Enquiries: tackling crime effectively, HMSO, London.

Audit Commission (2002) Route to Justice: improving the pathway of offenders through the criminal justice system, June, London.

Auld Report (2001) Review of the Criminal Courts of England and Wales: report, October, TSO, London.

Bailey, V. (ed.) (1981) Policing and Punishment in Nineteenth Century Britain, Croom Helm, London.

Baker, K. (2005) Assessment in Youth Justice: professional discretion and the use of ASSET, *Youth Justice,* 5: 123–130.

Baldwin-Edwards, M. and Hebenton, B. (1994) Will SIS be Europe's 'Big Brother'? in Anderson, M. and den Boer, M. (eds.).

Barr, R. (1962) The Scotland Yard Story, Hodder and Stoughton, London.

Bartrip, P. W. J. (1981) Public Opinion and Law Enforcement: the ticket of leave scares in mid-Victorian Britain, in Bailey, V. (ed.).

Bell, A. (2000) A check too far? *Solicitors Journal,* 24 March.

Bennetto, J. (1995) DNA database under fire after samples mix-up, *Independent on Sunday,* 22 October.

Bennetto, J. (1996a) Clampdown on illegal use of police computer, *The Independent,* 20 September.

Bennetto, J. (1996b) Report linking crime and jobs was 'censored', *The Independent,* 28 December.

Bentley, R. (2003) Sad inevitability of criminal records failure, *Computer Weekly,* 6 March.

Benyon, J., Turnbull, L., Willis, A., Woodward, R. and Beck, A. (1993) Police Co-operation in Europe: an investigation, Centre for the Study of Public Order, University of Leicester.

Berrett, J. (1932) When I was at Scotland Yard, Sampson Low, Marston and Co. Ltd.

Bichard Report (2004) A public inquiry report on child protection procedures in Humberside police and Cambridgeshire constabulary, particularly the effectiveness of relevant intelligence-based record keeping, vetting practices since 1995 and information sharing with other agencies, HC 653, The Stationery Office, London.

BJS (Bureau of Justice Statistics) (2003) Survey of State Criminal History Information Systems 2001, US Department of Justice, Washington DC.

BJS (Bureau of Justice Statistics) (2005) Improving Access to and Integrity of Criminal History Records, Department of Justice, Washington, DC.

Blair, T. (2002) Rebalancing of Criminal Justice (Speech) 18 June.

Boseley, S. (1984) List of errors that ended in child's death, *The Guardian,* 18 December.

Breed, B. (1987) Off the Record, John Clare Books, London.

Bresler, F. (1992) Interpol, Sinclair Stevenson, London.

Brindle, D. (1989) Jobs with young shut to offenders, *The Guardian,* 30 August.

Broadbent, G. and Vincenzi, C. (1990) World Cup 1990: law and order v. civil liberties and EEC rights, *Solicitors Journal,* 22 June: 698–702.

Bunyan, T. (1977) The History and Practice of the Political Police in Britain, Quartet Books, London.

Burney, E. (2005) Making People Behave: anti-social behaviour, politics and policy, Willan Publishing, Cullompton.

Butt, R. (2005) The trials of living with the 'feral youths' of Salford, *The Guardian,* 21 May.

Cabinet Office (1999) Modernising Government, Cm. 4310, The Stationery Office.

Campbell, D. (1980) Society Under Surveillance, in Hain, P. (ed.)

Campbell, D. (1998) Police urge talks on DNA database for whole nation, *The Guardian,* 6 May.

Campbell, D. and Connor, S. (1986) On the Record: surveillance, computers and privacy, Michael Joseph, London.

Cannings, D. (1990) Policing in Europe Towards 1992, Devon and Cornwall Constabulary.

Caplan, J. and Torpey, J. (eds.) (2001) Documenting Individual Identity: the development of state practices in the modern world, Princeton University Press, Princeton and Oxford.

Chief Secretary to the Treasury (2003) Every Child Matters, Cm. 5860, The Stationery Office, London.

CICA (Criminal Injuries Compensation Authority) (2001) The Criminal Injuries Compensation Scheme, 2001, London.

CICA (Criminal Injuries Compensation Authority) (2004) Guide to the 2001 Compensation Scheme, London.

Cohen, N. (1992) 'Extraordinary' crime records deal attacked, *The Independent*, 30 June.

Cohen, N. (2002) Capita punishment, *The Observer*, 8 September.

Cole, S. A. (2001) Suspect Identities: a history of fingerprinting and criminal identification, Harvard University Press, Cambridge MA.

Collins, T. (2003) NHS Courts £5bn IT disaster by following the LIBRA route, *Computer Weekly*, 7 February.

Collins, T. (2005) What national police IT fiasco has to teach us for the NHS modernisation programme, *Computer Weekly*, 5 July.

Commissioner of Police for the Metropolis (1903) Annual report for 1902, Cd. 1814, HMSO, London.

Commissioner of Police for the Metropolis (1925) Annual report for the year 1924, Cmd. 2480, HMSO, London.

Connor, S. (2001) Privacy fears put police off giving samples of DNA, *The Independent*, 7 May.

Council of Europe (1950) European Convention on Human Rights, Strasbourg.

Council of Europe (1959) Convention on Mutual Assistance in Criminal Matters (ETS 30), Strasbourg.

Council of Europe (1981) Convention for the Protection of Individuals with regard to Automatic Processing of Personal Data, Strasbourg Convention no. 108, Strasbourg.

Council of Europe (1984) The Criminal Record and Rehabilitation of Convicted Persons, Strasbourg.

Council of Europe (1988) Regulating the Use of Personal Data in the Police Sector (Recommendation No. (87) 15), Strasbourg.

Council of the European Union (2000) Council Regulation (EC) No. 2725/2000 of 11th December 2000 Concerning the Establishment of 'Eurodac' for the Comparison of Fingerprints for the Effective Application of the Dublin Convention (OJ L316, 15/12/2000 p. 1).

Council of the European Union (2002) EU Schengen Catalogue, Volumes 1 and 2, December, Brussels.

Council of the European Union (2005) Treaty between the Kingdom of Belgium, the Federal Republic of Germany, the Kingdom of Spain, the Republic of France, the Grand Duchy of Luxembourg, the Kingdom of the Netherlands and the Republic of Austria (The Prüm Convention), Brussels.

Council of the European Union (2006) Draft Council Resolution Concerning an Updated Handbook with Recommendations for International Police

Cooperation and Measures to Prevent and Control Violence and Disturbances in Connection with Football Matches with an International Dimension, in which at least one Member State is involved, Brussels 13 11 9/06 Limite Enfopol 159.

Council of the European Union (2007) Council Decision on the Exchange of Information Extracted from Criminal Records – Manual of Procedure, 6397/5/06 REV 5.

CPSI (Crown Prosecution Service Inspectorate) H. M. Inspectorate of Constabulary, H. M. Magistrates Courts Services Inspectorate, H. M. Inspectorate of Prisons, H. M. Inspectorate of Probation, Social Services Inspectorate (2000) Casework Information Needs within the Criminal Justice System (Volumes 1 and 2), Magistrates Courts Service Inspectorate, London.

CRB (Criminal Records Bureau) (2001) Code of Practice for Registered Persons and Other Recipients of Disclosure Information, Liverpool.

CRB (Criminal Records Bureau) (2004) Strategic Plan 2004/2005–2006/2007, Liverpool.

CRB (Criminal Records Bureau) (2005a) Regulations under Part V of the Police Act 1997: a consultation paper, July, Liverpool.

CRB (Criminal Records Bureau) (2005b) Regulations under Part V of the Police Act 1997: analysis of responses to the consultation document, November, Liverpool.

CRB (Criminal Records Bureau) (2005c) Customer Confidence in Criminal Records Bureau's vetting service at an all time high (Press Release) 15 July.

CRB (Criminal Records Bureau) (2006a) Five-Year Strategy and Business Plan 2006/07, Liverpool.

CRB (Criminal Records Bureau) (2006b) Fee Levels for 2006/2007 (Press Release) 22 December, Liverpool.

CRB (Criminal Records Bureau) (2007a) Fee Freeze as CRB Achieves Self-funding Status (Press Release) 5 February, Liverpool.

CRB (Criminal Records Bureau) (2007b) Overseas Convictions (Press Release) 10 January.

Critchley, T. A. (1978) A History of Police in England and Wales (2nd ed.) Constable, London.

Cullen, P. J. (1992) The German Police and European Co-operation, Department of Politics, University of Edinburgh, Edinburgh.

Curtis, P. (2002) Teacher checking system fails to impress, *The Guardian*, 22 May.

DCA (Department for Constitutional Affairs) (2006a) Increasing Penalties for Deliberate and Wilful Misuse of Personal Data – Consultation Paper, July, London.

DCA (Department of Constitutional Affairs) (2006b) Swifter Justice as Crown Courts enter Electronic Age (Press Release) 6 April.

Department of Transport (1992) Disclosure of Criminal Records: applicants for Hackney Carriage and Private Hire Vehicle Driver's Licences (Circular no. 2/1992).

Devlin, D. (1966) Police Procedure, Administration and Organisation, Butterworths, London.

DfES (Department for Education and Skills) (2006a) Review of the List 99 decision making process and policy implications, London.

DfES (Department for Education and Skills) (2006b) Safeguarding Children and Safer Recruitment in Education, London.

DfES (Department for Education and Skills), Home Office and Department for Work and Pensions (2005) Reducing Re-Offending through Skills and Employment, London.

DoH (Department of Health) (1991) Disclosure of Criminal Background: proprietors and managers of residential care homes and nursing homes (Circular no. LAC 4/1991).

DoH (Department of Health) (1995) Child Protection: messages from research, HMSO, London.

DoH (Department of Health) (2000) The Protection of Children Act 1999: a practical guide to the act for all organisations working with children, NHS Executive, London.

DoH (Department of Health) (2004) Protection of Vulnerable Adults Scheme – a Practical Guide, London.

DoH (Department of Health), Home Office, Department for Education and Employment (1999) Working Together to Safeguard Children: a guide to inter-agency working to safeguard and promote the welfare of children, The Stationery Office, London.

DPR (Data Protection Registrar) (1989) The Use of the Subject Access Provisions of the Data Protection Act to check the Criminal Records of Applicants for Jobs or Licences, Guidance Note 21, Wilmslow.

Draper, H. (1978) Private Police, The Harvester Press, Sussex.

Dyer, C. (2003) 'It's a fair thing to do', *The Guardian,* 18 March.

EC Directive (1995) The Protection of Individuals with Regard to the Processing of Personal Data and on the Free Movement of Such Data (Directive 95/46/EC).

Emsley, C. (1991) The English Police: a political and social history, Harvester Wheatsheaf, Hemel Hempstead.

Emsley, C. (1996) Crime and Society in England 1750–1900 (2nd ed.) Longman, London.

Ericson, R. V. and Haggerty, K. D. (1997) Policing the Risk Society, Clarendon Press, Oxford.

EU Council (1995) Convention based on Article K3 of the Treaty on European Union, on the establishment of a European Police Office. SN 3549/95 Limite, Brussels.

European Commission (2004) Proposal for a Council Decision on the exchange of information extracted from the criminal record (Com (2004) 664 final), Brussels.

European Commission (2005a) White Paper on exchanges of information on convictions and the effect of such convictions in the European Union (Com (2005) 10 final), Brussels.

European Commission (2005b) Proposal for a Council Framework Decision on the organisation and content of the exchange of information extracted from criminal records between Member States (Com (2005) 690 final), Brussels.

Europol (2006) Europol annual report, 2005 March, The Hague.

Evans, C. (2005) Charting crime, *Police Review,* 14 October.

Farrall, S. and Calverley, A. (2006) Understanding Desistance from Crime, Open University Press, Maidenhead.

FBI (Federal Bureau of Investigation) (1999) NCIC 2000 (Press Release) 15 July, US Department of Justice, Washington DC.

FBI (Federal Bureau of Investigation) (2006) Crime Index Sets Record (Press Release) 15 February, US Department of Justice, Washington DC.

FCO (Foreign and Commonwealth Office) (1991) Convention determining the State responsible for examining Applications for Asylum lodged in one of the Member States of the European Communities, Cm1623, HMSO, London.

Firmin, S. (1949) Scotland Yard: the inside story, Hutchinson and Co., London.

Flaherty, D. (1989) Protecting Privacy, in Surveillance Societies, University of North Carolina Press, Chapel Hill, NC.

Fletcher, D. R., Taylor, A., Hughes, S. and Breeze, J. (2001) Recruiting and Employing Offenders, Joseph Rowntree Foundation/York Publishing Services.

Fosdick, R. B. (1915) European Police Systems, The Century Company, New York.

Foucault, M. (1977) Discipline and Punish, Allen Lane, London.

Gallagher, F. (1992) Kent County Constabulary – its European perspective, in Anderson, M. and den Boer, M. (eds.).

Garda Siochana (2004) Working Group on Garda Vetting: report, February, Dublin.

Gardiner Report (1972) Living it Down: the problem of old convictions, Justice, NACRO and the Howard League, London.

Goldman, H. (1986) Co-ordination of Computerisation in the Criminal Justice System, Home Office, London.

Goldman, L. (1986) The Social Science Association 1857–1886: a context for mid-victorian liberalism, *English Historical Review*, C1: 95–134.

Good Friday Agreement (1998) The Agreement Reached in the Multi-party Negotiations (10 April 1998), Belfast.

Gordon, D. R. (1986) The Electronic Panopticon: a case study of the development of the national criminal records system, *Politics and Society*, 15.

Gordon, D. R. (1990) The Justice Juggernaut: fighting street crime, controlling citizens, Rutgers University Press, New Jersey.

Graham, V. (1995) Phoenix rises, *Police Review*, 2 June.

Grundy, S. (1990) Fast and friendly, *Police Review*, 17 August: 1626–1627.

H. M. Government (2006) Working Together to Safeguard Children: a guide to inter-agency working to safeguard and promote the welfare of children, TSO, London.

H. M. Inspectorate of Constabulary (1933) Police (Counties and boroughs England and Wales) Reports of H. M. inspectors of constabulary for the year ended 29th September 1932, 46, HMSO, London.

H. M. Prison Service (1994) Release of Prisoners Convicted of Offences Against Children or Young Persons under the age of 18, Guidance Note to: instruction to governors 54/1944.

H. M. Treasury (2002) Improving the Delivery of Justice (Press Release) 15 July.

Haggerty, K. D. (2006) Tear Down the Walls: on demolishing the panopticon, in Lyon, D. (ed.).

Hain, P. (ed.) (1980) Policing the Police, Volume 2, John Calder, London.

Halliday Report (2001) Making Punishments Work: report of a review of the sentencing framework for England and Wales, July, Home Office, London.

Haskins Report (1999) Review of Fit Person Criteria: a review of the criteria used to judge people's suitability for certain occupations, Better Regulation Task Force, Cabinet Office, May, London.

Hayes, B. (2005) A Failure to Regulate: data protection in the police sector in Europe in *Open Society*.

Hayes, D. (2003) Change the record, *Community Care*, 3–9 July.

Hayward, D. and Cusick, J. (1995) National plan for fingerprints is abandoned, *The Independent,* 29 March.

Hebenton, B. and Thomas, T. (1992) Police Attendance at Child Protection Conferences: a reappraisal, *Children and Society,* 6(4): 364–376.

Hebenton, B. and Thomas, T. (1994) The Closed World of Warner: a comment on 'choosing with care', *Practice,* 7(1): 55–62.

Hebenton, B. and Thomas, T. (1995) Policing Europe: co-operation, conflict and control, Macmillans, Basingstoke.

Hebenton, B. and Thomas, T. (1998) Transnational policing networks, *International Journal of Risk, Security and Crime Prevention,* 3(2): 99–110.

Hennessey, P. and Brownfield, G. (1982) Britain's Cold War Security Purge: the origins of positive vetting, *The Historical Journal,* 25: 965–973.

Henry, E. (1900) Classification and Uses of Fingerprints, HMSO, London.

Hewitt, D. (2004) An added duty of risk assessment, *New Law Journal,* 23 January.

Hewlett Packard (2005) HP Wins $48.5 Million Contract with European Commission (Press Release) 28 April.

HFEA (Human Fertilisation and Embryology Authority) (1991a) Code of Practice: explanation, London.

HFEA (Human Fertilisation and Embryology Authority) (1991b) Code of Practice, London.

Higgs, E. (2004) The Information State in England: the central collection of information on citizens since 1580, Palgrave Macmillan, Basingstoke.

Hillier, J. (1995) Crime-solving increase as computer is ignored, *Oxford Times,* 25 August.

HMIC (H. M. Inspectorate of Constabulary) (1905) Annual report for Scotland for year ending 31th December 1904, Cd. 2463, HMSO, London.

HMIC (H. M. Inspectorate of Constabulary) (1914) Report on the county and borough police forces year ending 29th September 1913, HC 193, HMSO, London.

HMIC (H. M. Inspectorate of Constabulary) (1932) Police Counties and Boroughs, England and Wales: report of H. M. inspector of constabulary for the year ended 29th September 1931, 36, HMSO, London.

HMIC (H. M. Inspectorate of Constabulary) (1933) Police Counties and Boroughs, England and Wales: reports of H. M. inspectorate of constabulary for the year ended 29th September 1932, 46, HMSO, London.

HMIC (H. M. Inspectorate of Constabulary) (1957) Police Counties and Boroughs, England and Wales: report of H. M. inspectors of constabulary for the year ended 30th September 1956, 210, HMSO, London.

HMIC (H. M. Inspectorate of Constabulary) (1959) Police Counties and Boroughs, England and Wales: report of H. M. inspectors of constabulary for the year ended 30th September 1958, 202, HMSO, London.

HMIC (H. M. Inspectorate of Constabulary) (1960) Police Counties and Boroughs, England and Wales: report of H. M. inspectors of constabulary for the period from 1st October 1958 to 31st December 1959, 257, HMSO, London.

HMIC (H. M. Inspectorate of Constabulary) (1964) Report of H. M. chief inspector of constabulary for the year 1963, 259, HMSO, London.

HMIC (H. M. Inspectorate of Constabulary (1968) Report of H. M. chief inspector of constabulary for the year 1967, 272, HMSO, London.

HMIC (H. M. Inspectorate of Constabulary (1999) 1998–1999 Inspection – Metropolitan Police Service: specialist operations, London.

HMIC (H. M. Inspectorate of Constabulary) (2000a) On the Record: thematic inspection report on police crime recording, the Police National Computer, and Phoenix Intelligence System Data Quality, July, London.

HMIC (H. M. Inspectorate of Constabulary) (2000b) Under the Microscope: thematic inspection report on scientific and technical support, July, Home Office, London.

HMIC (H. M. Inspectorate of Constabulary) (2002) Police National Computer data quality and timeliness (Second Report), Home Office, London.

HMIP (H. M. Inspectorate of Probation) (2000) Using Information and Technology to Improve Probation Service Performance, Home Office, London.

HMIP (H. M. Inspectorate of Prisons)/(HMIP (H. M. Inspectorate of Probation) 2001) Through the Prison Gate: a joint thematic review, Home Office, London.

Hollingsworth, M. and Norton-Taylor, R. (1988) Blacklist: the inside story of political vetting, The Hogarth Press, London.

Home Office (1938) Report of the Departmental Committee on detective work and procedure (Volume 3, Chapter V), HMSO, London.

Home Office (1952) Report of the working party on crime circulations and clearing houses (Circular no. 123/1952).

Home Office (1955) Police reports for government departments and other authorities (Circular no. 77/1955).

Home Office (1961) Compensation for Victims of Crimes of Violence, Cmnd. 1406, HMSO, London.

Home Office (1969) Police National Computer (Circular no. 152/1969), London.

Home Office (1970) Part I of the Children and Young Persons Act 1969: a guide for courts and practitioners, HMSO, London.

Home Office (1971) Reports to the courts on accused persons (Circular no. 59/1971) London.

Home Office (1973) Police Reports of convictions and related information (Circular no. 140/1973).

Home Office (1975a) Computers and Privacy, Cmnd. 6353, HMSO, London.

Home Office (1975b) The Rehabilitation of Offenders Act 1974 – Practice Direction (Circular no. 130/1975), London.

Home Office (1976) Non-Accidental Injury to Children: the police and case conferences (Circular no. 179/1976).

Home Office (1978) Citing of Police Cautions in the Juvenile Court (Circular ref. no. 49/1978).

Home Office (1982) Data Protection: the government's proposals for legislation, Cmnd. 8539, HMSO, London.

Home Office (1983) Disclosure of convictions to probation officers preparing social inquiry reports for Magistrates Courts and in respect of persons placed under their supervision (Circular no. IV/1983).

Home Office (1984) Recording of Criminal Convictions on the Police National Computer (Circular no. 86/A98'4), London.

Home Office (1986a) Police reports of convictions and related information (Circular no. 45/1986).

Home Office (1986b) Protection of Children: disclosure of criminal background of those with access to children (Circular no. HOC 4/1986).

Home Office (1988a) IT Strategy for the Police Service – Guidance to Forces, London.

Home Office (1988b) Protection of Children: disclosure of criminal background of those with access to children (Circular no. HOC 102/1988).

Home Office (1988c) Protection of Children: disclosure of criminal background of those with access to children (Circular no. HOC 8/1988).

Home Office (1989) Protection of Children: disclosure of criminal background of those with access to children (Circular no. 58/1989).

Home Office (1990a) Criminal Records: the government reply to the third report from the Home Affairs Committee session 1989–1990, Cm. 1163, HMSO, London.

Home Office (1990b) Crime, Justice and Protecting the Public, Cm. 965, HMSO, London.

Home Office (1991) The National Collection of Criminal Records: report of an efficiency scrutiny, London.

Home Office (1993a) Co-ordination of Computerisation in the Criminal Justice System: regional seminars Autumn 1992: composite report, April, CCCJS Unit, London.

Home Office (1993b) Protection of Children: disclosure of criminal background of those with access to children (Circular no. 47/1993).

Home Office (1993c) Disclosure of Criminal Records for Employment Vetting Purposes: a consultation paper by the Home Office, Cm. 2319, September, HMSO, London.

Home Office (1995a) Criminal Careers of those born between 1953 and 1973, Statistical Bulletin 14/95, Home Office, London.

Home Office (1995b) National DNA Database (Circular no. 16/1995).

Home Office (1995c) Liability in Law for Information kept on Phoenix, the Criminal Justice Record Service (Circular no. 29/1995), London.

Home Office (1995d) Phoenix – putting you in the Picture, London.

Home Office (1996a) Sentencing and Supervision of Sex Offenders – a Consultation Document, Cm. 3304, London.

Home Office (1996b) On the Record: the government's proposals for access to criminal records for employment and related purposes in England and Wales, Cm. 3308, HMSO, London.

Home Office (1996c) Finding the Form: employers get new access to criminal records (Press Release) 19 June.

Home Office (1996d) Explanatory Note on Document Produced under Title VI (Justice and Home Affairs) of the Treaty on European Union – Presidency proposal for a draft Convention Concerning the Establishment of the 'Eurodac' System for the Identification of Applications for Asylum, 6 June, London.

Home Office (1998a) Police National Computer (PNC) Printouts for Probation Service (Probation Circular no. 06/1998), London.

Home Office (1998b) Criminal Records Bureau to Strengthen Child Protection Safeguards (Press Release) 14 December.

Home Office (1999a) Prime Minister announces HI-Tech Drive Against Crime (Press Release) 28 September.

Home Office (1999b) The Rehabilitation of Offenders Act 1974 and Cautions, Reprimands and Final Warnings – a Consultation Paper, August, London.

Home Office (1999c) Report of the inter-departmental working group on preventing unsuitable people from working with children and abuse of trust, London.

Home Office (1999d) UK to Participate in Schengen Law Enforcement and Judicial Cooperation Work (Press Release) 12 March.

Home Office (2000a) Setting the Boundaries: reforming the law on sex offences, July.

Home Office (2000b) PM Hails High-Tech Drive Against Crime (Press Release) 31 August.

Home Office (2000c) Criminal Record Checks to Protect Children and Vulnerable Adults on the way (Press Release) 3 August.

Home Office (2001) Initial Guidance to the Police and Probation Services on Sections 67 and 68 of the Criminal Justice and Court Services Act 2000, London.

Home Office (2002a) Multi-Agency public protection arrangements, Annual Report 2001–2002, July, London.

Home Office (2002b) Breaking the Circle: a review of the Rehabilitation of Offenders Act 1974, July, TSO, London.

Home Office (2003a) Revised Arrangements for Police Checks, Crime Reduction and Community Safety Group (Circular no. 47/2003), London.

Home Office (2003b) Breaking the Circle: a summary of the views of consultees and the government response to the report of the review of the Rehabilitation of Offenders Act 1974, April, London.

Home Office (2003c) Government announces new measures to improve the Criminal Records Bureau (Press Release) 27 February.

Home Office (2003d) Criminal Records Bureau – Reform of the Disclosure Process: a consultation paper, London.

Home Office (2003e) Criminal Records Bureau – should applicants for disclosures be required to submit their fingerprints with their application? A consultation paper, London.

Home Office (2003f) Criminal Records Bureau – Basic Disclosure: routing applications for basic disclosure through registered bodies, A Consultation Paper, April, London.

Home Office (2003g) EU Asylum Fingerprint Database Begins Operating Today (Press Release) 14 January.

Home Office (2004a) National Policing Plan 2003–2006, TSO, London.

Home Office (2004b) Police Science and Technology Strategy 2004–2009, May, London.

Home Office (2004c) Building Communities, Beating Crime: a better police service for the 21st century, Cm. 6360, November, TSO, London.

Home Office (2004d) The Bichard Inquiry – Memorandum by the Home Office, London.

Home Office (2004e) Bichard Inquiry Recommendations: progress report, December, London.

Home Office (2005a) ViSOR: protecting the public from dangerous offenders (Press Release) 19 August.

Home Office (2005b) Guidance on Offences Against Children (Circular no. 16/2005).

Home Office (2005c) DNA expansion programme 2000–2005: reporting achievement, October, London.

Home Office (2005d) Code of Practice: the Police National Computer, National Centre for Policing Excellence, Wyboston.

Home Office (2005e) Code of Practice: National Intelligence Model, National Centre for Policing Excellence, Wyboston.

Home Office (2005f) Code of Practice on the Management of Police Information, National Centre for Policing Excellence, Wyboston.

Home Office (2005g) The report of the review of the Police Information Technology Organisation (PITO), February, London.

Home Office (2005h) Bichard Inquiry Recommendations: second progress report, November, London.

Home Office (2005i) Further Enhancements to the Criminal Record Bureau's Vetting Process (Press Release) 2 March.

Home Office (2005j) Criminal Records Bureau: local checks by police forces for the purpose of enhanced disclosures (Circular no. 5/2005).

Home Office (2006a) The Notifiable Occupations Scheme: revised guidance for police forces (Circular no. 6/2006).

Home Office (2006b) Bichard Inquiry Recommendations: third progress report, May, London.

Home Office (2006c) Maximising the opportunities for sharing DNA information across Europe – Seminar report, 24–26 October 2005, London.

Home Office (ACPO) Association of County Councils, Association of Metropolitan Authorities (1994) The National Strategy for Police Information Systems (10 Volumes), Home Office, London.

Home Office, ACPO, Association of Police Authorities, PITO (2002) Information Systems Strategy for the Police Service, Volumes 1 and 2 (Final Versions), London.

Home Office, Department of Health, Department of Education and Science and the Welsh Office (1991) Working Together under the Children Act 1989: a guide to arrangements for inter-agency co-operation for the protection of children from abuse, HMSO, London.

Home Office, Lord Chancellors Department, Attorney General's Office (2002) Justice for All, Cm. 5563, The Stationery Office, London.

Home Office/DHSS (Department of Health and Social Security) (1985) Disclosure of criminal convictions of those with access to children – First report, July, London.

Hood, R. (1992) Race and Sentencing: a study in the Crown Court, Clarenden Press, Oxford.

Hooley, P. (1994) Bosses to buy crime files on job-hunters, *Daily Express*, 19 December.

House of Commons (1990a) Criminal records, Home Affairs Committee, Third Report, Session 1989–1990, HC 285, HMSO, London.

House of Commons (1990b) Policing football hooliganism, Home Affairs Committee, Second Report, Session 1990–1991, HC 001, HMSO, London.

House of Commons (1990c) Practical police co-operation in the European community, Home Affairs Committee, 7th Report Session 1989–1990, HMSO, London.

House of Commons (2001a) Criminal records bureau, Home Affairs Committee, Second Report, Session 2000–2001, HC 227, The Stationery Office, London.

House of Commons (2001b) Government reply to the second report from the Home Affairs Committee Session 2000–2001, Home Affairs Committee, 5th Special Report, Session 2000–2001, C. 467, HC 467, The Stationery Office, London.

House of Commons (2004) Criminal Records Bureau: delivering safer recruitment? Public Accounts Committee, 45th Report of Session 2003–2004, HC 453, The Stationery Office, London.

House of Commons (2005) Police reform, 4th Report of Session 2004–2005 Volume 2, Oral and Written Evidence, HC 370–411, The Stationery Office, London.

House of Lords (1999) European Union Databases, European Union Committee, 23rd Report, HL 120, Session 1998–1999.

House of Lords (2000) Convention on mutual assistance in criminal matters between the member states of the European union – the final stages, Select Committee on European Union 12th Report, HL 93, Session 1999–2000.

Howard, G. (1953) Guardians of the Queen's Peace – the Development and Work of Britain's police, Odham's Press Ltd., London.

Hudson, B (1996) Understanding Justice: an introduction to ideas, perspectives and controversies in modern penal theory, Open University Press, Buckingham.

Hyder, K. (1988) The child care vetting crisis, *Police Review*, 5 August.

IBIS (Integrating Business and Information Systems) Unit (1999) Medium Term Strategic Plan for Information Systems in the Criminal Justice System, Home Office, London.

ICO (Information Commissioner's Office) (2006) What Price Privacy? The unlawful trade in confidential information, ICO, Wilmslow.

Intelligence and Security Committee (2005) Annual report 2004–2005, Cm. 6510, April, TSO, London.

IPCC (Independent Police Complaints Commission) (2004) Police Officers have Moral Duty to Protect Data Entrusted to them says Independent Police Complaints Commission Deputy Chair (Press Release) 15 July.

IRT (Independent Review Team) (2002) Main Findings from the Independent Review of the Criminal Records Bureau, Home Office, London.

Jensen, R. B. (1981) The international anti-anarchist conference of 1898 and the origins of Interpol, *Journal of Contemporary History*, 16: 323–347.

Jones, G. (2006) DNA database 'should include all', *Daily Telegraph*, 24 October.

Joseph, A. M. (2001) Anthropometry, the Police Expert and the Deptford Murders: the contested introduction of fingerprinting for the identification of criminals in Late Victorian and Edwardian Britain, in Caplan, J. and Torpey, J. (eds.).

JSA (Joint Supervisory Authority) (1998) Second annual report, March, Strasbourg.

Justice (2000) The Schengen Information System: a human rights audit, London.

Justice (2003) Criminal Justice Bill, Part II, Chapter 1, Evidence of Bad Character, House of Lords Briefing, London, June.

Kempner, R. M. W. (1946) The German national registration system as means of police control of population, *Journal of Criminal Law and Criminology*, 36: 362–368.

Kemshall, H. and Maguire, M. (2001) Public Protection, Partnership and Risk Penalty: the multi-agency risk management of sexual and violent offenders, *Punishment and Society*, 3(2): 237–264.

Kemshall, H. and McIvor, G. (eds.) (2004) Managing Sex Offender Risk, Jessica Kingsley Publishers, London.

Kersten, U. (2005) Enhancing International Law, Enforcement Co-operation: a global overview, paper presented at a workshop at the 11th UN congress on crime prevention and criminal justice, Bangkok, 18–25 April.

Kirby, T. (1989) Home Office plans register of criminals DNA profiles, *The Independent*, 24 May.

Kirby, T. (1990) Research into fingerprints abandoned, *The Independent*, 13 February.

Lam, H. and Harcourt, M. (2003) The Use of Criminal Records in Employment Decisions: the rights of ex-offenders, employers and the public, *Journal of Business Ethics*, 47: 237–252.

Lambert, S. (1993) UK 'does not need EC crime databank', *The Independent*, 7 September.

Laudon, K. (1986) Dossier Society: value choices in the design of national information systems, Columbia University Press, New York.

Laurie, P. (1970) Scotland Yard: a personal inquiry, The Bodley Head, London.

Law Commission (1996) Evidence in Criminal Proceedings: previous misconduct of a defendant, Consultation Paper no. 141.

Law Commission (2001) Evidence of bad character in criminal proceedings, Report No. 273, London.

Leigh, D. (1981) Police give computer secrets out, *The Observer*, 4 October.

Leppard, D. (1995) Tories' secret plan to sell off police records, *Sunday Times*, 5 February.

Liberty (1991) Report on the criminal record and information system, June, London.

Liberty (2002) Databasing – the DNA of innocent people – why it offers problems not solutions (Press Release) 13 September, London.

Lindop Report (1978) Report of the Committee on Data Protection, Cmnd. 7341, HMSO, London.

Linebaugh, P. (1991) The London Hanged: crime and civil society in the eighteenth century, Allen Lane, Penguin, London.

Linn, I. (1990) Application Refused: employment vetting by the state, The Civil Liberties Trust, London.

Lombroso, C. (1875) L'Uomo Delinquente, Milan, Hoepl.

London Borough of Lambeth (1987) Whose Child? The report of the public inquiry into the death of Tyra Henry, London.

Los, M. (2006) Looking into the Future: surveillance, globalisation and the totalitarian potential, in Lyon, D. (ed.).

Loucks, N., Lyner, O. and Sullivan, T. (1998) The employment of people with criminal records in the European Union, *European Journal on Criminal Policy and Research*, 6(2): 195–210.

Lundin, J. (1981) Police Act to stop computer leaks, *The Observer*, 8 November.

Lustgarten, L. and Leigh, I. (1994) In from the Cold: national security and Parliamentary democracy, Clarendon Press, Oxford.

Lyon, D. (1994) The Electronic Eye, Polity Press, Cambridge.

Lyon, D. (2001) Surveillance Society: monitoring everyday life, Open University Press, Milton Keynes.

Lyon, D. (ed.) (2006) Theorizing Surveillance: the panopticon and beyond, Willan Publishing, Cullompton.

MacDonald, J. (2000) Pioneering work on offenders, *Yorkshire Post*, 12 August.

Maguire, M. and John, T. (1995) Intelligence, Surveillance and Informants: integrated approaches, Police Research Group Crime Detection and Prevention Series Paper 64, Home Office, London.

Manifesto Club (2006) The Case Against Vetting: how the child protection industry is poisoning adult – child relations, October, London.

Martienssen, A. (1953) Crime and the Police, Penguin Books, London.

Maruna, S. (2001) Making Good: how ex-convicts reform and rebuild their lives, American Psychological Association, Washington DC.

McCartney, C. (2006) Forensic Identification and Criminal Justice: forensic science, justice and risk, Willan Publishing, Cullompton.

McEwan, J. (2002) Previous Misconduct at the Crossroads: which 'way ahead'? *Criminal Law Review,* 180–191.

McLynn, F. (1989) Crime and Punishment: eighteenth century England, Routledge, New York.

McWilliams, W. and Pease, K. (1990) Probation practice and an end to punishment, *Howard Journal of Criminal Justice,* 29(1): 14–25.

Mills, H. (1996) Job checks 'risk' for offenders, *The Independent,* 20 June.

Morris, N. (2007a) Home Office blunder leaves serious offenders off police crime records, *The Independent,* 10 January.

Morris, N. (2007b) Eight left off police records 'could have reoffended', *The Independent,* 15 January.

Morris, S. (2003) Vetting failures let caretaker slip through net, *The Guardian,* 18 December.

Morrish, R. (1940) The Police and Crime-Detection To-day, Oxford University Press, London.

Moylan, J. (1934) Scotland Yard and the Metropolitan Police, G. P. Putnam's Sons Ltd., London.

NACRO (National Association for the Care and Resettlement of Offenders) (1990) Declaring Convictions, London.

NACRO (National Association for the Care and Resettlement of Offenders) (2005) Integrated Resettlement: putting the pieces together, London.

NACRO (National Association for the Care and Resettlement of Offenders) (2006) Getting Disclosures Right: a review of the use and misuse of criminal record disclosures, with a guide to best practice and assessing risk, London.

NAO (National Audit Office) (2003) New IT System for Magistrates Courts: the libra project, HC 237, Session 2002–2003, January, TSO, London.

NAO (National Audit Office) (2004) Criminal Records Bureau – Delivering Safer Recruitment? HC 266, Session 2003–2004, February, TSO, London.

NCCL (National Council for Civil Liberties) (1988) NCCL Urges Reform of Police Checks System (Press Release) 26 September.

NCIS (National Criminal Intelligence Service) (1999) Police support Home Secretary's Announcement on Schengen Participation (Press Release) 12 March.

NCSC (National Care Standards Commission) (2002) Government Removes 1 August Criminal Checks Deadline for Care Home Sector (Press Release) 31 July, London.

NCVYS (National Council for Voluntary Youth Services) (2003) Voluntary Youth Sector Responds to Government Measures to Improve the Criminal Records Bureau (Press Release) 28 February.

NPS (National Probation Service) (2006) Keeping Communities Safe: multi-agency public protection arrangements (Press Release) 20 October.

Nuffield Council on Bioethics (2006) Forensic Use of bioinformation: ethical issues – consultation paper, London.

O'Keefe, D. (1992) The Schengen Convention: a suitable model for European integration? Year book of European Law II, Clarendon Press, Oxford.

O'Neill, E. (2006) Mark of innocence, *The Guardian*, 18 April.

OCJR (Office of Criminal Justice Reform) (2006) PROGRESS: IT support for case progression (leaflet) June, London.

Oliver, I. (1978) The Metropolitan Police Approach to the Prosecution of Juvenile Offenders, Peel Press, London.

Open Society (2005) Ethnic Profiling by Police in Europe, Justice Initiatives, London.

Orr-Munro, T. (2001) Quest for data, *Police Review*, 22 March.

Orwell, G. (1949) Nineteen Eighty-four: a novel, Secker and Warburg, London.

Parratt, L. (1999) Criminal Record Certificates: a recipe for disaster? *Liberty*, Spring, London.

Parton, N. (1985) The Politics of Child Abuse, Macmillans, Basingstoke.

Parton, N. (2006) Safeguarding Childhood: early intervention and surveillance in a late modern society, Palgrave Macmillan, London.

PCMG (Police Checks Monitoring Group) (1988) There is a Better Way, London.

Penal Affairs Consortium (1999) The Rehabilitation of Offenders Act 1974: the case for review and reform, November, London.

Petrow, S. (1994) Policing Morals: the metropolitan police and the Home Office 1870–1914, Clarendon Press, Oxford.

Pickover, D. (2001) A sample of common sense, *Police Review*, 2 February: 23–24.

PITO (Police Information Technology Organisation) (1996) A Review of Phoenix Input Standards and Data Quality, London.

PITO (Police Information Technology Organisation) (2001) National Fingerprint Jigsaw is Complete (Press Release) 26 April.

PITO (Police Information Technology Organisation) (2006) PNC Monthly Hits Top 10 million (Press Release) 9 February.

PITO (Police Information Technology Organisation) (n.d.) Introducing PNCD and its Services, London.

Platt, S. (1988) Police check delays put children at risk, *New Society*, 19 February.

Powers, R. (1987) Secrecy and Power: the life of J. Edgar Hoover, The Free Press, New York.

Pringle, P. (1955) Hue and Cry, Museum Press Ltd., London.

Programme of Action (1990) Reinforcement of Police Co-operation and of the Endeavours to Combat Terrorism or Other Forms of Organised Crime, June, TREVI, Dublin.

Protocol France No. 1 (1992) Protocol between the Government of the United Kingdom of Great Britain and Northern Ireland and the Government of the French Republic concerning Frontier Controls and Policing, Co-operation in Criminal Justice, Public Safety and Mutual Assistance relating to the Channel Fixed Link, Cmnd. 1802, HMSO, London.

Radcliffe Report (1962) Security procedures in the public service, Cmnd. 1681.

Radzinowicz, L. (1956) A History of English Criminal Law and its Administration from 1750, Volume 3: the reform of the police, Stevens and Sons Ltd., London.

Radzinowicz, L. and Hood, R. (1986) A History of English Criminal Law and its Administration from 1750 – Volume 5: the emergence of penal policy, Stevens and Sons, London.

Readhead, I. (2006) Data control, *Police Review*, 6 January: 18–19.

Redmayne, M. (1998) The DNA Database: civil liberty and evidentiary issues, *Criminal Law Review,* 437–454.

Reiner, R. (1992) The Politics of the Police (2nd ed.) Harvester Wheatsheaf, Hemel Hempstead.

Robertson, J. (2006) £750,000 payout to fingerprint detective, *The Scotsman,* 8 February.

Rule, J. B. (1973) Private Lives and Public Surveillance, Allen Lane, London.

Runciman Report (1993) The Royal Commission on Criminal Justice, Cm. 2263, HMSO, London.

Russell, J. (1998) Phoenix Data Quality, Police Research Group, Special Interest Series: paper 11, Home Office, London.

Samuels, A. (2002) Rehabilitation of Offenders Act 1974, *Justice of the Peace,* 166: 685–686.

Schengen Convention (1990) Applying the Schengen Agreement of 14 June 1985 between the Governments of the Benelux Economic Union, the Federal Republic of Germany and the French Republic on the gradual abolition of checks at their common borders, June.

Schutte, J. (1991) Schengen: its meaning for the free movement of persons in Europe, *Common Market Law Review,* 28: 549–570.

Scott, H. (1954) Scotland Yard, Andre Deutsch, London.

Scout Association (1999) Criminal Records Bureau: concerned voluntary youth charities brief MPs (Press Release) 23 June.

Sengoopta, C. (2003) Imprint of the Raj: how fingerprinting was born in Colonial India, Pan Books, London.

SEU (Social Exclusion Unit) (2002) Reducing re-offending by ex-prisoners, Office of the Deputy Prime Minister, London.

SIA (Security Industry Authority) (2006) Licensing Private Security, London.

Simons, M. (2000) Errors rife in police data file, *Computer Weekly,* 27 April.

Singh, R. (1988) Infertility treatment and the courts, *Family Law,* 299–303.

Smith, J. (1999) Prior Criminality and Employment of Social Workers with Substantial Access to Children: a decision board analysis, *British Journal of Social Work,* 29: 49–68.

Smith, P. T. (1985) Policing Victorian London: political policing, public order and the London metropolitan police, Greenwood Press, London.

Spencer, M. (1990) 1992 And All That: civil liberties in the balance, The Civil Liberties Trust, London.

SSI (Social Services Inspectorate) (1999) Someone Else's Children: inspections of planning and decision making for children looked after and the safety of children looked after, Department of Health, London.

Steele, J. (1996) PC Lovers ran official checks on wife's friend, *Daily Telegraph,* 18 June.

Stephen, J. F. (1973) A History of the Criminal Law of England, Franklin, New York.

Stevenson, S. J. (1986) The habitual criminal in 19th century England, *Urban History Yearbook,* 37–60, University of Leicester.

Suff, R. (2005) Checking out the activities of the criminal records bureau, *IRS Employment Review,* 483: 42–48.

Sullivan, D. (1998) Employee violence, negligent hiring and criminal record checks, *St. John's Law Review,* 72: 580–591.

Surveillance Studies Network (2006) A Report on the Surveillance Society: for the Information Commissioner, September, London.

Tendler, S. (1996a) Computer hitch halts profiles of criminals, *The Times*, 16 September.

Tendler, S. (1996b) Police anger over database disorder, *The Times*, 10 September.

The Chief Constables of West Yorkshire, South Yorkshire and North Wales Police and the Information Commissioner, Information Tribunal, 2005 (accessible at www.informationtribunal.gov.uk).

Thomas, T. (2001) The National Collection of Criminal Records: a question of data quality, *Criminal Law Review*, 886–896.

Thomas, T. (2004) Sex Offenders: registers and monitoring, in Kemshall, H. and McIvor, G. (eds.)

Thomas, T. (2006) The Criminal Records Bureau and its Registered Bodies: new regulations for a 'disparate and unwieldy' customer network, *Journal of Social Welfare and Family Law*, 28(3–4): 359–366.

Thomas, T. and Hebenton, B. (1991) To Minimize Future Risk: circular 88(102) and the politics of protection, *Journal of Social Welfare and Family Law*, 2: 128–141.

Thompson, J. (1996) Communications breakdown, *Police Review*, 1 November.

Travis, A. (1993) Ministers propose private criminal records agency, *The Guardian*, 10 September.

Travis, A. (1995) Ministers plan police record sales agency, *The Guardian*, 16 January.

Travis, A. (1998) 10m face criminal vetting, *The Guardian*, 15 December.

Treaty of Canterbury (1986) Treaty between the United Kingdom of Great Britain and Northern Ireland and the French Republic concerning the Construction and Operation by Private Concessionaires of a Channel Fixed Link with Exchange of Notes, Cmnd. 9745, HMSO, London.

Trickett, A., Osborn, D., Seymour, J. and Pease, K. (1992) What is different about high crime areas? *British Journal of Criminology*, 32: 81–90.

Uggen, C. (2000) Work as a Turning Point in the Life Course of Criminals: a duration model of age, employment and recidivism, *American Sociological Review*, 67: 529–546.

UN (United Nations) (1959) Convention between Denmark, Finland, Norway and Sweden concerning the waiver of passport control at the intra-Nordic frontiers. Signed at Copenhagen on 12 July 1957. (Treaty Series No. 4660), New York.

Unell, J. (1992) Criminal Records Checks within the Voluntary Sector: an evaluation of the pilot schemes, Volunteer Centre, United Kingdom.

Utting Report (1997) People Like Us: the report of the review of the safeguards for children living away from home, The Stationery Office, London.

von Hirsch, A. (1986) Past or Future Crimes: deservedness and dangerousness in the sentencing of criminals, Manchester University Press, Manchester.

von Hirsch, A. (2002) Record-enhanced sentencing in England and Wales, *Punishment and Society*, 4(4): 443–457.

von Hirsch, A. and Wasik, M. (1997) Civil Disqualifications Attending Conviction: a suggested conceptual framework, *Cambridge Law Journal*, 53(3): 599–626.

Wacks, R. (1989) Personal Information: privacy and the law, Clarendon Press, Oxford.

Walker, N. (1965) Crime and Punishment in Britain, Edinburgh University Press, Edinburgh.

Walker, S. R. (1970) The police national records computer, *The Police Journal*, March, XLIII(3): 111–116.

Warner Report (1992) Choosing with Care: the report of the committee of inquiry into the selection, development and management of staff in children's homes, HMSO, London.

Wasik, M. (1987) Guidance, Guidelines and Criminal Record, in Wasik, M. and Pease, K. (eds.).

Wasik, M. and Pease, K. (eds.) (1987) Sentencing Reform: guidance or guidelines? Manchester University Press, Manchester.

Wasserman, G. (1989) Putting crime into context – interview, *Siemens Magazine.com* 5/89.

Watt, N. (2000) 3m face DNA tests in Blair crime initiative, *The Guardian*, 1 September.

Waugh, P. (1991) The Use of Computers in the Administration of Justice in the United Kingdom, in Yearbook of Law, Computers and Technology, Volume 5, Butterworths, London.

West Yorkshire Police (2006) Pocket Computers Put Police 'In the Picture' (Press Release) 28 March.

Westin, A. (1967) Privacy and Freedom, The Bodley Head, London.

Wiener, M. J. (1990) Reconstructing the Criminal: culture, law and policing in England 1830–1914, Cambridge University Press, Cambridge.

Wilmot Report (1987) Study proposal on the need for integrated communications networks, ACPO, London.

Woodhall, E. T. (1936) Secrets of Scotland Yard, John Lane, The Bodley Head, London.

YJB (Youth Justice Board)/ACPO (Association of Chief Police Officers) (2005) Sharing Information on Children and Young People at Risk of Offending: a practical guide, London.

Younger Report (1972) Report of the committee on privacy, Cmnd. 5012, HMSO, London.

Zenk, G. (1979) Project SEARCH, Greenwood Press, California.

Names Index

Subject Index